Heaven's Dew

Mary Ann Grady

ISBN: 1541188101
ISBN-:9781541188105

DEDICATION

To the one who set me free, Jesus
To the one who ran to me, my Abba Father
To the one who gently whispers to me, the Holy Spirit

To the one who captured my heart and loves me
unconditionally, Jim, my husband
To the one who is always teaching me new things,
Jess, our firstborn
To the one who shows kindness to all,
Rach, our middle daughter
To the one who extends grace to all he meets,
Jacob, our son

I will praise you, Lord, among the nations;
I will sing of you among the peoples.
For great is your love, reaching to the
heavens; your faithfulness
reaches to the skies.
Be exalted, O God, above the heavens;
let your glory be over all the earth.
Psalm 57:9-11 NIV

"There is no excess of goodness.
You cannot go too far in the
right direction."
C.S. Lewis

ACKNOWLEDGMENTS

Thank you
To these who have been my shepherd
George Dodson, Fredonia Hill
Johnny Hendricks, Woodland Heights
Frankie Rainey, Crestmont
Robert Morris, Gateway

Cover design: Jess Grady Mauldin
Thank you, Jess, for your great design.
Catcitycreative.com

Witness in love, not a word!
When dew falls it makes no sound.
You cannot know when it falls by listening for it.
In the same way our stillness, our utter
quietness, displays to the world God's splendor.
Be like the dew so others will be blessed.

January 1
My eyes were blind, I didn't know who you were

But blessed are your eyes because they see,
and your ears because they hear.
Matthew 13:16 NIV

"Our eyes were blind, we could not see, we didn't know who you were". These lyrics to a song say much about our world. My eyes were blind for so many years. I could not see! What I did see caused me much destruction and heartache.

But one day my eyes were opened. I could see. I could really see for the very first time. I saw the one who gave everything for me. I saw the one who created me and formed me. I saw the one who loved me, who had always loved me, I just didn't know. I saw the one who had been so patiently waiting for me to come to Him. I saw the world in a new way. I found hope and love and joy and peace and life everlasting.
Once I was blind but now I can see. Now I know who He is, my Father, my Savior, my Counselor, my Prince of Peace, my Friend.

As you begin the new year . . .
May He reveal Himself to you in new ways.
May He teach you things you thought were not possible.
May He forever change you
May you see, really see, all that He is and all that He has for you.
Blessings on you in this new year!

The path of the righteous is like the morning sun, shining ever brighter
until the full light of day.
Proverbs 4:18 NIV

January 2
He has a word for you

So Jacob called the place Peniel, saying, "It is because I saw God face to face, and yet my life was spared." The sun rose above him as he passed Peniel, and he was limping because of his hip.
Genesis 32:30-31 NIV

Our son, Jacob, was sixteen when he was diagnosed with an inoperable malignant brain tumor. Our world was forever changed. Through incredible doctors and months of chemo and radiation God healed our son. Several years later God showed me the verse above. I was blown away by what I read. God gave me a specific word of healing and comfort and hope, for our son, for our family. The location in the brain of our son's tumor was on the peniel gland! Jacob, in the bible, called the place where he met God, Peniel!

Jacob, in the bible, walked away with a limp and that was his reminder of meeting God.

Jacob, our son, walked away with slight peripheral double vision and that is his reminder of God sparing his life.

God has a word for you.
Just as He gave me this very specific and personal word
about our son, Jacob. He has a specific and personal
word for you.
Take the time to search His word.
He will show you and you will be forever changed!

He loves you

January 3
Become like a child

Then people brought little children to Jesus for him to place his hands on them and pray for them. But the disciples rebuked them. Jesus said, "Let the little children come to me, and do not hinder them, for the kingdom of heaven belongs to such as these." When he had placed his hands on them, he went on from there.
Matthew 19:13-15 NIV

Dallas Willard wrote this in his book Hearing God.

"How hard it is for us to come to an adequate conception of the lowliness of God! His greatness is precisely what makes him ready to hear and speak personally with his creatures. Jesus' actions and words made clear how accessible God is to the weak and downtrodden, even children. One characteristic of children is their relative unimportance, but the humanly unimportant ones are important to God. God being who God is, and revealed in the person of Jesus Christ, we should be surprised if he does not speak to us."
(Hearing God Devotional week 12 day 4)

Become like a child. Seek him.

Do whatever it takes to find him.

Climb high enough to see Him.

Ask for help if you need it.

He wants you to see Him.

He wants to speak to you.

He loves you

"When Zacheus was a wee little boy he climbed up in the tree."

January 4
Jesus knew His words had power and authority

On that day, when evening had come, he said to them, "Let's go over to the other side." Leaving the multitude, they took him with them, even as he was, in the boat. Other small boats were also with him. A big windstorm arose, and the waves beat into the boat, so much that the boat was already filled. He himself was in the stern, asleep on the cushion, and they woke him up, and told him, "Teacher, don't you care that we are dying?" He awoke, and rebuked the wind, and said to the sea, "Peace! Be still!" The wind ceased, and there was a great calm.
Mark 4:35-39 WEB

Jesus knew the plan was to go over to the other side. He knew there would be a storm. He knew His words had power because His Father had given Him all authority. He knew what He was to do. Just speak the words and even the wind and the waves would obey Him. He was not surprised. He knew where His power came from.
All authority comes from our Heavenly Father. He has given it to us.

God knows what lies ahead for you.

He knows the plans He has for you.

Plans to prosper you and not harm you.

Plans to give you a hope and a future.'

There may be a storm ahead for you.

But you can trust in the one who has calmed

every storm.

You will make it to the other side.

All power has been given to Jesus.

January 5
Just do it

While he was in Bethany, reclining at the table in the home of Simon the
Leper, a woman came with an alabaster jar of very expensive perfume,
made of pure nard. She broke the jar and poured
the perfume on his head.
Mark 14:3 NIV

What the world sees as crazy God sees as beautiful. What crazy thing do
you want to do for Jesus? Do it. The world may laugh but Jesus will be
touched by your act. Jesus was resting, at a Pharisee's home. Mary knew
in her heart what she wanted to do. She broke the expensive jar of
perfume and poured it on Jesus' head. No one but Jesus understood.
Those around her rebuked her harshly for her act. Everyone tried to
reason it out.

Jesus saw her with His heart. Jesus knew her heart. Jesus stood up for
her. He spoke words of encouragement over Mary. God used Mary in an
incredible way, to prepare Jesus' body for burial. Mary did not know the
significance of her act, she only knew what she was to do.

Whatever God has told you to do. Just do it!
You may never know the long reaching affects of your act.
Sometimes your act will cause extreme emotion.
It's okay to let others see that.
They may not understand but Jesus does and He is blessed.
Your act, the one God has placed on your heart to do,
will bring you peace.

Luke 7:36-50
He loves you.

January 6
Who fills everything in every way

He who descended is the very one who ascended higher than all the
heavens, in order to fill the whole universe.
Ephesians 4:10 NIV

We all are apart of His one body.
This body is the fullness of Him.
This fullness is given all grace.
This grace has filled the whole universe.

We are to be Him, representing His grace, all that He is, to this world.
He has done it, we only need to be! Let Jesus fill you with all that He is so
that the world might see Him through you.

There is not a place you can go that He is not there.

He has filled the whole universe.

You can rest in His presence.

Now you are the body of Christ, and each one of you
is a part of it.
1 Corinthians 12:27 NIV

He loves you

January 7
The wisdom that comes from above

But the wisdom that comes from heaven is first of all pure; then peace loving, considerate, submissive, full of mercy and good fruit, impartial and sincere. Peacemakers who sow in peace reap a harvest of righteousness.
James 3:17-18 NIV

God's wisdom is good.
　　It brings life and hope and direction and peace.

God's wisdom harms no one!
　　It produces peace.
　　It is always considerate of others.
　　It is full of mercy.
　　It always produces good fruit.
　　It shows no partiality.
　　It is sincere.

God's wisdom is first pure. It cannot have any of the other qualities until it is first pure.
　　Are your words pure when you speak to others?
　　Are your motives pure when you do for others?
　　Do your actions come from a pure heart?

We have all sinned and fallen short but Jesus took all of our sins upon Himself when He was nailed to the cross. So we now can speak from a pure heart. We can do from a pure heart. We can act from a pure heart, There is such freedom in Jesus.

January 8
He gives us songs in the night

By day the Lord directs his love, at night his song is with me,
a prayer to the God of my life.
Psalm 42:8 NIV

Songs in the night:
He gives the songs to you.
You will laugh again.
You will know joy again.
He will direct you.
You will want to give him thanks again.
You will sing again.

Be ready to sing the song He gives to you.

In order for God to give us these songs, there must be the darkness of night. But the day will come and the sun will rise again!

I remembered my songs in the night. My heart meditated
and my spirit asked.
Psalm 77:6 NIV

He loves you

January 9
He created you to enjoy life

Trust in the Lord and do good; dwell in the land and enjoy safe pasture.
Psalm 37:3 NIV

One of my favorite movies is "Second Hand Lions". The movie is about two older men who live together in a run down dilapidated house. They are very set in their ways and not very happy. Then one day an unexpected guest comes to live with them. He's a young boy, the son of their niece, who is a very poor example of a mother.
Through this boy the old men learn how to live and love. When the little boy becomes a man and returns for their funerals, his words are "They lived! They really lived!" I love that!

May you and I learn how to really live in Him.

Trust comes first.

Learning to dwell is next.

Enjoyment is what He wants for us.

He gave His all, His only son, Jesus,

just for you and me.

I am the gate; whoever enters through me will be saved.
They will come in and go out, and find pasture.
John 10:9 NIV

He loves you

January 10
In Him we live and move

'For in him we live and move and have our being.' As some of your own
poets have said, 'We are his offspring.'
Acts17: 28 NIV

In Him
We live. We move. We have our being
We are His offspring
He carries us. He gives us breath
He holds our life in His hand. And He knows all our ways.

When my tiny little grandson was born at 2 pounds we did not know if he
could breathe on his own. His little lungs were not developed and every
breath was such a struggle for him. It was so very difficult to watch. I just
wanted desperately to breathe for him. But I could not. The NICU doctors
and nurses were wonderful. They knew just what he needed. They knew
every machine and its purpose. They knew every beep and what it
meant. Those sounds became comforting to me over time. But in all of
this there was still a fear. God very gently reminded me He had my tiny
grandson in the palm of His hand and that He was the one who would give
him breath! And He did! He kept him safe in the NICU for 78 days!
My grandson isn't so tiny now, he is a healthy, happy, fearless little three
year old! He is my constant reminder of God's testament to His word.

He gave you life. He will carry you. He will give you breath,
even in the times you feel like you can't go on.
He holds you. He knows all your ways.
You are His.

In his hand is the life of every creature and the breath of all mankind.
Job 12:10 NIV

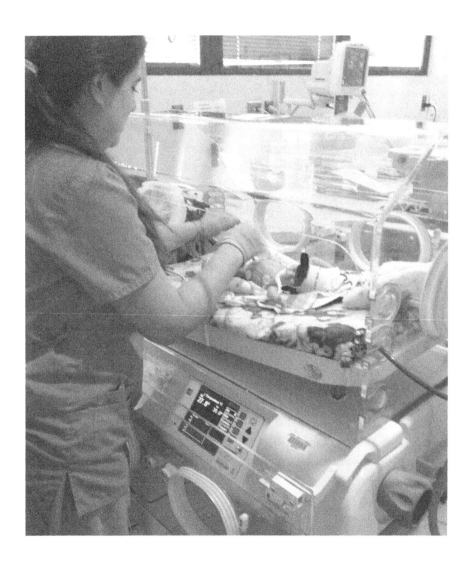

He loves you

January 11
Delight in the Lord

Take delight in the Lord, and he will give you the desires of your heart.
Psalm 37:4 NIV

To delight is to please someone greatly.
God has something for you.
He wants to give it to you.
He knows you.
He knows what makes you happy.
He put those desires in you.
Take from Him all He is offering you.
He alone knows how to fulfill your desires.
He alone will give you what you long for. He alone will satisfy you.
He alone delights in giving you the desires of your heart.
It's not the things of this world that will delight you but rather it is the things of God. Seek Him and receive from Him.

You have granted him his heart's desire and have not withheld the request of his lips.   Psalm 21:2 NIV

January 12
Your righteous reward

Commit your way to the Lord; trust in him and he will do this He will make
your righteous reward shine like the dawn, your vindication
like the noonday sun.
Psalm 37:5-6 NIV

Commit all that you are
All that you desire
All that you seek
To Him

Trust only in Him
And He will do this:

He will bless both you and your children
His righteousness will be not only with you but with your children and your
children's children!
His wealth and His riches will be in their houses, all their houses!

The wealth of all that He is, the riches of:
Love and joy
Peace and patience
Hope and perseverance
Kindness and goodness
Life everlasting

But from everlasting to everlasting the Lord's love is with those who fear
him, and his righteousness with their children's children.
Psalm 103:17 NIV

He loves you

January 13
Find your wings

They shall mount up with wings as eagles. Isaiah 40:31 NIV

Mark Harris, a worship leader at our church, Gateway, wrote this song entitled, "Find Your Wings". The words are so good.

"I pray that God would fill your heart with dreams. And that faith
gives you the courage to dare to do great things
I'm here for you whatever this life brings. So let my love give you roots
and help you find your wings
May passion be the wind that leads you through your days
And may conviction keep you strong, guide you on your way
May there be many moments that make your life so sweet
Oh, but more than memories
I pray that God would fill your heart with dreams and that faith gives
you the courage to dare to do great things"

"Those who wait upon the Lord shall obtain a marvelous addition to their resources: they shall obtain wings! They become endowed with power to rise above things. Men who do not soar always have small views of things. Wings are required for breadth of view. The wing-life is characterized by a sense of proportion. To see things aright we must get away from them. An affliction looked at from the lowlands may be stupendous; looked at from the heights, it may appear little or nothing. This "light affliction, which is but for a moment, works in us a far more exceeding and eternal weight of glory." What a breadth of view!" (Excerpt From: L. B. E. Cowman. "Springs in the Valley.")

Wait upon The Lord! He will give you wings.
Wings are required for the breadth of the view.
Rise above it all and you will see from a new perspective.
God will give you a new vision, a vision through His eyes.
You will begin to see what He sees.
He longs for you to soar above on wings as eagles.

January 14
Our God is able

Then the king arose very early in the morning, and went in haste to the den of lions. When he came near to the den to Daniel, he cried with a lamentable voice; the king spoke and said to Daniel, Daniel, servant of the living God, is your God, whom you serve continually, able to deliver you from the lions? Then Daniel said to the king, O king, live forever. My God has sent his angel, and has shut the lions' mouths, and they have not hurt me; because as before him innocence was found in me; and also before you, O king, have I done no hurt. Then was the king exceedingly glad commanded that they should take Daniel up out of the den. So Daniel was taken up out of the den, and no kind of harm was found on him, because he had trusted in his God.
Daniel 6:19-23 WEB

There is nothing that is too difficult for our God!
Nothing!
He can shut the mouths of lions.
He can calm the raging seas.
He can breathe life into the dead.
He can make a way where there seems to be no way.
He can give hope when all hope is lost.
He can heal a broken heart.
He can move a mountain into the sea.
He can give peace in the storm.

He is able to make all grace abound toward you

So that in all ways, in everything you do, you will abound.

Just trust Him, He is able!

In all things

At all times

Having all that you need

You will abound in every good work

And God is able to bless you abundantly, so that in all things at all times, having all that you need, you will abound in every good work.
2 Corinthians 9:8 NIV

January 15
There is no place God is not

When Jacob awoke from his sleep, he thought, "Surely the Lord is in this place, and I was not aware of it." He was afraid and said, "How awesome is this place! This is none other than the house of God; this is the gate of heaven."
Genesis 28:16-17 NIV

This is a quote from Dallas Willard's book, "Hearing God".
"There is no place where God is not."
(Hearing God week 14 day 3)
Even if you make your bed in the depths He is there.
Even if you are placed in a prison in a foreign land He is there.
He is everywhere!
We are never ever alone.

In 2014, a woman named Meriam Ibrahim was imprisoned in Sudan for her belief in Jesus. She refused to convert to Islam and for that she was imprisoned. She and her 20-month-old son were confined to a dirty prison cell. She was eight months pregnant. Her legs were shackled. She had to give birth under these horrible conditions. And yet God was there!

So Father, you were in that tiny prison cell in Sudan.
You were with Meriam Ibrahim and her little boy and her baby.
Her bed had been made for her in the depths.
She did not choose this yet she had been faithful to stand for You.
She did not reject her Christianity.
An amazing woman of faith
Your word says even there you will guide her.
Your right hand held her fast.
There was so much darkness there.
It seemed like there was no light at all.
But even there the darkness was not dark to you.
Darkness is as light to you.
You are the light, the light of the world.
You Father are the one who releases the captives!
You remove their shackles.

You open prison doors.
You set the captives free.
You use these as a witness, which causes many others, that are so deceived, to come to know you, Jesus!
Thank you for what you did in this tiny prison cell in Sudan!

Where can I go from your Spirit? Where can I flee from your presence? If I go up to the heavens, you are there; if I make my bed in the depths, you are there. If I rise on the wings of the dawn, if I settle on the far side of the sea, even there your hand will guide me, your right hand will hold me fast. if I say, "Surely the darkness will hide me and the light become night around me," even the darkness will not be dark to you; the night will shine like the day, for darkness is as light to you.
Psalm 139:7-12 NIV

He loves you

January 16
He teaches you what is best for you

This is what the Lord says---your Redeemer, the Holy One of Israel: "I am the Lord your God, who teaches you what is best for you, who directs you in the way you should go."   Isaiah 48:17 NIV

There is a way that is best for you.
It is often not the way you would normally choose.
He will teach you His way.
It may be totally different than any way you've ever gone before.
He will direct you in the way you should go.
He will go before you. He knows your path well.
You need only to trust Him. His ways are safe and secure.
Listen for His directions. Be still and listen for His gentle voice.
Follow in the direction He leads you. The end result will always be good for you.

The Lord will guide you always; he will satisfy your needs in a sun-scorched land and will strengthen your frame. You will be like a well watered garden, like a spring whose waters never fail.   Isaiah 58:11 NIV

The Voyage

(words by Amanda Cook) Bethel Music

"You're afraid, but you can hear adventure calling.

There's a rush of adrenaline to your bones.

What you make of this moment changes everything.

What if the path you choose becomes a road.

What if the path you take becomes your home.

The wind is high, but the pressure's off

I'll send the rain wherever we end up.

Set your sights, set them far beyond the familiar

in the rising tides. Feel the rhythm of your heart.

Lift your head.

Now the wind and waves don't matter.

The path you choose becomes a road. The ground you

take becomes your home. The wind is high, but the

pressures off. I'll send the rain wherever we end up. I am

the wind in your sails."

He loves you

January 17
He will remind you of everything I have said

But the Advocate, the Holy Spirit, whom the Father will send in my name, will teach you all things and will remind you of everything I have said to you. Peace I leave with you: my peace I give you. I do not give to you as the world gives. Do not let your hearts be troubled and do not be afraid.
John 14:26-27 NIV

The Holy Spirit will teach you all things.

That's His job.

He will remind you of everything Jesus has said to you.

He will guide you.

He will give you peace.

The world does not have this, nor do they understand it.

Do not let your heart be troubled.

Do not be afraid.

You must remain in Him.

But when he, the Spirit of truth, comes, he will guide you into all the truth. He will not speak on his own; he will speak only what he hears, and he will tell you what is yet to come.
John 16:13 NIV

He loves you

January 18
The law will never give life

Is the law, therefore, opposed to the promises of God? Absolutely not! For if a law had been given that could impart life, then righteousness would certainly have come by the law. But Scripture has locked up everything under the control of sin, so that what was promised, being given through faith in Jesus Christ, might be given to those who believe.
Galatians 3:21-22 NIV

You will never be able to fulfill the law.
The law will never give life.
You will only know life, real life, through faith in Jesus.
His blood has covered you.
You are alive in Him.
You need not try to perform anymore.
His blood is sufficient for you.
There is freedom only in Him.
In Him we live and move and have our being.
In Him we become alive, really alive!

He loves you

January 19
He is our guide

For this God is our God forever and ever; he will be our guide
even to the end.   Psalm 48:14 NIV

Years ago when I was in college I signed up to go on a spelunking trip. I knew nothing at all about cave exploring! Nothing! My roommate and I decided to go. When we got to the site of the adventure we saw no evidence of a cave. There were however two guides, each with hats on that had lights on them. There were probably about ten others ready to go on this adventure too. We followed the guides to the entrance to the cave. I don't remember much about the entrance.

I do however remember the tunnel. It was very narrow and long and dark. We were told we had to lie down and put our arms straight out in front of us and our legs straight behind us. Then the only way to move through the tunnel was to inch our way through. I remember thinking this is going to be difficult but I wasn't afraid at all. It was my turn and I inched my way through just as the guides said. When we got through the tunnel we came to a huge room. You could stand up and the ceiling was very tall. It covered a great expanse. The only problem was that all we could see was what the light from the headlamps of the two guides shown. We were at their mercy. But I was young and I totally trusted these two young guides who I did not know at all!

We made it through our exploration and came back up to the light. It was nice to smell fresh air and see the sunlight. I was amazed when I looked at my clothes. Nasty!! I did not realize the whole time I was walking and crawling I was going through bat droppings. My clothes were covered as well as my shoes. I was proud that I made it through. I did throw my clothes and shoes away. And I never went on another spelunking adventure again!

God is our guide even to the end. We may not always see Him but we know He is there. At times we may not be given much light but we can know He will lead us to our appointed place. He will protect us. We may pick up a little dirt along the way but that's okay too. It is our reminder of what we have been through. There is always an end to each adventure and there is always light at the end of the tunnel. He is our faithful guide.

January 20
We are to be His light in this world

"You are the light of the world. A city set on a hill cannot be hidden."
John 5:14 NIV

I have always loved candles and the way their wicks flicker.
I love old street lamps and the ways they seem to have a glow around them.
But I love, love, love lighthouses! They stand so tall above all that surrounds them.
Their strong light provides the hope for the ships that need to be shown their way.
They provide comfort for these on the land as a familiar sight.
Their light never goes out. It is always shining!
I love stars. Their lights can be seen all over the world.

We are to shine as lights in this world.
You may only feel like a small candle that seems unimportant to you but the light that your small candle puts out is just the light that someone else will need to find their way.
Maybe He is using you as a street lamp that shines in the night for many who need your light to find their way.
Maybe He has made you into a lighthouse - you are to be a beacon of hope to the many people who have lost their way. They've been tossed around by incredible storms and they've lost all hope of ever finding their way.
Maybe He made you into a star, a light that shines in the darkness. Stars' lights shine long after they are gone. They continue to give hope for others.
Father, use us to be a light.
May our light always shine so that others may see you Abba Father!

"Let your light shine before men in such a way that they may see your good works, and glorify your Father who is in heaven.
John 5:16 NIV

January 21
God does not condemn

Who then is the one who condemns? No one. Christ Jesus who died---more than that, who was raised to life---is at the right hand of God and is also interceding for us.   Romans 8:34 NIV

There is no condemnation for those who are in Christ Jesus.
Jesus not only died for us, He was raised to life for us.
And He is sitting at the right hand of God, His righteous right hand . .
Interceding for you and for me.
Nothing can separate us from the love of the Father.
Nothing, neither height nor depth.

He does not condemn, He only loves.

He loves you

January 22
He is with you always

And teaching them to obey everything I have commanded you. And surely
I am with you always, to the very end of the age."
Matthew 28:20 NIV

*"Sir Ernest Shackleton and two of his companions spent thirty-six hours
among the snow mountains of New Georgia, seeking for a station that
meant life or death to them and their waiting crew on Elephant Island.
Writing of that journey, he says, "It seemed to me, often, that we were
four, not three." He refers to the "guiding Presence" that went with them.*

*Paul was not peculiarly privileged when he saw the Living One while en
route to Damascus.*
*Kahlil Gibran, the Syrian, explaining his remarkable modern painting of
Jesus, said: "Last night I saw His face again, clearer than I have ever
seen it."*
*Handel, composer of the "Hallelujah Chorus," declared: "I did see God on
His throne."*
*During the terrible stress of war many affirmed positively that they saw
"The White Comrade."*
Excerpt From: L. B. E. Cowman. "Springs in the Valley." Zondervan
June 26

Many today express these same sentiments. They have seen him in a
dream or a vision. Jesus has revealed Himself to them.

He is with you always.

He said, "Look! I see four men walking around in the fire, unbound and
unharmed, and the fourth looks like a son of the gods."
Daniel 3:25 NIV
He loves you

January 23
We should go up and take possession

When they reached the Valley of Eshkol, they cut off a branch bearing a
single cluster of grapes. Two of them carried it on a pole between them,
along with some pomegranates and figs.
Numbers 13:23 NIV

God told Moses to send twelve Israelites to go and explore the land of
Canaan. They were to look at everything, the land, the fruit of the land,
the cities, how they were fortified, the people, were they strong or weak.
They did what Moses asked and they brought back fruit that was so
incredibly big that it took two people to carry just one cluster of grapes on
a pole! The fruit was indeed good!
Even though the visible evidence was right before their eyes and God had
promised them this land, ten of the explorer's eyes were on something
else, the physical size of their enemy,
But Caleb and Joshua's eyes were on God. They saw with the eyes of
their hearts. They knew what a powerful God they served. They had
complete trust in Him. They knew the battle was not theirs but Gods. He
would fight for them. They knew the victory was theirs. God had a new
home for them and they wanted it!
But the other ten explorers could not see what Caleb and Joshua saw.
The enemy was too big to them. They did not believe in the power of
God. They did not see with the eyes of their hearts.
They were so against taking this land, that they began to spread bad
reports about it, so much so that what they said was not even true. Their
reports damaged not only their hearts but also all who heard it. Their
physical eyes told them "We are small, we cannot fight this battle. The
enemies are giants!" They believed this so much that their own size
diminished in their hearts.
They lost sight of who God was and His power.
What are you looking at? What do you see?
Are you seeing what only your eyes can see or are you looking through
God's eyes?

Let God give you His perspective. It is always right.

Fix your eyes on God. Allow Him to show you.

January 24
His appointed time

Then an angel of the Lord appeared to Zechariah, standing at the right side of the altar of incense. When Zechariah saw him, he was startled and was gripped with fear. Luke 1:11-12

Zechariah had been chosen on that day at that time to go into the temple to burn incense. It was his appointed time to meet God.
God had a word just for him.
He was alone, all the other worshippers were praying outside.
Gabriel, an angel of The Lord appeared to Zechariah, the husband of Elizabeth.
Gabriel was standing on the right side of the altar of incense.
Zechariah was scared, yet Gabriel comforted him.
His words were an answer to Zechariah's prayer.
A prayer that he had prayed for many years!
Gabriel told him the words from God about his future son.
He did not tell him who he was or who sent him until after he had spoken the words God had for Zechariah.
The words must have been for Zechariah more than he could have ever hoped. Not only would he have a son but he would be powerful in The Lord. He would be filled with the Holy Spirit before he was born.
He would go before Jesus in the spirit and power of Elijah.
To make ready the people for The Lord.
Gabriel then identified himself.
He was standing in the presence of God, His kingdom here.
He was sent to tell him the good news.
Zechariah was left speechless!

When God has a word for you:

It may startle you

It may come when you least expect it

It may come when you are all alone

It may be more than you could have ever hoped was possible

You can believe it and you can walk in it. His kingdom is here!
Luke 1:8-22 NIV

January 25
Into Your arms

Into your hands I commit my spirit; deliver me, Lord, my faithful God.
Psalm 31:5 NIV

Andy Malone was the worship leader at Woodland Heights, the church in which my husband was youth pastor. He was also a seminary student. Andy and his baby boy died in a terrible fire in their home. His wife and older two boys lived. The boys were both very young also. We were always told that they found the baby lain across a threshold that went into another room. They speculated that Andy thought he was laying the baby outside the house into safety. In his confused, smoke ridden state he believed he was putting him in a place where he would be safe.

Recently I read the "The Divine Conspiracy" by Dallas Willard. While reading this book God very gently said to me. Andy was laying his baby in a safe place. I was there, he was handing him to me. I did rescue Andy and his baby. His baby was forever free and safe in my arms. Just as I was in the fire with Daniel, I was in the fire with Andy. Andy saw me and I reached out to him. He died in peace knowing I was there with him.

Thank you Father for this new picture of death. We are never alone!

When the perishable has been clothed with the imperishable, and the mortal with immortality, then the saying that is written will come true: "Death has been swallowed up in victory." "Where, O death, is your victory? Where, O death, is your sting?"
1 Corinthians 15:54-55 NIV

Death has no sting, only victory,

for those who know Him.

He loves you

January 26
He will free you

When I was hemmed in, Thou hast freed me often.
Psalm 4:1 KJV

During the Civil War, Abraham Lincoln, once said: "I have been driven many times to my knees by the overwhelming conviction that I had nowhere else to go. My own wisdom and that of all about me seemed insufficient for the day."

He can be trusted.
He will find a way for you
He will free you
Every time you feel yourself hemmed in
Remember He is the one that sets the captives free
He is the one that has gone before you
He is the one that defeats your enemies
He is the one that will bring you to freedom

So if the Son sets you free, you will be free indeed.
John 8:36

It is for freedom that Christ has set us free. Stand firm, then, and do not let yourselves be burdened again by a yoke of slavery.
Galatians 5:1

He loves you

January 27
I will lead you

I instruct you in the way of wisdom and lead you along straight paths.
When you walk, your steps will not be hampered; when you run, you will
not stumble. Hold on to instruction, do not let it go;
guard it well, for it is your life.
Proverbs 4:11-13 NIV

I will instruct you.
I will lead you.
When you walk, your steps will not be hampered
When you run, you will not stumble
Listen and hold on to His words
Guard them well
It is your life
Whether you walk or whether you run, you will be protected
He will lead you through it all
He has a path for you
You need only listen, walk and trust Him
He will always go with you.

January 28
He will not always plow

When a farmer plows for planting, does he plow continually? Does he keep on breaking up and working the soil? When he has leveled the surface, does he not sow caraway and scatter cumin? Does he not plant wheat in its place, barley in its plot, and spelt in its field? His God instructs him and teaches him the right way.   Isaiah 28:24-26 NIV

God will not always plow in your life.
He has a purpose behind His plowing.
He breaks up the dead and lifeless dirt of the heart.
He can then plant His seeds.
Seeds that produce life, abundant life.
He will not go on forever doing this.
He has a purpose.
His plan is wonderful.
His wisdom is magnificent.
One day you will look back and be amazed at the beautiful harvest that has come from your life.

January 29
Run the race with perseverance

Therefore, since we are surrounded by such a great cloud of witnesses, let us throw off everything that hinders and the sin that so easily entangles. And let us run with perseverance the race marked out for us, fixing our eyes on Jesus, the pioneer and perfecter of faith. For the joy set before him he endured the cross, scorning its shame, and sat down at the right hand of the throne of God.
Hebrews 12:1-2 NIV

The Cowtown Marathon is held each year in Fort Worth. We've lived in this area for many, many years and have never gone to watch the race. (Nor have we ever participated in it! I'm like the saying I read somewhere that 'if you ever see me running you better run too because a bear can't be too far behind'!). We went to cheer on three friends. My daughter and grandson made signs for their family member. One sign had the words, Tap Here to Power Up (with a Mario Button on it).
We clapped and cheered from the sidelines as the runners ran by. As I stood and watched I began to notice the faces of each runner. Each one was different. Each one was running their race in the way they had trained or in the way that they thought was best. (Now bear in mind we were at mile 19!! But they were much closer to the end than the beginning.) As I clapped I noticed some heads turned and smiled, some turned and thanked us, some could not look, they could only focus on what lay ahead, some tapped the sign and smiled, some even chatted with the runner beside them, and one looked at the sign and said, "No thanks, I've got the Lord and pointed up". It made me smile to see them smile. But it also made me emotional thinking about all the time and effort they had taken just to prepare for this race and now to run it. Some ran for different causes. The one we knew ran for his aunt who had been diagnosed with Alzheimer's, another lady was running her 292nd marathon and she had just completed chemotherapy for breast cancer! Amazing the strength and perseverance people have!
As I thought about all these different runners, I wondered. . . How many feel like they are running this 'race of life' alone or with little support or they are running to try and put their past behind them or they are running for the next big job or the next big medal? How many people in life have

never felt a pat on the back or a word of encouragement or sensed the love of someone.

My hope would be that as you run this 'race of life' that you would hear the cheers of others, that you would know the Father's love, that you would have the strength to finish the race. For those who know Jesus, there is a finish line! There is a reward at the end. The reward far outweighs anything you could have accomplished here on earth. It's a reward of life everlasting with the one who gave His all for you!

Everyone who competes in the games goes into strict training.
They do it to get a crown that will not last, but we do it
to get a crown that will last forever.
1 Corinthians 9:25 NIV

He loves you

January 30
Let the weary rest

God will speak to this people, to whom he said,
"This is the resting place, let the weary rest".
Isaiah 28:11 NIV

Let the weary rest.
God knows you are tired.
He knows you've fought this battle a long time.
He's seen you grow weary.
He knows that it's hard to stand, much less press on.
There will be a resting place for you.
He has designed it just for you.
He will restore your strength.
You will hope again.

The Lord will fight for you; you need only to be still."
Exodus 14:14 NIV

"Come to me, all you who are weary and burdened, and I will give you
rest. Take my yoke upon you and learn from me, for I am gentle and
humble in heart, and you will find rest for your souls. For my yoke is easy
and my burden is light."
Matthew 11:28-30 NIV

He loves you

January 31
He heals

He welcomed them and spoke to them about the kingdom of God,
and healed those who needed healing.
Luke 9:11 NIV

Our first baby was born via an emergency caesarean. We were young
and scared and like most couples, knew nothing about caring for a
baby. But we learned moment by moment or maybe I should say, cry by
cry or diaper by diaper, what she needed. After a few weeks of trying to
feed her I knew something wasn't right. She cried much. We finally
discovered she was allergic to my milk and she needed s special
formula. We changed to this formula and thought everything would be
better. But soon she began to get very sick. We learned she now had
pneumonia! My baby was only three months old and she had
pneumonia! She had to be hospitalized. They put her in this giant metal
baby bed and then placed an even bigger oxygen tent over the
bed. When the oxygen went in the bed I could barely see my tiny
baby. They said she had to have breathing treatments too. Each time
she did these treatments she cried, big cries but the nurses said that was
good because the more she cried the deeper she inhaled the medicine. It
was so hard for me to watch and hear. But I had to remind myself it was
all for her good.

After seven days we got to take our baby home. God had healed her and
we were so very thankful.
Sometimes you may have to go through some hard times but God will
give you the "medicine", the "treatment" you need to make you better, to
heal you.

Maybe you heart is hurt and need His love
Maybe you have an illness and need His healing
Maybe you have a scar from the past and need His touch

Whatever you need He has it for you.
And the best part is, it's free!   You only need ask Him.

February 1
That great shepherd of the sheep

Now may the God of peace, who through the blood of the eternal covenant brought back from the dead our Lord Jesus, that great Shepherd of the sheep, equip you with everything good for doing his will, and may he work in us what is pleasing to him, through Jesus Christ, to whom be glory for ever and ever. Amen.
Hebrews 13:20-21 NIV

My grandson recently went to New Zealand to visit his dad's family. His great granddad owns a sheep farm. While James was there he got to go in the sheep pen.
He loved it! His dad has told us about growing up around sheep.
He said they had two dogs that always herded the sheep. The dogs knew the exact sound to make to keep the sheep together. The sheep knew what that exact sound meant. They followed the sound of the dog's bark. The sheep trusted the dog. The dogs knew the sheep would follow them.

So it is with our shepherd, Jesus.
He is our great shepherd.
He leads us where we should go.
He knows us by name.
He knows everything about us.
He knows what is best for us.
He will equip us with everything good for doing His will.
He will work in us what is pleasing to Him.

He loves you

All we need to do is listen
for His voice and follow.
But you first have to
know His voice.

He loves you

February 2
You are a treasure

"The kingdom of heaven is like treasure hidden in a field. When a man found it, he hid it again, and then in his joy went and sold all he had and bought that field."   Matthew 13:44 NIV

My pastor, Robert Morris, spoke from this verse. He titled his message, "You are the treasure". He said the traditional meaning of this verse is that the kingdom is the treasure. That we find the treasure and we are to give everything to keep that treasure.

But in reality God found us. We can't buy it, it isn't for sale. We can't afford it. The new meaning is that the field is the world. The man is Jesus. The treasure is you. Jesus is the one that gave everything to buy it, the whole world.

Our sweet grandsons were at our house and we were all in the living room playing while this message was streaming on TV. We did not know it but our four-year-old grandson was listening to it. He said, "He found a treasure", to which I replied "You are that treasure."' I was on the floor with them and I hugged him and then I hugged our two-year-old grandson and said, "You are a treasure too." He quickly said, "Gandad a tweser. Mamae a tweser." Those six little words made me smile and melted my heart and gave me such hope. My grandsons heard! May they always realize what a treasure they are. Such a treasure that Jesus gave everything just for them.
Then I thought if a two year old and a four year old can understand this then why can't we?
God gave it all, His only son, just for you.

Don't listen to what the world says.
YOU are His treasure.
He gave it all just for YOU.
May you walk (and talk and move and breathe) in the realization of this incredible love that He has just for you.

For where your treasure is, there your heart will be also.
Matthew 6:21 NIV

He loves you

February 3
Show His Grace

But he said to me, "My grace is sufficient for you, for my power is made perfect in weakness. " Therefore I will boast all the more gladly about my weaknesses, so that Christ's power may rest on me.
2 Corinthians 12:9 NIV

His grace, the grace He bestows on us is not just a word,
or a one time act or a pat on the back
or a nod of the head or a few short words.

It is a lifestyle.
It is all consuming.
It leaves no one behind.
It cares for all.
It is extended to the happy as well as the hurting.
It never fails.
It never stops.
It is amazing.

All who experience it, really experience it,
never want to live without it.
They want to share this incredible grace with others.
They want others to know, really know
His amazing grace!

He loves you

Amazing Grace
John Newton 1779

"Amazing grace! How sweet the sound
That saved a wretch like me!
I once was lost, but now am found;
Was blind, but now I see.

'Twas grace that taught my heart to fear,
And grace my fears relieved;
How precious did that grace appear
The hour I first believed.

Through many dangers, toils and snares,
I have already come;
'Tis grace hath brought me safe thus far,
And grace will lead me home.

The Lord has promised good to me,
His Word my hope secures;
He will my Shield and Portion be,
As long as life endures.

Yea, when this flesh and heart shall fail,
And mortal life shall cease,
I shall possess, within the veil,
A life of joy and peace.

The earth shall soon dissolve like snow,
The sun forbear to shine,
But God, who called me here below,
Will be forever mine.

When we've been there ten thousand years,
Bright shining as the sun,
We've no less days to sing God's praise
Than when we'd first begun.

February 4
Press on

Not that I have already obtained all this, or have already arrived at my goal, but I press on to take hold of that for which Christ Jesus took hold of for me.   Philippians 3:12 NIV

Press on!
Take hold of what Christ has for you.
Reach out
Don't let it go
Forget what is behind
There is a new path ahead
Go for it
Press on
God has called you
He's gone before you on the path
He doesn't see what lies behind you
He only sees what is ahead, what He has planned for you
Press on!

February 5
In whom He believed

Against all hope, Abraham in hope believed and so became the father of many nations, just as it had been said to him, "So shall your offspring be."
Romans 4:18 NIV

In whom he believed

He believed in the God who gives life to the dead.

He believed in the God who calls into being things that were not.

Against all hope, Abraham in hope believed.
God's word became truth in his life.
Without weakening in his faith, he believed.
He did not waver in his faith.
But was rather strengthened in his faith.
He gave glory to God.
He knew God, really knew God.
He knew His God had the power to do what He had promised.
So it was credited to him as righteousness.

What do you believe your God has the power to do?

Do you know the God of Abraham?

If so, you can believe all of His promises.

You can know He will do what He has said.

Being fully persuaded that God had power to do what he had promised.
Romans 4:21

February 6
The place of His feet is glorious

So Moses thought, "I will go over and see this strange sight---why the bush does not burn up."
Exodus 3:3 NIV

"The incidents of which Jesus' work was made up are, humanly speaking, very humble and unpretentious. Human details fill the compass of His vast experience and work. He might have stilled a tempest every night. He could have walked upon the sea or flown over it, had the need existed. He could have transfigured Himself before Pilate and the astonished multitude in the Temple. He could have made visible ascensions at noon every day, had He been minded so to do.

The most faithful cannot compare with Jesus in lowliness of manner: He taught only one woman at Jacob's well; He noticed a finger-touch on the hem of His garment; He stooped to take little children up in his arms and bless them; even so small a thing as a cup of cold water, He said, would yield its recompense of a heavenly reward.

It may be on a kitchen floor,
Or in a busy shopping store,
Or teaching, nursing, day by day,
Till limb and brain almost give way;
"Yet if, just there, by Jesus thou art found,
The place thou stand on is Holy Ground.
M. COLLEY

I will make the place of my feet glorious," said the Lord. Be it never so rough, be it never so steep, be it never so miry—the place of His feet is glorious!"
(L. B. E. Cowman. "Springs in the Valley." July 13)

Where am I standing today?
Do I notice the touch?
Am I willing to teach just one?
Do I stop and take just one in my arms and bless them?
Have I given such a small thing as a cup of water?
These things will yield a heavenly reward

He sees
He knows
He is pleased

Always look to see where your feet are standing

When the Lord saw that he had gone over to look, God called to him from within the bush, "Moses! Moses!" And Moses said, "Here I am." "Do not come any closer," God said. "Take off your sandals, for the place where you are standing is holy ground."
Exodus 3:4-5

February 7
Do not be afraid, I am with you

That night the Lord appeared to him and said, "I am the God of your father Abraham. Do not be afraid, for I am with you; I will bless you and will increase the number of your descendants for the sake of my servant Abraham." Isaac built an altar there and called on the name of the Lord.
Genesis 26:24-25 NIV

When Isaac heard God speak it gave him hope.
He wanted to remember this place,
so he built an altar there.
He even pitched his tent in that very spot where God spoke to him.

Those places in which God speaks are comforting.

You will want to stop and stay awhile there.

You might even want to dwell there.

Others will see that God is with you.
You need not perform.
They will see that you are different.
They will see.

Do not be afraid, He is with you.

He loves you

February 8
He makes my feet like the feet of a deer

The Sovereign Lord is my strength; he makes my feet like the feet of a
deer, he enables me to tread on the heights.
Habakkuk 3:19 NIV

Animals that climb mountains have such agility.
They are able to climb to very steep heights, places where there are no
paths.
They know where their strength comes from.
They don't hesitate, they just climb.

He is your strength.

He makes your feet strong.

He makes your feet do things that would normally be impossible.

He makes it possible for you to climb to great heights.

He gives you the ability to do things you never dreamed you

could do.

He makes you stand and press on and climb every mountain.

The words from one of the songs from the movie,
"The Sound of Music" are:
"Climb every mountain
Forge every stream
Follow every rainbow
Until you find your dream"
"The Sound of Music" is such a great movie.
It's the perfect picture of God giving a family strength to do the impossible.
They did 'climb every mountain' until they found their freedom! They
forged a new path for their lives.
God gave them His strength. He will do the same for you.

February 9
His Voice

A spirit glided past my face, and the hair on my body stood on end. It stopped, but I could not tell what it was. A form stood before my eyes, and I heard a hushed voice: "Can a mortal be more righteous than God? Can a man be more pure than his Maker?"
Job 4:15-17

"Just as Elijah was spoken to by God in a "still, small voice" on Mount Horeb, Eliphaz the Temanite "heard a hushed voice" (Job 4:16). In other versions, "still small voice" (KJV) is translated "a gentle whisper" (NIV) and "a sound of sheer silence" (NRSV). Each expression places the emphasis on the unobtrusiveness of the way God communicated."
Hearing God by Dallas Willard week 19 day 5

A hushed voice

A still, small voice

A gentle whisper

A sound of sheer silence

God is such a gentleman.

He will never intrude.

He wants to speak to you but you have to be oh so still to hear Him.

He speaks in hushed whispers, in a still, small voice, in the sound of sheer silence.

Be still and listen.

You will hear His gentle whisper.

He loves you

February 10
His commands are not burdensome

This is how we know that we love the children of God: by loving God and carrying out his commands. In fact, this is love for God: to keep his commands. And his commands are not burdensome.
1 John 5:2-3 NIV

We carry out His commands if we love God.
This is love for God...to keep His commands.
His commands are not burdensome.

I never knew that.
It took me years to understand that His commands are not burdensome.
It has been so freeing.
I no longer have 'to do' just to be doing, I can just 'be'.

'Be' who He created you 'to be' and when you do that
His commands are a joy.
They are not what the world says you are 'to do' but
rather what God says you are 'to be'.

He loves you

February 11
We spread the aroma of Jesus

But thanks be to God, who always leads us as captives in Christ's triumphal procession and uses us to spread the aroma of the knowledge of him everywhere. For we are to God the pleasing aroma of Christ among those who are being saved and those who are perishing.
2 Corinthians 2:14-15 NIV

There are many different kinds of essential oils.
They are used for many different purposes. . .
For relief from pain, for soothing aching joints, for calming anxiety and stress, for peaceful sleep and on and on. Most of the oils have a pleasant aroma to them. They not only provide benefits but they also have a pleasing aroma.

We emit an aroma too.
Some people have pleasant aromas, people want to be around them.
Some people have aromas that are not pleasant, people do not want to be around them!
What aroma are you spreading?
Is it one that is pleasant to others?
Or is it an aroma that turns others away?
Does it prove beneficial or harmful to others?

The aroma of Jesus provides life and hope and health and healing.
Are you being used to spread His aroma?
Is the aroma that is being offered up to God by your life, pleasing to him? Does it draw others to Jesus?

May His aroma always be evident in our lives.

He loves you

February 12
The battle is not yours

He said: "Listen, King Jehoshaphat and all who live in Judah and Jerusalem! This is what the Lord says to you: 'Do not be afraid or discouraged because of this vast army. For the battle is not yours, but God's.
2 Chronicles 20:15 NIV

Jehoshaphat was king. He was responsible for the safety of his people. He had been warned about a vast army that was coming to attack his people. He was alarmed but knew what he must do first.
Pray and fast!
All the people came together to pray and fast.
The fathers and mothers and all the children and the babies.
Jehoshaphat proclaimed before the people who God was.
He also reminded God of how He had helped in the past.
He knew God was powerful and could defeat their enemies.
He knew they had no power on their own.
He knew they must keep their eyes on God.
He knew the battle was not theirs but Gods.

When you face a battle remember to pray first.

Remember who God is, The great I Am.

Remember what God has done for you in the past.

Remember the battle is not yours.

Remember God will fight for you.

You will one day rejoice in this victory.

Take some time to read about Jehoshaphat and this battle. Be encouraged as you read, that if God can do it for this king and his people then He can and will do it for you.

2 Chronicles 20:1-30

He loves you

February 13
His word is a treasure

For no matter how many promises God has made, they are "Yes" in
Christ. And so through him the "Amen" is spoken by us
to the glory of God.
2 Corinthians 1:20 NIV

When I was young I often dreamed of finding treasures.
These treasures were usually found in big houses.
In these big houses there were rooms that were hidden that I found that
contained many treasures.
I loved having these dreams.
I have loved looking for treasures, whether in an antique shop, an old junk
store or in my husband's grandparents house. The anticipation was such
fun.
In the last few years, God has shown me the purpose for those dreams.

His word is a treasure! The more I search it out, the more treasures I find.
These treasures have given me new life, new hope, new strength to go
on, new love, new joy and new purpose to live. I have found my true
identity in His word.
I love these precious treasures.

I love sharing these treasures with others,
May you find His treasures too!

He loves you

February 14
The word of God is alive and active

For the word of God is alive and active. Sharper than any double-edged
sword, it penetrates even to dividing soul and spirit, joints and marrow; it
judges the thoughts and attitudes of the heart.
Hebrews 4:12 NIV

The word of God is alive!
The power of His word is so much more powerful than we can
comprehend.
It continues to work in the hearts of man.
It never dies.

If only we could fully understand the power of the word of God.

The word of God is constantly at work.
It never returns void.
It always accomplishes what it was sent for!
It will achieve its purpose.

If you want to find hope for your life read His word.

It can and will do amazing things in and for you.

So is my word that goes out from my mouth: It will not return to me empty,
but will accomplish what I desire
and achieve the purpose for which I sent it.
Isaiah 55:11 NIV

He loves you

February 15
He loves to be gracious to you

Yet the Lord longs to be gracious to you; therefore he will rise up to show you compassion. For the Lord is a God of justice.
Blessed are all who wait for him!
Isaiah 30:18 NIV

He longs to be gracious to you.
He is deeply moved by you.
He will rise up.
He will show you compassion.
Wait for Him.
He is not slow, but He is very patient.
You will be blessed if you wait for Him.

Blessed are all who wait for Him.

The Lord is not slow in keeping his promise, as some understand slowness. Instead he is patient with you, not wanting anyone to perish, but everyone to come to repentance.
2 Peter 3:9 NIV

He loves you

February 16
Find out what pleases God

For you were once darkness, but now you are light in the Lord. Live as
children of light (for the fruit of the light consists in all goodness,
righteousness and truth) and find out what pleases the Lord.
Ephesians 5:8-10 NIV

You were once in darkness before you met Jesus.
Now you are in the light.
The fruit of the light is all goodness, all righteousness and all truth.
Find out what pleases God.
Do not have anything to do with the darkness.
Expose everything to the light.
Everything that is illuminated becomes a light,
a lamp, a candle, a torch.
These all need a match to illuminate them.
Will you be that match that illuminates the world?
Will you allow Christ to shine through you?

Take the time to find out what pleases God.

59

February 17
Make music from the heart

Speaking to one another with psalms, hymns, and songs from the Spirit.
Sing and make music from your heart to the Lord, always giving thanks to
God the Father for everything, in the name of our Lord Jesus Christ.
Ephesians 5:19-20 NIV

This world has become so cruel.
People speak to others so rudely.
With social media, Christians are often bashing other Christians.
The "light" they are sending out is not producing more light but rather
darkness.
Others are not being drawn to the source of all light, Jesus.

Wouldn't it be heavenly if every person would speak to one another with a
song from the Spirit.
These songs would give life and hope and peace, because that is who the
Spirit is.
He cannot put people down.
He can only love.

Are the words that you speak to others

ones that will edify?

Always try to make music from your heart.

Others will hear.

He loves you

February 18
To believe in order to see

I remain confident of this: I will see the goodness of the Lord
in the land of the living.
Psalm 27:13 NIV

*"Faith is to believe what we do not see, the reward for this faith is to see
what we believe."*
Saint Augustine

The world says: Seeing is believing.
God wants us to: Believe in order to see.

What do we miss each day by not believing?

If we but believe...

We will see the goodness of The Lord.

We will see His right hand at work everywhere.

We will see Him in all of creation:

When a bird sings

When a child laughs

When a flower blooms

When a tree sways in the wind

When a stranger smiles

Teach us to believe that we might see ALL that you have for us.

Then Jesus told him, "Because you have seen me, you have believed;
blessed are those who have not seen and yet have believed."
John 20:29 NIV

February 19
A refuge for His people

The Lord will roar from Zion and thunder from Jerusalem; the earth and the heavens will tremble. But the Lord will be a refuge for his people, a stronghold for the people of Israel.   Joel 3:16 NIV

He is our refuge, our ever-present help in times of trouble.

He is our stronghold. His fortress is secure for us.

He is our safe hiding place, the one who protects us from the enemy and the storms of life.

His safe place is like granite, unbending, immovable, solid as a rock.

We can always run to Him.

His safe place is always open for us.

"The sky turns black, sun and moon go dark, stars burn out. God roars from Zion, shouts from Jerusalem. Earth and sky quake in terror. But God is a safe hiding place, a granite safe house for the children of Israel. Then you'll know for sure that I'm your God, Living in Zion, my sacred mountain. Jerusalem will be a sacred city, posted: 'no trespassing.'
Joel 3:15-17 MSG

February 20
David led with skillful hands

He chose David his servant and took him from the sheep pens; from tending the sheep he brought him to be the shepherd of his people Jacob, of Israel his inheritance. And David shepherded them with integrity of heart; with skillful hands he led them.
Psalm 78:70-72 NIV

God chose David.
He took him from the sheep pens.
He took him from tending the sheep to shepherding His people.
Davis shepherded with integrity of heart.
With skillful hands he led them.

When God chose David He knew all the choices David would make before he made them.
Yet he still chose him to shepherd His people.
He knew about Bathsheba.
He knew David would have Bathsheba's husband killed.
God knew and yet He chose David.
He knew David's heart.
He called him a man of integrity!
What a gracious and forgiving God we serve.
Hc sees beyond all of our weaknesses.
He's knows the potential we have.

He will use us mightily if we will only allow Him.

God chose you.

He loves you

February 21
Before he finished praying

Before he had finished praying, Rebekah came out with her jar on her shoulder. She was the daughter of Bethuel son of Milkah, who was the wife of Abraham's brother Nahor.
Genesis 24:15 NIV

Before he finished praying...
Without saying a word, he watched her closely
To see if his journey was successful
He bowed down and worshiped The Lord
He praised and thanked God for his answer

The servant then retold all that God had done for him.
He testified of God's goodness and answer to his prayer.
Those listening knew he was from God and they could trust him.
They knew what he said was from God.

Before he finished praying,

God had already answered his prayer.

Before he finished praying

Genesis 24:1-67

He loves you

February 22
I am going to wake him up

After he had said this, he went on to tell them, "Our friend Lazarus has
fallen asleep; but I am going there to wake him up."
John 11:11 NIV

Such a beautiful picture of what God does when He sets us free.
We wake up
The grave clothes are taken off
We walk in freedom
Never to be the same again
To live forever with him
Total freedom in him

Just as God heard Jesus He hears you, every time!
You can have confidence in that.
And when He hears, He answers,
In miraculous ways
Setting a person free, forever free from the chains that have bound them
their whole life.
Free to walk in newness!
The grave clothes are taken off.
Forever free!

John 11:13-44

He loves you

February 23
Pray large prayers

Until now you have not asked for anything in my name. Ask and you will
receive, and your joy will be complete.
John 16:24 NIV

When the woman with the issue of blood touched the hem of Jesus
garment she was instantly healed.

Totally miraculously healed!

There was not a trace of her illness left. She believed and merely reached
out and touched the bottom of his garment.

What would happen if we didn't just touch the hem of His garment but we
totally embraced Him, all that He is, each time we prayed.

There is no limit to the possibilities of prayer!

Help us to embrace you God and pray large prayers.

And a woman was there who had been subject to bleeding
for twelve years, but no one could heal her.
She came up behind him and touched the edge of his cloak,
and immediately her bleeding stopped.
Luke 8:43-44

He loves you

February 24
I will watch for you

You are my strength, I watch for you; you, God, are my fortress.
Psalm 59:9 NIV

You are my strength.
I watch for you.
You are my fortress.
I will sing of your strength,
I will sing of your love.
You are my fortress.
You are my refuge in times of trouble.
You are my strength.
I will sing praise to you,
You are my fortress,
My God on whom I can rely.

I will watch for you.

Watch and wait but remember to look and listen.
Look for Him. He is all around you.
He is in the morning sunrise.
He is in the song of a bird.
He is in the laughter of a child.
He is in the setting of the sun.
He is all around you.
Watch for Him.

He loves you

February 25
How good and pleasant it is when God's people live together in unity

How good and pleasant it is when God's people live together in unity! It is
like precious oil poured on the head, running down on the beard, running
down on Aaron's beard, down on the collar of his robe.
Psalm 133:1-2 NIV

How good and pleasant it is when God's people live together in unity
It is like precious oil on the head.
So much oil that it runs down on the beard
Even down on the collar of his robe
It is if the dew of Hermon were falling on Mount Zion.
There you will find God's blessing,
Life evermore
When God's people live together in unity
How very good and pleasant it is!

Unity - being united or joined as a whole
How much unity do we see right now, in our world, in our country, in our
state, in our town, in our home?
There is so much division! When the people are divided they cannot
stand but when they are united they can stand.

There is such strength in unity.
God designed it to be that way.
It is refreshing.
It is life giving,
They will be blessed by God.
It pleases God!

It is as if the dew of Hermon were falling on Mount Zion. For there the
Lord bestows his blessing, even life forevermore.
Psalm 133:3 NIV

February 26
He is a sun and a shield

For the Lord God is a sun and shield; the Lord bestows favor and honor;
no good thing does he withhold from those whose walk is blameless.
Psalm 84:11 NIV

God is a sun.
He is a shield.
He bestows favor.
He bestows honor.
He withholds no good thing from those whose walk is blameless.
We are blameless because Jesus bore all our sin.
He is our light.
He protects us from the enemy.
He gives favor.
He shows honor.
He will not withhold anything good from you.
You need only walk in His truth and He will be the light for your path.

He loves you

February 27
There is no shame, your face is radiant

Those who look to him are radiant; their faces are never covered
with shame.
Psalm 34:5 NIV

Several years ago God told me to tell my story.
He said my face was no longer covered with shame.
So I say to you, if you've met Jesus then tell your story.
Your face is not covered with shame.
God has wiped away all your shame.
You are radiant in His eyes.
Thank God for what He has done.
Thank God for the ways He will use your story.

All your concerns about how your story will be received are now washed
away.
God has spoken to you in His very still, small voice.
It is not your concern how people receive your story, it is God's concern.
He will speak, you need only to be faithful to Him.
Thank you, Abba Father.

I sought the Lord, and he answered me; he delivered me
from all my fears.
Psalm 34:4 NIV

He loves you

February 28
He guides

Abide in me as I abide in you. Just as the branch cannot bear fruit by itself, unless it abides in the vine, neither can you unless you abide in me.
John 14:4 NIV

In "Take Another Look at Guidance', Bob Mumford writes: "God wants to bring us beyond the point where we need signs to discern His guiding hand. Satan cannot counterfeit the peace of God or the love of God dwelling in us. When Christ's abiding presence becomes our guide, then guidance becomes an almost unconscious response to the gentle moving of His Holy Spirit within us."

When you abide "it's like you are so in sync with Christ that his next movements are plain to you - and you immediately follow. Ask God to help you live that way."
(Excerpt from Hearing God by Dallas Willard week 23 day 4)

To abide - to stay, to dwell, to remain
When we abide in Him He becomes our dwelling place.
He becomes our home, the place where we find direction for our lives,
peace for today, hope for tomorrow.
The longer we remain in Him the more we want to live with Him.
He becomes our guide for everything.
He speaks and we follow.
We abide and He abides in us.
He always leads us.

He makes me lie down in green pastures, he leads me
beside quiet waters.
Psalm 23:2 NIV

He loves you

March 1
Yet He stayed two more days

Yet when he heard that Lazarus was sick, he stayed
where he was two more days.
John 11:6 NIV

*"What a startling word: "Yet"! Jesus refrained from going not because He
did not love them but because He did love them. It was His love alone that
kept Him from hurrying at once to their beloved yet grief-stricken home.
Only the power of divine love could have held back the spontaneity of the
Savior's tenderheartedness until the angel of pain had finished his work."*
(L. B. E. Cowman. "Springs in the Valley.")

So often my heart's cry is to rescue someone from their pain.
Yet, God has shown me that is not always the best thing for them.
Sometimes distance is what is needed so that they can become who You
created them to be. Children of virtue: compassion, love, perseverance,
hope, joy, peace, faithfulness, humility, and patience.
Help us to listen and know when to go and when to stay.

Yet He stayed two more days.
Thank you for the freedom in this for us.

It was that Mary who had anointed the Lord with ointment, and wiped his feet with her hair, whose brother, Lazarus, was sick. The sisters therefore sent to him, saying, "Lord, behold, he for whom you have great affection is sick." But when Jesus heard it, he said, "This sickness is not to death, but for the glory of God, that God's Son may be glorified by it." Now Jesus loved Martha, and her sister, and Lazarus. When therefore he heard that he was sick, he stayed two days in the place where he was.
John 11:2-6 WEB

An incredible story:
Mary the one who poured perfume on Jesus feet
God chose Mary and her sister Martha, to be the ones to witness their brother being raised from the dead
Jesus loved both Mary and Martha and Lazarus
He chose these three for God's glory
so that God's son would be glorified through them
They were chosen.

He loves you

March 2
Light is sweet

Light is sweet, and it pleases the eyes to see the sun.
Ecclesiastes 11:7 NIV

Light brings hope in a darkened world,
Light gives direction when you've lost your way.
Light reveals what is all around.

Light often means the storm is passing.

We vacationed on the island of St. John in the US Virgin Islands. We were to have left the island by ferry on Saturday. We knew a tropical storm, Bertha, had been forming in the ocean.

We found out Friday that it was to hit our island on Saturday.
In order to fly out on Saturday we had to take the ferry to the island of St. Thomas where the airport was. On Saturday morning, we were told the ferry was not running. There would be no way to get to the airport on the other island. We were there to stay.

As we waited and wondered what this storm would do, we watched the ocean and sky.
There was no light, the gray clouds covered the blue sky. The ocean began to have bigger and bigger waves. The palm trees began to sway and bend as the winds got stronger and stronger.
We felt we would be okay but we all were rather apprehensive about this storm and the damage it might do. Our neighbors began to close their shutters, covering their windows, protecting them from the power of the storm. We were thankful that the house we had rented was high up on the mountain and not down on the beach. We saw the powerful force of nature at work. We were blessed that our power did not go out. The storm lasted most of the day from the early hours of sunrise until late in the afternoon. The skies had been gray all day with no sunlight. Then we began to see just a little light break through the dark clouds.

The storm was passing!

The light was indeed sweet to see.
It was pleasing to our eyes to see the sun.
We knew we would be okay and that we would be able to leave the
island.

He loves you

March 3
He talks with me

I will listen to what God the Lord says; he promises peace to his people,
his faithful servants---but let them not turn to folly.
Psalm 85:8 NIV

*"Instead of each of us making a prayer-speech to Him, let's talk things
over with Him, including Him in it, as we do when we have a
conversation."*
(Hearing God by Dallas Willard week 24 day 1)

I love that I can talk things over with God.
He loves to talk with me.

The words from an old hymn, "He Walks with Me", say it all:

"He talks with me and He walks with me,

He tells me I am a His own and

The joy we feel as we tarry here

None other has ever known."

Thank you Father that you enjoy talking with us!

This is the confidence we have in approaching God: that if we ask
anything according to His will, He hears us. And if we know that He hears
us, whatever we ask, we know that we have what we asked of Him.
1 John 5:14-15 NIV

He loves you

March 4
We can escape this world

His divine power has given us everything we need for a godly life through
our knowledge of him who called us by his own glory and goodness.
Through these he has given us his very great and precious promises, so
that through them you may participate in the divine nature, having
escaped the corruption in the world caused by evil desires.
2 Peter 1:3-4 NIV

His divine power has given us everything we need
Through our knowledge of Him
He called us by His own glory and goodness

He has given us His very great and precious promises.
So that through them we may participate in His divine nature.
Because of them we can escape the corruption of this world
Caused by evil desires.

His power has given us everything we need.
So that we can escape this corrupt world
We *can* escape this world

The enemy tries to lure us with his many lies.
Constantly berating us, telling us we are nothing,
We will never be enough, we will never find happiness
There is no hope, it will always be like this.

Many hear these voices.
They cannot get past them.
They were always there.

Yet there is an answer for each of us.
A very gentle, kind, loving voice
A whisper of a voice
A voice that longs to rescue us from the madness and despair

He loves you

March 5
All my longings lie open before You

All my longings lie open before you, Lord; my sighing is not hidden from
you. My heart pounds, my strength fails me; even the light
has gone from my eyes.
Psalm 38:9-10 NIV

God knows your every longing.
He hears your every sigh.
He knows every beat of your heart.
He knows when your strength is gone.
He knows when your eyes have grown dim and all hope seems lost.
He knows all of this.

Yet, He wants to fulfill those longings.
He desires to comfort your sighings.
He wants to keep your heart from pounding.
He longs to put the light back in your eyes.

He wants to give joy to your heart.

He wants to be your all.

He will restore the light for you.

The precepts of the Lord are right, giving joy to the heart. The commands
of the Lord are radiant, giving light to the eyes.
Psalm 19:8 NIV

He loves you

March 6
Strengthening and encouraging them to remain true to their faith

Strengthening the disciples and encouraging them to remain true to the faith. "We must go through many hardships to enter the kingdom of God," they said.   Acts 14:22 NIV

"If you aspire to be a person of consolation, if you want to share the priestly gift of sympathy, if you desire to go beyond giving commonplace comfort to a heart that is tempted, and if you long to go through the daily exchanges of life with the kind of tact that never inflicts pain, then you must be prepared to pay the price for a costly education—for like Christ, you must suffer."
Frederick William Robertson

Frederick William Robertson only lived 37 years but in those 37 years He lived, really lived, for Christ.

Aspire to be that person.
The one who consoles.
The one who gives sympathy.
The one who encourages when someone is tempted.
The one who listens but never inflicts pain.
The one who is willing to suffer for another's sake.
Always strengthening and encouraging them to remain true to the faith.

*To console, to sympathize, to comfort and to listen
these are what God desires for us,
His children, to do. Not in our own strength but in His.*

So many in this world are hurting.
So many in this world are dying.
So many in this world have lost their hope.
So many in this world just need someone to listen.
He loves you

March 7
He knows our steps

A person's steps are directed by the Lord. How then can anyone understand their own way?
Proverbs 20:24 NIV

There is such freedom in this truth.
He knows our steps,
He directs our steps.

We need only follow.
We don't have to figure it all out.
We don't have to understand it.
We don't have to know what lies ahead,
We don't have to know what tomorrow holds.

We need only know that He knows.

We can trust Him with all our tomorrows.

He is there for you.
He will always be there for you.

He stilled the storm to a whisper, the waves of the sea were hushed. They were glad when it grew calm, and He guided them to their desired haven.
Psalm 107:29-30

He loves you

He loves you

March 8
Find your purpose

Moses said to the Lord, "Pardon your servant, Lord. I have never been eloquent, neither in the past nor since you have spoken to your servant. I am slow of speech and tongue."
Exodus 4:10 NIV

"Find your purpose and fling your life out into it; and the loftier your purpose is, the more sure you will be to make the world richer with every enrichment of yourself."
Phillip Brooks

Moses' thinking while he's talking to God:
"Pardon your servant, Lord!
In case you don't remember God
I have never been eloquent when I talk, in the past or now.
Did you not hear me when I spoke to you God?
I am slow of speech and tongue.
I hear myself and many others have told me this.
There must be some mistake here, God do you know who I am?"

The Lord's reply:
"Who gave you your mouth, Moses?
Who makes people deaf or mute?
Who gives them sight or makes them blind?
Am I not the one?
Enough said, Moses.
I am God, I created you, I know you, I chose you.

Now go!
I will help you speak, Moses,
I will teach you what to say.

I know you.

I knit you together in your mother's womb.
I held you while you floated down the Nile to your new home.

I know the plans I have for you.
Trust me in this.
I will speak through you,
I will teach you what to say.
You need only to trust Me."

Find your purpose.
Fling your life into it,
The loftier your purpose
The more sure you will be to make the world richer
With every enrichment of yourself

Find your purpose
Put everything into it
Go for the gold
The world will be a richer place
Because you have given your all

C. S. Lewis, the great man of God who wrote "The Chronicles of Narnia" and so many other incredible works, said,

"The question is not what we intended ourselves to be, but what He intended us to be whcn He made us."

Find your purpose

He loves you

March 9
Give what you have

And if anyone gives even a cup of cold water to one of these little ones
who is my disciple, truly I tell you, that person will certainly
not lose their reward.
Matthew 10:42 NIV

*"What shall I do? I expect to pass through this world but once. Therefore
any good work, kindness, or service I can render to any person or animal,
let me do it now. Let me not neglect or delay to do it,
for I will not pass this way again."*
an old Quaker saying

*"Give what you have, for you never know—to someone else it may be
better than you can even dare to think."*
Henry Wadsworth Longfellow

Give what you can.
A touch
A kind word
A scripture
A smile
A hug
A song

Whatever you give, give in Jesus name
You will never know the far- reaching results it will have.

God sees every touch, every kind word, every sharing of
scripture, and every smile.
He loves you

God is not unjust; he will not forget your work and the love you have
shown him as you have helped his people and continue to help them.
Hebrews 6:10 NIV

March 10
God met with him

God met with him, and Balaam said, "I have prepared seven altars, and on each altar I have offered a bull and a ram." The Lord put a word in Balaam's mouth and said, "Go back to Balak and give him this word."
Numbers 23:4-5 NIV

God met with Balaam.
The Lord put a word in his mouth.
The Lord said now go back and give Balak this word.

God loves to meet with you,
He loves to talk with you.
He loves spending time with you.
You only need to be still and listen.
He may give you a word just for you.
Or He may give you a word for someone else.
Your job is to just be still and listen.
So often people think that God only gives words of rebuke or correction.
But the opposite is so true.

His words are gentle and kind, filled
with such love and encouragement.
Listen, do you hear Him?

He was oppressed and afflicted, yet he did not open his mouth; he was led like a lamb to the slaughter, and as a sheep before its shearers is silent, so he did not open his mouth.
Isaiah 53:7

He loves you

March 11
Sorrowful, yet always rejoicing

Sorrowful, yet always rejoicing, poor, yet making many rich; having nothing, and yet possessing everything.
2 Corinthians 6:10

"Sorrow was beautiful, but his beauty was the beauty of the moonlight shining through the leafy branches of the trees in the woods. His gentle light made little pools of silver here and there on the soft green moss of the forest floor. And when he sang, his song was like the low, sweet calls of the nightingale, and in his eyes was the unexpectant gaze of someone who has ceased to look for coming gladness. He could weep in tender sympathy with those who weep, but to rejoice with those who rejoice was unknown to him.
Joy was beautiful, too, but hers was the radiant beauty of a summer morning. Her eyes still held the happy laughter of childhood, and her hair glistened with the sunshine's kiss. When she sang, her voice soared upward like a skylark's, and her steps were the march of a conqueror who has never known defeat. She could rejoice with anyone who rejoices, but to weep with those who weep was unknown to her.

Sorrow longingly said, "We can never be united as one, "No, never," responded Joy, with eyes misting as she spoke, "for my path lies through the sunlit meadows, the sweetest roses bloom when I arrive, and songbirds await my coming to sing their most joyous melodies."
"Yes, and my path," said Sorrow, turning slowly away. "leads through the dark forest, and moonflowers, which open only at night, will fill my hands. Yet the sweetest of all earthly songs— the love song of the night—will be mine. So farewell, dear Joy, farewell."

Yet even as Sorrow spoke, he and Joy became aware of someone standing beside them. In spite of the dim light, they sensed a kingly Presence, and suddenly a great and holy awe overwhelmed them. They then sank to their knees before Him.
"I see Him as the King of Joy," whispered Sorrow, "for on His head are many crowns, and the nail prints in His hands and feet are the scars of a great victory. And before Him all my sorrow is melting away into deathless

love and gladness. I now give myself to Him forever."

"No, Sorrow," said Joy softly, "for I see Him as the King of Sorrow, and the crown on His head is a crown of thorns, and the nail prints in His hands and feet are the scars of terrible agony. I also give myself to Him forever, for sorrow with Him must be sweeter than any joy I have ever known."

"Then we are one in Him," they cried in gladness, "for no one but He could unite Joy and Sorrow. "Therefore they walked hand in hand into the world, to follow Him through storms and sunshine, through winter's severe cold and the warmth of summer's gladness, and to be "sorrowful, yet always rejoicing."
(Streams in the Desert by L.B.E. Cowman August 19)

He is the king of joy for on His head are many crowns.
The nail prints in His hands are the scars of a great victory.
All your sorrow is melted away into love and gladness.
He is the king of sorrow for on his head is the crown of thorns.
The nail prints in his hands are the scars of terrible agony.
Sorrow with him is sweeter than any joy you will ever know.

We are one in Him.
He is the only one that can unite joy and sorrow.
Hand in hand, sorrowful, yet always rejoicing.

God has seen every tear you've ever shed.

He has seen every smile.

He knows you. He loves you.

No matter where you are, either in the valley of sorrow

or on the mountaintop of joy He is there with you.

He will never, ever leave you or forsake you.

Sorrow will flee.

Joy will come in the morning.

March 12
The power of the word

Where the word of a king is, there is power.
Ecclesiastes 8:4 KJV

Dallas Willard wrote in his book Hearing God:
"The phrase "still, small voice" might seem to suggest that what lies at the heart of a relationship with God is something weak and marginal. But that is far from the truth. One who hears God's voice is operating from the foundation and framework of all reality, not from the fringe.

This is true because God uses the words of his voice to do the work of creating, of ruling and of redeeming. To hear the words of God's voice is to be in relationship with God as a colaborer in the work of creating, ruling and redeeming."
(Hearing God week 24 day 6)

The words of God's voice create, rule and redeem.
When you listen you will hear the words of God's voice
if you are in a relationship with Him.
You are a colaborer with God when you use His words.
He is the one that gives power through His words.
We are the conduit that His power passes through
for creating, ruling and redeeming.
Don't you want to be the one who helps to pass the life on to others?

There is nothing more lasting or far-reaching than to know you have given hope.

For the word of God is alive and active. Sharper than any double-edged sword, it penetrates even to dividing soul and spirit, joints and marrow.
Hebrews 4:12 NIV

He loves you

March 13
You brought me to a spacious place

He brought me out into a spacious place; he rescued me
because he delighted in me.
Psalm 18:19

"What is this "spacious place"? What can it be but God Himself—the
infinite Being through whom all other beings find their source and their end
of life? God is indeed a "spacious place." And it was through humiliation,
degradation, and a sense of worthlessness that David was taken to it."
Madame Guyon

He brought you to a spacious place.
He rescued you because he delighted in you.

God has a spacious place for you.
He delights in you.
He loves to bless you.

Sometimes the road to this 'spacious' place may be difficult at
times. There may be humiliation or loss but He will always take you there.

This spacious place is good.

It is good to remain there.

It is good and pleasant place.

It will become your forever home.

He will be there with you.

He loves you

March 14
God will provide an escape

The soldiers planned to kill the prisoners to prevent any of them from swimming away and escaping. But the centurion wanted to spare Paul's life and kept them from carrying out their plan. He ordered those who could swim to jump overboard first and get to land. The rest were to get there on planks or on other pieces of the ship. In this way everyone reached land safely.   Acts 27:42-44 NIV

The rest were to get there on planks or other pieces of the ship....
In this way everyone reached land safely.
God did send a "life jacket" for them, just as He did for you.
When we are struggling the most
And all hope for survival seems gone. . .
Then we must relax and look for our "plank or pieces of the ship" to hold on to.
God will provide a way of escape.
Look for it. Grab it. Hold on to it.
Relax in His anchor
He will never fail you.
You will be forever secure in Him.

March 15
God can change a person

And Saul approved of their killing him. On that day a great persecution
broke out against the church in Jerusalem, and all except the apostles
were scattered throughout Judea and Samaria. Godly men buried
Stephen and mourned deeply for him. But Saul began to destroy the
church. Going from house to house, he dragged off both men and women
and put them in prison.
Acts 8:1-3 NIV

Saul approved of the stoning of Stephen.
Saul...who later became Paul.
Saul began to destroy the church.
He had Christian men and women put in prison.
He dragged them, men and women, from their homes.
He did not know Jesus.
He believed what he was doing was right.
Follow the law they said!
He knew it well, too well.

Yet, God met Saul and he became Paul,

in the midst of all of this and

he was forever changed, forever!

God can meet even the vilest offender and

change them forever.

We must never forget that!

March 16
The heavens declare

The heavens declare the glory of God; the skies proclaim the work of his hands. Day after day they pour forth speech; night after night they display knowledge. There is no speech or language where their voice is not heard. Their voice goes out into all the earth,
their words to the ends of the world.
Psalm 19:1-4 NIV

Dallas Willard wrote in his book "Hearing God"...
"The word of God is God speaking and communicating. When God speaks, he expresses his mind, his character and his purposes. Thus he is always present with his word.

But words of God are more than "words," as we think of them. All expressions of God's mind are "words" of God. Anything God does to express his mind are "words" of God. This is true whether God uses things that are outside the human mind (as in natural phenomena expressed in Psalm 19:1-4, other human beings, the incarnate Christ - the Logos - or the Bible) or inside the human mind (our own thoughts, intentions and feelings). God creates, rules and redeems through these words."
(Hearing God by Dallas Willard week 25 day 5)

When I look at a sunset now I see God speak.
He is the creator of all.
The amazing thing is He loves to speak to us His children.
Whether it's through a beautiful sunset or a bird singing or a perfect flower.
He spoke it all into existence for us, for our good pleasure.
What a loving God! He loves to bless us!

He loves you

March 17
God uses us

In Damascus there was a disciple named Ananias. The Lord called to him
in a vision, "Ananias!" "Yes, Lord," he answered.
Acts 9:10 NIV

Ananias was a disciple of Jesus.
The Lord called to him in a vision.
He answered, he knew who was speaking to him.
He was familiar with God's voice.
Ananias knew who Saul was,
He reminded God of what Saul had done to the Christians.

But God said go!
So Ananias obeyed, he went.
He even put his hands on Saul.
He told Saul about who he had seen.
He prayed for Saul that he would see and that he would be filled with the
Holy Spirit.
Immediately scales fell from Saul's eyes.
Immediately Saul could see.
Immediately Saul got up.
Immediately Saul was baptized.
Immediately Saul became Paul, a new creature in Christ.
Immediately!

Ananias obeyed and Saul was forever changed!

Sometimes God may call us to do what seems impossible. The enemy
may whisper to us that it will never work. He may even try to cause fear
and doubt to enter in. But one thing is for sure, if God has told us to do it,
His power will be made evident in our lives.

Allow God to use you! You will never regret it.

He loves you

March 18
To see, to hear, to speak His words

The angel of the Lord came and sat down under the oak in Ophrah that
belonged to Joash the Abiezrite, where his son Gideon was threshing
wheat in a winepress to keep it from the Midianites. When the angel of the
Lord appeared to Gideon, he said, "The Lord is with you, mighty warrior."
Judges 6:11-12 NIV

The angel of The Lord came and sat down under an oak tree. The tree
belonged to Gideon's family.
The Lord immediately spoke to Gideon, words of encouragement.
Gideon's reply was, "If God is with us, why has all this bad happened to
us? Why has God abandoned us?"
God told Gideon he was to be the one to save his people.
Gideon only saw himself through his own eyes, the least in his family, and
his family as the weakest.
Yet God saw him as a mighty warrior. There is a difference in looking
through God's eyes versus our own eyes.

Gideon asked for a sign to confirm what God had said.
God graciously gave him a sign.
Gideon knew he had seen God face to face!
God spoke "Peace" over him. Gideon received that and called that place
(where he built an altar) "The Lord is Peace".

We need to be like Gideon:
To see as God's sees
To hear what God speaks
To receive and believe what God speaks
To walk in faith and stand on His words

God sees you so differently than you see yourself.
He sees you as a mighty warrior!
You can walk in that truth today.
Judges 6:11-24

March 19
Just believe

While Jesus was still speaking, some people came from the house of Jairus, the synagogue leader. "Your daughter is dead," they said. "Why bother the teacher anymore?" Overhearing what they said, Jesus told him, "Don't be afraid; just believe."
Mark 5:35-36 NIV

Jesus heard what the others said. He knew Jarius heard it too.
Jesus didn't want their words to cause fear for Jarius about his daughter.

Jesus comforted with His words, as only He can.
Don't be afraid!
Just believe!

Don't believe what others say
Don't let fear take hold of you
Just believe!

Believe in the one who raised His son from the dead

Believe in this same power that is available

for you today

Just believe!

He loves you

March 20
He is infinite in . . .

Great is our Lord and mighty in power; his understanding is infinite.
Psalm 147:5 NIV

There is no limit with God.
He is infinite (without limit or restriction) in:
Understanding
Power
Creativity
Love
Joy
Hope
Wisdom
Knowledge
Mercy
Grace
Compassion
Strength

He never grows weary.

His love never fails.

His mercies are new every morning.

All that you need He is....today, tomorrow and forever!

The steadfast love of the Lord never ceases. His mercies never come to
an end. They are new every morning, great is your faithfulness.
Lamentations 3:22-23 ESV

He loves you

March 21
He took him aside

He took him aside, away from the crowd.
Mark 7:33 NIV

"To see Paul in prison is to see another side of life. Have you noticed how he handled it? He seemed to be looking over the top of his prison wall and over the heads of his enemies. Through it all, he saw only the hand of God at work. To him, the prison became a palace, with its corridors resounding with shouts of triumphant praise and joy.

Forced from the missionary work he loved so well, Paul built a new pulpit—a new witness stand. And from his place of bondage arose some of the most encouraging and helpful ministries of Christian liberty. What precious messages of light came from the dark shadows of his captivity.

Also think of the long list of saints who have followed in the footsteps of Paul and were imprisoned for their faith. For twelve long years, John Bunyan's voice was silenced in an English jail in Bedford. Yet it was there he wrote the greatest work of his life, Pilgrim's Progress—read by more people than any other book except the Bible. He once said, "I was at home in prison, and my great joy led me to sit and write and write." And the darkness of his long captivity became a wonderful dream to light the path of millions of weary pilgrims."
(Streams in the Desert by L. B. Cowman August 27)

He took him aside.
If you've ever been in a place of darkness you were never alone. He was always with you. Sometimes those are the places we can hear Him the best. In the quietness we can hear His gentle whispers.

"Be still and know that I am God." He will give you a song in the night.

He loves you

March 22
You need only ask

Then Moses led Israel from the Red Sea and they went into the Desert of
Shur. For three days they traveled in the desert without finding water.
When they came to Marah, they could not drink its water because it was
bitter. So the people grumbled against Moses, saying, "What are we to
drink?" Then Moses cried out to the Lord, and the Lord showed him a
piece of wood. He threw it into the water, and the water
became fit to drink.
Exodus 15:22-25 NIV

The Israelites had just seen an incredible miracle - God had parted the
waters of the Red Sea. The Israelites walked through as God held the
waters up!!! It must have been such an amazing sight!

After this Moses led them into the desert, where for three days they
traveled with no water. They began to grumble against Moses, their
leader, God's chosen one.
They had just seen God rescue them from their enemy, using His power
to part the waters. Yet three days later they are grumbling again! What
they wanted, water, they had just seen in abundance. Was it too hard for
them to remember just three days prior how God had rescued them? If
He could part the Red Sea, could he not provide water for them to
drink? Could it be they only needed to stop and ask? And that is what
Moses did and God changed what was once bitter water to refreshing
drinking water. The provision was there all along they just needed to
ask.

Then they came to Elim, where there were twelve springs and seventy
palm trees, and they camped there near the water.
Exodus 15:27 NIV

God led them to a place to camp, where there was an abundance of
springs with fresh water.
And He gave them shade, abundant shade! God will provide, you need
only ask!

March 23
He will guide you to your desired haven

Then they cried out to the Lord in their trouble, and he brought them out of
their distress. He stilled the storm to a whisper; the waves of the sea were
hushed. They were glad when it grew calm,
and he guided them to their desired haven.
Psalm 107:28-30 WEB

Two years ago I thought I might die. We were on the island of St. John
and we decided to swim out to a very small island to snorkel. I got caught
in a very strong current and fear began to engulf me and I began to panic.
Yet God were there. The waves began to get bigger and the current was
so strong, much stronger than I was. I could not get the attention of my
husband. I called his name four times but his head was under water and
he could not hear me. He was swimming farther and farther away. He
was the only one that would save me, I thought. Then I remembered I did
have my little belt on that was to help me float. My head was staying
above water. I could breathe. I was not going to drown but the current was
carrying me away in the wrong direction and I could not get out of it.
Finally my husband heard my cry and he swam to me. He pulled me to
safer waters where I could touch the rocks on the island. There were
barnacles sticking out of the rocks. I did not care if I cut myself all I wanted
was to hold on to the rock. I knew the rock was secure, even with the
waves lapping all around and the current pulling me away I knew the rock
would not move.
We rested on the rock and then swam to the sandy beach on the other
side of the island. It was an adventure! One that I am thankful I did but
probably will never do again!

God is that way. He is your rock. He never moves. He is always secure.
He is your firm foundation. The waves of life may try to swallow you, the
currents may try to take you away but our rock is always there. God will
provide lifesavers along the way too. We can trust them too. Get close
to those you know that walk with God. They will be there for you to give
you a hand or a kind word of encouragement or a little push in the right
direction.

Thank you Father for showing us that we are stronger than we think we are. We really can do "all things through Christ who strengthens us".

"Remember, our faith is always at its greatest point when we are in the middle of the trial, and confidence in the flesh will never endure testing. Fair-weather faith is not faith at all."
Charles H. Spurgeon

God will bring you out of your distress and He will guide you to your desired haven. You can trust Him.

Psalm 107:23-27 NIV
Some went out on the sea in ships; they were merchants on the mighty waters. They saw the works of the Lord, his wonderful deeds in the deep. For he spoke and stirred up a tempest that lifted high the waves. They mounted up to the heavens and went down to the depths; in their peril their courage melted away. They reeled and staggered like drunkards; they were at their wits' end.

He loves you

March 24
He sent out His word
He sent out his word and healed them; he rescued them from the grave.
Psalm 107:20 NIV

He sent out His word. He healed them. He rescued them from the grave.
God in His infinite mercy wants to do this in your life. He wants to heal you
of all your pain and hurt. He wants to sit with you to encourage you. He
loves you so!

He loves you

March 25
He will reveal Himself to you

Thomas answered him, "My Lord and my God!" Jesus said to him,
"Because you have seen me, you have believed. Blessed are those who
have not seen, and have believed."
John 20:28-29 WEB

When we believe He shows us more and more of Himself.
He revealed Himself to Thomas in a physical way so that Thomas would
believe. He reveals Himself to us in so many ways:
Through His creation
Through the smile of a baby
Through the freshly picked flower of a child
Through the sunset with a million shades of orange
Through the whisper of His voice
Be still and watch and listen. He will reveal Himself to you!

March 26
His hand is strong

The Lord makes firm the steps of the one who delights in him; though he may stumble, he will not fall, for the Lord upholds him with his hand.
Psalm 37:23-24 NIV

He makes our steps firm if we delight in Him.

We may stumble, but we will not fall.
He will uphold us with His hand.

Just as a child is learning to walk, he stretches out his hand to come to you.
He is afraid to do it on his own
But he knows with your help he can do it.
He completely trusts you.

Our God is the same.

He longs for you to come to him.

His hand is strong!

Become like a child!

He loves you

He loves you

March 27
His word will accomplish its purpose

"For my thoughts are not your thoughts, neither are your ways my ways,"
declares the LORD. "As the heavens are higher than the earth, so are my
ways higher than your ways and my thoughts than your thoughts. As the
rain and the snow come down from heaven, . . . so is my word that goes
out from my mouth: It will not return to me empty, but will accomplish what
I desire and achieve the purpose for which I sent it."
Isaiah 55:8-11 NIV

Words from "Hearing God" by Dallas Willard. . .
*"The word of God is characterized by overwhelming power, whether it is
manifested in nature or in the incarnate Christ. Words of God are the
expression of God's thoughts, which are as high above mere human
thoughts as the heavens are above the earth. The power of the word
coming out of God's mouth is like the powerful forces of nature - the rain
and seed bringing forth plants, seed and bread to nourish the hungry
(55:10). No wonder these words will accomplish what God desires!"*
(Hearing God by Dallas Willard week 27 day 1)

His word created the whole world.
He spoke and it came to be.
His word brought life from the dust.
He spoke and man was formed.
His word brought water from rock.
He spoke and water gushed forth.
His word brought protection from the fire.
He spoke and they were not burned.
His word brought life evermore for all that would believe.
He spoke and Jesus arose from the dead.

*His word will always accomplish what He desires.
It will never return void! Never!*

He loves you

March 28
He met them where they were

Immediately he made his disciples get into the boat, and to go ahead to
the other side, to Bethsaida, while he himself sent the multitude
away. Seeing them distressed in rowing, for the wind was contrary to
them, about the fourth watch of the night he came to them, walking on the
sea, and he would have passed by them, for they all saw him, and were
troubled. But he immediately spoke with them, and said to them, "Cheer
up! It is I! Don't be afraid." He got into the boat with them; and the wind
ceased, and they were very amazed among themselves, and marveled.
Mark 6:45, 48, 50-51 WEB

Jesus made his disciples get in the boat.
He stayed to dismiss the crowd. The disciples obeyed.

They were tired, they had just fed 5,000 people.
Jesus knew they were tired so He made them get into the boat away from
the crowd. To a place of solitude on the water.

Jesus went to pray alone.
Later that night Jesus saw the disciples straining at the oars. The wind
was against them and He knew they were tired. Jesus went to them,
walking on the water. But they did not recognize Him. They were scared.

He spoke to them. He even identified Himself.
He spoke words of encouragement to them.
He even climbed into the boat with them.
They were amazed.

He met them where they were.

Jesus will do the same for you.

He knows when you are tired. He knows the work you've done. He will
provide a place of rest for you. He will speak words of encouragement to
you. He will even "climb into the boat with you".

He loves you

March 29
It is good to praise

Lord, our Lord, how majestic is your name in all the earth! You have set
your glory in the heavens. Through the praise of children and infants you
have established a stronghold against your enemies,
to silence the foe and the avenger.
Psalm 8:1-2 NIV

*"There is a legend of a man who found the barn where Satan kept his
seeds ready to be sown in the human heart, and on finding the seeds of
discouragement more numerous than others, learned that those seeds
could be made to grow almost anywhere. When Satan was questioned he
reluctantly admitted that there was one place in which he could never get
them to thrive. "And where is that?" asked the man. Satan replied sadly,
"In the heart of a grateful man."*
*The Psalmist realized that gratitude plays an essential part in true
worship. He sang praises to God at all times; often, in his darkest
moments. When in his despair he called on God, his praises soon mingled
with his cries of anguish, showing the victory accomplished by his habitual
thankfulness.*
Sometimes a light surprises the Christian while he sings."
(Excerpt From: L. B. E. Cowman. "Springs in the Valley." September 3)

Sometimes it seems hard to praise.
The world seems so dark at times.
Everywhere we look there are bad things happening.
There is disease and famine and terror and yet God is here.
He has not left us alone.
His light still shines in the darkness.
We can make that light continue to shine in us through praise.

Praise opens up a place for the light to come in.

It may only be as bright as a candle at first but God will honor our attempts
and light will eventually break forth.

He loves you

March 30
He remains the same

You will roll them up like a robe; like a garment they will be changed. But
you remain the same, and your years will never end."
Hebrews 1:12 NIV

God remains the same.
His years will never end.
He is the same yesterday.
He is the same today.
He will be the same forever.

He never changes.
His love for you never changes.
His thoughts of you never change.

He has good thoughts about you.
He knows you like no one else ever has.
He loves you like no one else ever will.

There is no limit to God.

He was and is and always will be.

He remains the same.

Jesus Christ is the same yesterday and today and forever.
Hebrews 13:8 NIV

He loves you

March 31
The strength of iron

Thou hast enlarged me when I was in distress.
Psalm 4:1 KJV

People often say, "I know what you are going through." As I've grown older I've realized how sometimes shallow these words can be. The only way we can really relate to others suffering is by going through pain ourselves.

These words by George Matheson are so good.
"If you want your sympathy for others to be enlarged, you must be willing to have your life narrowed to certain degrees of suffering. Joseph's dungeon was the very road to his throne, and he would have been unable to lift the iron load of his brothers had he not experienced the iron in his own life. Do not say that the darkness of the prison has shackled you, for your shackles are wings—wings of flight into the heart and soul of humanity. And the gate of your prison is the gate into the heart of the universe. God has enlarged you through the suffering of sorrow's chain."

"If Joseph had never been Egypt's prisoner, he would have never been Egypt's governor. The iron chain that bound his feet brought about the golden chain around his neck."
("Streams in the Desert" L.B. Cowman September 8)

How often I have pleaded with God to take some difficulty away. I did it when two of my children had very difficult brain issues. One with a brain cyst and one with a malignant brain tumor. Yet God did not take this away but rather he made us all stronger through it. We each became different people because of what we went through. He gave us wings to fly above all of this.
He used these dark times to give us a heart of compassion and understanding for others. We can truly say, the iron chain that bound us has become for us, our nuggets of gold that we can give away to others.

You intended to harm me but God meant it for good.
Genesis 50:20

April 1
He can do the impossible

Then Moses raised his arm and struck the rock twice with his staff.
Water gushed out, and the community and their livestock drank.
Numbers 20:11 NIV

God spoke face to face with Moses.
Moses heard God speak.
God spoke the words the people needed to hear.
God would provide for their needs.
God told Moses what to say to provide the water.
Moses spoke and the water came forth from the rock.
Miraculous water, abundant water, water to not only meet the needs of the people but their livestock as well
Water from rock!
What did happen inside that rock for water to burst forth?
It was just an ordinary rock
Yet God spoke and he used that ordinary rock to meet the needs of the people

What seems impossible to us

is never impossible with God

You never know what God may use to meet your needs!

Isaiah 41:18 NIV
I will make rivers flow on barren heights, and springs within the valleys. I will turn the desert into pools of water, and the parched ground into springs.

He loves you

April 2
The foundation was laid

With praise and thanksgiving they sang to the Lord: "He is good; his love toward Israel endures forever." And all the people gave a great shout of praise to the Lord, because the foundation of the house of the Lord was laid.
Ezra 3:11 NIV

They sang and they gave a great shout of praise to the Lord.
All of this because the foundation was laid.

They knew the importance of a foundation.
They knew what the foundation stood for.
They knew that everything was to be laid on this foundation.
With a firm foundation anything can stand.
Jesus is our firm foundation.
He does not change like shifting sand.
He is our cornerstone.

I taught Kindergarten for many years. I watched over the years as the firm foundation was slowly being taken away from the children. All the things that I knew, that were so important for building a firm foundation for these children, were being taken away. I knew what would happen to those children who never got that firm foundation. What would they stand on in the future? It would not be good. My heart broke because they would not have that firm foundation. I could not teach them what they so desperately needed. And I could not talk of Jesus and the love He had for them.
But, the one thing they could not take away from me was Jesus. I would be Jesus to the children. I might be the only "Jesus" some would ever see or hear!
How important a firm foundation is!
It is worth singing over.
It is worth shouting over.
He is good. His love to us does endure forever!

He loves you

April 3
To see God in everything

Lord, our Lord, how majestic is your name in all the earth!
You have set your glory in the heavens.
Psalm 8:1 NIV

I see Him everywhere
From the light that beams through the curtains
To the incredible colors of the sunset
From the tall oak trees
To the tiniest blade of grass
From the deer grazing in the meadow
To the smallest gecko
From the sounds of nature
To the instruments of musicians
From the bluest blue of the sky
To the darkest black of the night
God, you are in everything
You have made yourself to be seen by all
May we see you more and more
In all of these things You have made

April 4
The music of His love

I will give thanks to you, Lord, with all my heart; I will tell of all your
wonderful deeds. I will be glad and rejoice in you; I will sing the praises of
your name, O Most High.
Psalm 9:1-2 NIV

*"David could never have sung his sweetest songs had he not been sorely
afflicted. His afflictions made his life an instrument on which God could
breathe the music of His love to charm and soothe the hearts of men."*
(Excerpt From: L. B. E. Cowman. "Springs in the Valley." September 20)

To soothe the hearts of men
So many people need to have their hearts soothed.
They are constantly seeking something to make them feel better.

Maybe it's fame or fortune or possessions or 'likes on facebook' or some
form of alcohol or drugs. We see it everyday in the news or on the
Internet.

*What many don't know is that Jesus is their only source
of hope. We can be that instrument that God uses to
soothe the souls of men. Sing your song to the world.
They are longing to hear.*

He loves you

April 5
Come to me

"Come to me, all you who are weary and burdened,
and I will give you rest."
Matthew 11:28 NIV

Come to me
Withdraw to me
I will speak to your heart
I will give you rest
You will learn from me
I am gentle
I am humble
I will speak so very gently to your heart
You will find rest
Just come to me

But Jesus often withdrew to lonely places and prayed.
Luke 5:16 NIV

April 6
Strengthen your brothers

"Simon, Simon, Satan has asked to sift all of you as wheat. But I have prayed for you, Simon, that your faith may not fail. And when you have turned back, strengthen your brothers."
Luke 22:31-32 NIV

Satan wants to sift us as wheat.
But Jesus has prayed for us that our faith may not fail.

Satan wants to:. . .
Sift
Strain
Destroy

But . . .
Jesus has prayed
He understands our weaknesses
He knows the attacks of the enemy

When our faith is strengthened then we are to
strengthen our brothers.
Many need what He has shown you.

I have fought the good fight, I have finished the race, I have kept the faith.
2 Timothy 4:7 NIV

He loves you

April 7
Whoever believes

Whoever believes in me, as Scripture has said, rivers of living water
will flow from within them."
John 7:38 NIV

Whoever believes . . .rivers of living water will flow from within them
Whoever drinks . . .a spring of water welling up to eternal life
With joy . . .you will draw water from the wells of salvation
Like a well-watered garden, like a spring whose waters never fail
Whoever believes in me . . .will never be thirsty
Whoever believes . . .rivers of living water will flow from within them

A full circle of living water.

But whoever drinks the water I give them will never thirst. Indeed, the
water I give them will become in them a spring of water
welling up to eternal life."
John 4:14 NIV

Whoever believes

He loves you

April 8
He fashioned you

Now the one who has fashioned us for this very purpose is God, who has given us the Spirit as a deposit, guaranteeing what is to come.
2 Corinthians 5:5 NIV

God formed you. He made you. He designed you for this very purpose.
For this very purpose!
Daily, He has a purpose for your life.
He fashioned you so that you might fulfill this purpose every moment of every day.
You can trust Him with all of your days, with every moment of every day.
He knows your purpose. He knows you.
He fashioned you so that you might accomplish this purpose in Him.
He fashioned you!

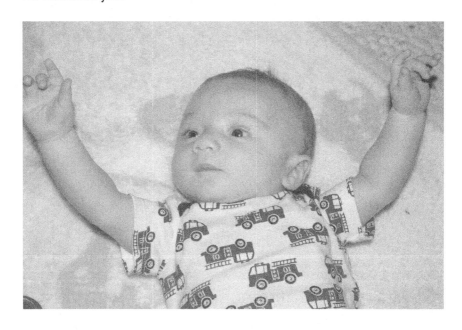

He loves you

April 9
Open the eyes of our heart

So we fix our eyes not on what is seen, but on what is unseen, since what is seen is temporary, but what is unseen is eternal.
2 Corinthians 4:18 NIV

We fix our eyes on what is unseen.
This ability to see the unseen is a gift from God.
He alone opens the eyes of your heart.
He alone shows you secret things, hidden treasures not seen by the human eye, rather seen by the eyes of your heart.
He reveals these eternal truths to you.

Oh that we might see more!

Open our eyes Father!

For now we see only a reflection as in a mirror; then we shall see face to face. Now I know in part; then I shall know fully, even as I am fully known.
1 Corinthians 13:12 NIV

He loves you

April 10
Hidden treasures

"It's all right," he said. "Don't be afraid. Your God, the God of your father, has given you treasure in your sacks; I received your silver." Then he brought Simeon out to them.
Genesis 43:23 NIV

Your God has given you treasures, treasure in your sacks.
So often, we think we must bribe God.
Yet God in His infinite kindness gives us gifts we know nothing of until we begin to search.
When we search we uncover hidden treasures.
We often think these are undeserved.
I haven't done enough, what if this was a mistake, it was probably meant for someone else!
All these thoughts enter our heads and we wonder.
Could it be, did God really want to do this for me, did He really want to bless me?
We need to learn how to always have an open heart to receive all He wants to give us!

Help us to receive all you have for us.
Help us to search for these hidden treasures.

He loves you

April 11
God does speak

For God does speak---now one way, now another---though no one perceives it. In a dream, in a vision of the night, when deep sleep falls on people as they slumber in their beds
Job 33:14-15 NIV

God does speak
In a dream
In a vision of the night
In your sleep
In your heart

He speaks for a purpose
His words are gentle and kind
He speaks to encourage and give you direction
He speaks so that you might know the path He has for you
The path that gives you joy
The path that causes you to be all that He created you to be
The path that gives you freedom in Him
The path that leads you to Him
The good path
The right path

Listen for His words and follow

He loves you

April 12
The music of life lies in your soul

"I have told you these things, so that in me you may have peace. In this world you will have trouble. But take heart! I have overcome the world."
John 16:33 NIV

Music is in the soul. Your own soul
This music, your music isn't determined by your circumstances but rather by what lies in your heart.

All that you are lies within you
Jesus has put it there
He is the lifter of your head
He is the song in the night
He is the joy in the morning
He is the calm in the storm
He is the one that puts laughter in your heart

Laughter is the music of my heart

Some people play violins
Some people sing operas
Some people paint landscapes
Some people build skyscrapers
Some people write novels
But I prefer laughter
It makes my heart so happy

You may have peace
In the laughter
In the tears
Peace
His peace that passes all understanding

He loves you

April 13
Broken pieces

*They all ate and were satisfied, and the disciples picked up twelve
basketfuls of broken pieces that were left over.
Luke 9:17 NIV*

Broken pieces
The world is full of broken pieces.
So many
Several years ago a movie came out called "Ragamuffin". It was the story
of Rich Muffins, the Christian singer's life.
He wrote and sang incredible music. Yet I never knew there was such
sadness and pain in his life.
From his early years his father never said anything kind to him. He was
never pleased with what his son did and he made it known to him. His
father actually said, "You break everything you touch!" His dad did not
like that his son could play the piano and sing, all his dad saw was that his
son could not do the farm work. Rich tried so hard to please his father but
it was never enough. Rich could not get past all of this hurt.
The love of a father
So often you find your identity in this.
Rich only saw himself as a failure.
Everyone he loved left him.
But he saw it as his own fault.
How I hurt for him as I watched his story unfold on screen.
I don't know if he ever fully grasped His Abba Father's unconditional love.
I'm so thankful Rich knows today because He is with Jesus now.

The world is full of broken pieces just like Rich.
But there is hope
There is a Father that is waiting for you to receive His love
It is unconditional.
He loves you just as you are!
Let him put the broken pieces back together.

He loves you

April 14
Faithful friends

The one who calls you is faithful, and he will do it.
1 Thessalonians 5:24 NIV

Every morning I sit in the same chair in the same room to meet Jesus.
I love my time with him.
I love my chair and I love my room.
The room is high and is surrounded by beautiful oak trees and pine trees.
My faithful friends are always there waiting on me too.
Each day they have the same nice smiles.
They never change.
They are always faithful.
They are always there.
That's the way my Abba Father is too.
He never changes
He is always faithful
He is always there waiting for me
Thank you Father for faithful friends
Friends from my children's childhood
Jacob's beloved Barky
Gram's big brown bear
My Kindergarten Brown bear
Polar Bear that's been hanging around waiting on grandchildren for many years

All faithful
Never moving unless the gentle hands of one of my grandsons hugs them and chooses another place for them to sit.
So faithful!

He loves you

He loves you

April 15
He longs to be compassionate to you

Yet the Lord longs to be gracious to you; therefore he will rise up to show
you compassion. For the Lord is a God of justice.
Blessed are all who wait for him!
Isaiah 30:18 NIV

Blessed are all who wait on Him.
You will weep no more.
When you cry for help He will be gracious.
As soon as He hears you, He will answer.
Your teachers will be hidden no more.
You will see them with your own eyes.
If you turn to the left or the right you will hear a voice behind you
Saying, this is the way, walk in it.

Such a compassionate God
He waits on you
He longs to be gracious to you
He wants you to see Him.
He wants you to hear Him.
Such a compassionate God

People of Zion, who live in Jerusalem, you will weep no more. How
gracious he will be when you cry for help! As soon as he hears, he will
answer you. Although the Lord gives you the bread of adversity and the
water of affliction, your teachers will be hidden no more; with your own
eyes you will see them. Whether you turn to the right or to the left, your
ears will hear a voice behind you, saying, "This is the way; walk in it."
Isaiah 30:19-21 WEB

He loves you

April 16
Tethered to Jesus

"I am the vine; you are the branches. If you remain in me and I in you, you will bear much fruit; apart from me you can do nothing."
John 15:5 NIV

When I was young we played a game called "tether ball". A ball was attached to a rope and the rope was attached to a tall pole. There were two players playing, each trying to hit the ball back to the opposing side. You could hit the ball as many times as you wanted. The rope would eventually wind around the pole until it would be impossible to hit the ball anymore. The ball remained attached to the rope, which remained attached to the pole.

We are like that tether ball. The world is constantly trying to sling us around. Go this way, no go this way. Say this, no say that. Think this, no think that. Often we may feel tossed around but we must remember Jesus never loses His hold on us. We are forever attached to the rope, Jesus, our lifeline and He is forever attached to the pole, His Father. We are forever secure in Him!

"When you feel at the end of your tether, remember God is at the other end!"
(Excerpt From: L. B. E. Cowman. "Springs in the Valley.")

He loves you

April 17
The power of nature

The heavens declare the glory of God; the skies proclaim the work of his hands. Day after day they pour forth speech; night after night they reveal knowledge. They have no speech, they use no words; no sound is heard from them. Yet their voice goes out into all the earth, their words to the ends of the world. In the heavens God has pitched a tent for the sun.
Psalm 19:1-4 NIV

When you look at the sky, what do you see, what do you hear?
God is speaking to you.
He is sharing His beauty with you.
He is blessing you.
He is so faithful that He does it day after day after day.
He speaks through all of nature,
Through the sky and its clouds
Through the bird and its song
Through the storm and its rainbow
Through the butterfly and its wings
He is constantly speaking to you

Are you watching?
Are you listening?
He created it all for you.

He loves you

He loves you

April 18
Encourage one another

Therefore encourage one another and build each other up,
just as in fact you are doing.
1 Thessalonians 5:11 NIV

In 1988 our world changed. Our middle daughter was diagnosed with Type 1 diabetes. Everything about our daily life changed, from meals to snacks to monitoring blood sugar, not just during the day, but 24 hours a day. Life became very difficult and complicated trying to adjust to this "new normal" that I did not like! My sweet little girl now had to live with this horrible disease for the rest of her life. I could not take it away. Her dad could not take it away. And even though we asked God for a miracle He did not take it away.

What He did do was make her strong, really strong. Her name means "strong ram" and she has become that. She has lived with diabetes for 28 years now and she is strong not just in taking care of herself but she is strong in her faith. She knows who carries her.

When she was diagnosed we were a part of a wonderful church and an amazing home group. Those people became our support, they rallied around us. They prayed for us, they encouraged us. We needed them during this very difficult time in our lives.

We have always been a part of a church, a body of believers, a people that love Jesus and love each other.

It's so important to have that fellowship with other believers, so that when you go through hard times, and you will, you will have others to hold you up, to be there for you, to build you up and to encourage you.

All the believers were together and had everything in common. They sold property and possessions to give to anyone who had need. Every day they continued to meet together in the temple courts. They broke bread in their homes and ate together with glad and sincere hearts, praising God and enjoying the favor of all the people. And the Lord added to their number daily those who were being saved.

Acts 2:44-47 NIV

April 19
He wants your heart

Have mercy on me, O God, according to your unfailing love; according to
your great compassion blot out my transgressions. Wash away all my
iniquity and cleanse me from my sin.
Psalm 51:1-2 NIV

David wrote this verse when the prophet Nathan came to him after he had
committed adultery with Bathsheba.

Even then he knew God could make him clean
Even then he knew God could create in him a pure heart
Even then he knew God could renew his spirit
Even then he knew God could restore his joy
Even then he knew God would use him again
Even then he knew sacrifice was not what God wanted
Even then David knew what God wanted
He wanted his heart
God wants the same of you. No matter what you've done He still loves
you.
He longs to have your heart.

My heart is steadfast, God, my heart is steadfast.
I will sing, yes, I will sing praises.
Wake up, my glory! Wake up, lute and harp!
I will wake up the dawn.
I will give thanks to you, Lord, among the peoples.
I will sing praises to you among the nations.
For your great loving kindness reaches to the heavens,
and your truth to the skies.
Be exalted, God, above the heavens.
Let your glory be over all the earth.
Psalm 51:7-12 WEB

He loves you

April 20
Delight someone today

Moses told his father-in-law about everything the Lord had done to Pharaoh and the Egyptians for Israel's sake and about all the hardships they had met along the way and how the Lord had saved them. Jethro was delighted to hear about all the good things the Lord had done for Israel in rescuing them from the hand of the Egyptians.
Exodus 18:8-9 NIV

Moses told his father-in-law, Jethro, about everything the Lord had done for them and how He saved them.
Jethro was delighted to hear about all the good things the Lord had done.

It is good to share with others what God has done and is doing for you.
You never know who needs to hear just what you have to say.
Your words of encouragement may just be what someone else needs to believe, or to move forward or just to stand.

Share what you know.
Delight someone else's heart today
God loves to hear His children talk about His
faithfulness.

He said, "Praise be to the Lord, who rescued you from the hand of the Egyptians and of Pharaoh, and who rescued the people from the hand of the Egyptians. Now I know that the Lord is greater than all other gods, for he did this to those who had treated Israel arrogantly."
Exodus 18:10-11 NIV

He loves you

April 21
Be an area where God plays

Therefore, get rid of all moral filth and the evil that is so prevalent and
humbly accept the word planted in you, which can save you.
James 1:21 NIV

In the book "Hearing God" by Dallas Willard, he writes about the word of
God being implanted in us. "Each individual personality remains in the
uniqueness, beauty and goodness of its natural life. But a holy radiance
rests upon it and shines through it because it is now the temple of God,
the area over which the larger and higher power of God plays."

Our personalities remain the same,
But something very unique is added to them:
A holy radiance shines through.

A spiritual life comes through the word of God. That word redirects the
natural life to promote God's kingdom, "an area where God plays".

What an amazing thought,
To be the one in which His holy radiance shines through.
To be the area where His power plays!

So often we think of God as a rule maker.
The world portrays God as a taskmaster, you must do this, you can't do
that and on and on.
Yet the real picture of God is of a compassionate Father. One who loves
His children so much that He takes the time to laugh and play with them.

He loves you

April 22
The trees hear His voice

The men were amazed and asked, "What kind of man is this? Even the winds and the waves obey him!"   Matthew 8:27 NIV

I LOVE aspen trees. Each summer when our children were young we would take a trip to the mountains in New Mexico. We always hiked up a mountain or two, sometimes with a child on our backs, later with a child or two in hand and then eventually each child hiking on their own. One of my favorite memories of these mountains were the aspen trees. I loved their colors and the ways they seemed to almost twinkle when a gentle breeze touched them.
I stand in awe when I realize that it's God's voice that caused them to move and glisten!
He created it all! Even the winds and the waves and the water hear His voice, and the aspen trees too!

"Where is your faith?" he asked his disciples. In fear and amazement they asked one another, "Who is this? He commands even the winds and the water, and they obey him." Luke 8:25 NIV

April 23
Be light in a darkened world

For you were once darkness, but now you are light in the Lord.
Live as children of light.
Ephesians 5:8 NIV

The world is so very dark it seems.
Everywhere you turn you see and hear of such darkness.
The world needs your light, the light of Jesus to shine through you.
You are that light! Live as that light.
Let others see His goodness, righteousness and truth.

Find out what pleases God.
Expose the fruitless deeds of darkness.
Do not even mention what the disobedient do in secret.

Everything exposed by the light becomes visible
Everything that is illuminated becomes a light
Be a light in a darkened world

For the fruit of the Spirit is in all goodness and righteousness and truth,
proving what is well pleasing to the Lord. Have no fellowship with the
unfruitful deeds of darkness, but rather even reprove them. For the things
which are done by them in secret, it is a shame even to speak of.
But all things, when they are reproved, are revealed by the light, for
everything that reveals is light
Ephesians 5:9-13 WEB

He loves you

April 24
God will provide

They came to the place which God had told him of. Abraham built the altar there, and laid the wood in order, bound Isaac his son, and laid him on the altar, on the wood. Abraham stretched out his hand, and took the knife to kill his son. Yahweh's angel called to him out of the sky, and said, "Abraham, Abraham!" He said, "Here I am." He said, "Don't lay your hand on the boy or do anything to him. For now I know that you fear God, since you have not withheld your son, your only son, from me." Abraham lifted up his eyes, and looked, and saw that behind him was a ram caught in the thicket by his horns. Abraham went and took the ram, and offered him up for a burnt offering instead of his son.
Genesis 22:9-13 WEB

When they reached the place . . .
Abraham built an altar
Abraham looked up
Abraham saw His provision for the sacrifice
Abraham went over
Abraham took the ram
Abraham sacrificed the ram
God provided
The Lord will provide!

On the mountain of The Lord it was provided!
God will provide!

When our son was diagnosed with an inoperable malignant brain tumor, my world stopped, nothing else mattered but my son. I began to cry out to God day and night. I began to trust God in ways I never had before. And He was so faithful. He never left me. He was with us every minute of every day of this journey. Shortly after he was diagnosed, a biopsy had to be performed to find out exactly what kind of brain tumor it was. The biopsy was very difficult to do with many possible lasting side effects. As our family and friends sat in the waiting room waiting to hear the report from the neurosurgeon God brought the above scripture to my mind and heart. He spoke very gently to me. "I will provide a ram for your son!"

I had no idea exactly what that meant but I did know that God was saying He would take care of our son. I had an incredible peace from that moment on that our son would live. And our son did live! It was not an instant miracle as we had hoped. Instead He used incredible doctors and nurses and chemotherapy and radiation to bring our son back to total health. (His kind and brilliant oncologist, Dr. Stark Vance, is pictured below with our son and grandson.)

God did provide! And God has blessed us so much more than we could have ever imagined.

Abraham called the name of that place Yahweh Will Provide. As it is said to this day, "On Yahweh's mountain, it will be provided."
Genesis 22:14 WEB

137

April 25
His good, pleasing, perfect will

Do not conform to the pattern of this world, but be transformed by the renewing of your mind. Then you will be able to test and approve what God's will is---his good, pleasing and perfect will.
Romans 12:2 NIV

Let yourself be set apart from this world.
Choose to follow after God and not be conformed to this world.
God can transform your mind. He can change it.
When you allow God to change you, you will begin to hear His voice.
When you hear His voice you will begin to know God's will for your life.
His good and pleasing and perfect will for you.

Then you will find true happiness and contentment in Him.
He longs to show you.

In him the whole building is joined together and rises to become a holy temple in the Lord. And in him you too are being built together to become a dwelling in which God lives by his Spirit.
Ephesians 2:21-22 NIV

He loves you

April 26
No one can take away your joy

So with you: Now is your time of grief, but I will see you again and you will
rejoice, and no one will take away your joy.
John 16:22 NIV

If you want joy, look for Jesus.
Once you find Him and see His face you will never be the same.

He will give you what you need.
When He does, no one will be able to take away what He gives you.
No one!

He is the one that makes your joy complete.
Sorrow may last for a night but joy does come in the morning.

In that day you will no longer ask me anything. Very truly I tell you, my
Father will give you whatever you ask in my name. Until now you have not
asked for anything in my name. Ask and you will receive,
and your joy will be complete.
John 16:23-24

He loves you

April 27
Let God use you

Let perseverance finish its work so that you may be mature
and complete, not lacking anything.
James 1:4 NIV

*"Look with Edison at his deafness, with Milton at his blindness, with
Bunyan at his imprisonment, and see how patience converted these very
misfortunes into good fortunes.*
*Michelangelo went to Rome to carve statues, and found that other artists
had taken over all the Carrara marble—all but one crooked and
misshapen piece. He sat down before this and studied with infinite
patience its very limitations, until he found that by bending the head of a
statue here, and lifting its arms there, he could create a masterpiece: thus
The Boy David was produced.*
*Let us sit down in front of our very limitations, and with the aid of patience
dare to produce, with God's help, a masterpiece!"*
(Excerpt From: L. B. E. Cowman. "Springs in the Valley." October 21)

God has something He wants you to do.
It will be different than anything anyone else has ever done.
He has given only you this ability.
He wants you to:
Sit down with your limitations
With patience
And God's help
Dare to produce a masterpiece!
God is waiting.
The world is waiting.

He loves you

April 28
Holy and blameless

To make her holy, cleansing her by the washing with water through the word, and to present her to himself as a radiant church, without stain or wrinkle or any other blemish, but holy and blameless.
Ephesians 5:26-27 NIV

Christ loved you so much that He gave up everything just for you.
You need only believe.
He will make you holy.
He will cleanse you through His word.
He will one day present you as His radiant bride,
without stain or blemish.
You were chosen by Him before the foundation of the world.
Once you understand this great love God has for you,
ask Him to let you see yourself the way He sees you.
You will love what you see.

Even as he chose us in him before the foundation of the world, that we would be holy and without defect before him in love; having predestined us for adoption as children through Jesus Christ to himself, according to the good pleasure of his desire. To the praise of the glory of his grace, by which he freely gave us favor in the Beloved.
Ephesians 1:4-6 WEB

He loves you

April 29
When kindness appeared

But when the kindness and love of God our Savior appeared.
Titus 3:4 NIV

When the kindness and love of God appeared
Everything changed....
Hope became real
Joy became evident
Love was made visible
Everything changed
Everything!
For you and for me
For the whole world, for those who believe!

After teaching Kindergarten for 25 years one thing became evident to me,
if you want to reach a child you must love them first.
Over the years I've had many parents tell me over and over how bad their
child was or the bad things their child had done or you won't be able to
control my child! But I found once the parent was gone and it was just the
child and me, I could control them. It was all because I loved them first
and I spoke kindly to them. Once they knew I cared and I was going to be
kind to them and I would love them, their whole countenance began to
change.

But when the kindness and love of God appeared...

He loves you

April 30
His good promises

Not one word has failed of all the good promises he gave.
1 Kings 8:56 NIV

"Someday we will understand that God has a reason behind every no He gives us through the course of our lives. Yet even in this life, He always makes it up to us. When God's people are worried and concerned that their prayers are not being answered, how often we have seen Him working to answer them in a far greater way! Occasionally we catch a glimpse of this, but the complete revelation of it will not be seen until later. (L.B.E. Cowman, "Streams in the Desert", October 23)

Sometimes it seems when we pray God doesn't hear or the enemy says God doesn't care about your little worries. But that is so not true. God does care about every little detail of our lives. In fact he cares so much that He wrote a book just for us, a book that tells in great detail every promise He has for us.

Promises . . .

Give hope

Bring life

Cause joy

Create light

Expel darkness

Show wisdom

Give peace

Reveal His deep love

And His promises never fail!

May 1

Rest

Whoever dwells in the shelter of the Most High will rest in the shadow of the Almighty. Psalm 91:1 NIV

Rest. We all need it. Not just a physical rest but rest for our souls, rest for our minds and even rest for our hearts. We need only dwell in His presence and we will find that rest. That rest that gives peace and restores strength and gives hope. He is our refuge and our fortress. He is the one we can trust. Rest. Lean back in His arms and let Him hold you. His arms are secure. His strength is sufficient.

"My Presence will go with you, and I will give you rest."
Exodus 33:14 NIV

May 2
He is there

Where could I go from your Spirit?
Or where could I flee from your presence?
If I ascend up into heaven, you are there.
If I make my bed in the depths, behold, you are there!
If I take the wings of the dawn,
and settle in the uttermost parts of the sea;
Even there your hand will lead me,
and your right hand will hold me.
If I say, "Surely the darkness will overwhelm me;
the light around me will be night"
even the darkness doesn't hide from you,
but the night shines as the day.
The darkness is like light to you.
Psalm 139:7-12 WEB

We kept our three sweet grandsons for the weekend. What fun we had but we got so tired! Three in diapers! At night, we put the older two, on a pallet on the floor, their first time to sleep together on the floor. They were both only two. When my husband put them down they did okay and then the older one began to cry. I went to talk to him and he wanted me to lay down with him. So I did. He kept opening his eyes to make sure I was still there. After a few minutes I told him I had to get up. He shook his head no. I said no, I have to go. He said no! I said you are a big boy and you will be okay. He put his little head up and said, No, I not a big boy! He just wanted me to stay with him. Sweet boy! I prayed for them and sang Jesus Loves Me and he finally went to sleep.

How many times have I felt like that?
Often I've been afraid and I needed to know I wasn't alone.
The world says, stay strong, you can do it!
But that's not what God says
He says I will never leave you or forsake you.
If you go into the depths I will be with you.
If you make your bed on the far side of the sea I will be with you.
He is there!

May 3
By day God directs His love

By day the Lord directs his love, at night his song is with me,
a prayer to the God of my life.
Psalm 42:8 NIV

Did you know you are God's love?
An amazing thought, isn't it?
To be called His love

By day He directs you
He cares so much about you that He has a plan for you every day
At night He gives you a song, His song
He puts it in your heart
It's a song of a Redeemer's love
Your Redeemer, the one who gave everything for you!

Think about that as you walk through your day
Dwell on that as you listen to His song in the night

May you know His direction each day
May you hear His song at night
May He fill your heart with gladness
And joy everlasting!

I will praise the Lord, who counsels me;
even at night my heart instructs me.
Psalm 16:7 NIV

I remembered my songs in the night.
My heart meditated and my spirit asked.
Psalm 77:6 NIV

May 4
We are God's handiwork

For we are God's handiwork, created in Christ Jesus to do good works,
which God prepared in advance for us to do.
Ephesians 2:10 NIV

We are God's handiwork, not man's.
I recently watched the show "Sixty Minutes" on TV. This particular
episode was about the recent breakthroughs in testing in the DNA of
embryos. In their findings they were discovering what genes certain
embryos carried that could eventually cause diseases like cystic fibrosis
and cancer and many other diseases. They felt like it was an incredible
breakthrough in eliminating these diseases in children. They took one cell
from each embryo to determine if they carried these certain genes and if
they did, then they would not use that embryo to implant in the mothers
womb! What happened to the "defective embryos"? Are we playing God?

Another scientist had patented his findings and started a similar company
where they could do gene DNA testing to find the "good" embryo and the
"good" sperm that would be compatible to create a "good healthy
baby". The scientist said he thought in the future there would be people
who would opt out of a sexual relation to have a child and do it this way
instead!

We are not God, nor should we play God. We are God's handiwork
created by God to do good works, which He prepared for us in advance
If either our son or daughter had been tested as embryos, what would
have happened to our own son, who had a malignant brain tumor and our
daughter, who has diabetes? Would they have been considered "not
good" and been discarded!!
God help us!
What would our world lose because of this?

When they see among them their children, the work of my hands, they
will keep my name holy; they will acknowledge the holiness of the Holy
One of Jacob, and will stand in awe of the God of Israel.
Isaiah 29:23 NIV

May 5
The battle is not mine

He said: "Listen, King Jehoshaphat and all who live in Judah and
Jerusalem! This is what the Lord says to you:
Do not be afraid or discouraged because of this vast army.
For the battle is not yours, but God's."
2 Chronicles 20:15 NIV

God says:
Listen
Do not be afraid
Do not be discouraged because of this vast army
The battle is not yours, but mine

God is listening to the beat of your heart
You will not be afraid, what can man do to you?
Greater is He that is in you than he that is in the world
You will not be discouraged
Though satan meant it for evil God will use it for good!

God will fight for you.
You need only stand still and watch as He fights
the battle for you.

"Be strong and courageous. Do not be afraid or discouraged because of
the king of Assyria and the vast army with him,
for there is a greater power with us than with him.
2 Chronicles 32:7 NIV

He loves you

May 6
On the appointed day

On an appointed day, Herod dressed himself in royal clothing, sat on the throne, and gave a speech to them. The people shouted, "The voice of a god, and not of a man!" Immediately an angel of the Lord struck him, because he didn't give God the glory, and he was eaten by worms and died. But the word of God grew and multiplied.
Acts 12:21-24 WEB

On the appointed day...
It may look like the enemy has won
It may seem as if the battle is too big
It may appear that all hope has been lost

Immediately...
An angel appeared and struck the enemy down
The enemy was destroyed
The enemy was never seen again

But....
The word of God continued to spread and flourish

On the appointed day for you it may look like:
he has won
the battle is too big
all hope is lost

Immediately God will:
Strike your enemy down
Your enemy will be destroyed
You will never see him again
But in all of this...
His word will continue to spread and flourish

On the appointed day!

He loves you

May 7
He knows the way

Thy way is in the sea, and thy path in the great waters.
Psalm 77:19

"There is an infinite variety in the paths God makes, and He can make them anywhere! Think you not that He, who made the spider able to drop anywhere and to spin its own path as it goes, is not able to spin a path for you through every blank, or perplexity, or depression? God is never lost among our mysteries. He sees the road, "the end from the beginning." God takes us out into the deeps; but He knows the track! He knows the haven! and we shall arrive."
C. A. FOX
"Springs in the Valleys" L.B.E. Cowman, November 2

His paths are beyond tracing out.
He knows the way.
He sees the road.
He knows the end from the beginning.

You need only follow.
You will never be alone.

He stilled the storm to a whisper,
the waves of the sea were hushed.

They were glad when it grew calm,
And He guided them to their desired haven.

Psalm 107:29 -30

He loves you

May 8
The wings of one touched the other

Their wings were joined to one another; they didn't turn when they went;
each one went straight forward.
Ezekiel 1:9 WEB

Each wing touched another one's wing
They were together
They were of one accord
They held each other up
They had one mission in mind
They did not turn to the left or to the right
They flew straight ahead

On the wings of eagles...

We move forward in one accord...touching

Such were their faces. Their wings were spread out above.
Two wings of each one touched another, and two covered their bodies.
Each one went straight forward: where the spirit was to go,
they went; they didn't turn when they went.
Ezekiel 1:11-12 WEB

Their wings spread upward as they touched
Wherever the Spirit would go,
they would go in one accord
The beauty of these creatures in harmony
with one another and
following the Spirit wherever it may lead
The beauty of the body of Christ

May 9
Look for the forest

Then he turned to his disciples and said privately,
"Blessed are the eyes that see what you see".
Luke 10:23 NIV

"You can't see the forest for the trees."
'Forest' is the American saying.
In the UK they say "You can't see the wood for the trees".
Saying it to someone means that they are so involved in the details of
something that they forget or do not realize the real purpose or importance
of the thing as a whole.

Sometimes when you concentrate on the minute details of a problem, you
lose sight of the overall picture, in other words you focus on the
unimportant, rather than on the important things. You miss the big picture.

I think we often do this. We get so involved in our day-to-day life that we
forget our forever life. Maybe we just need to step back and look
again. We need to ask God what He sees. He sees so much more than
we do.

Oh that we might see the forest, what He sees!
Oh that we might gaze upon another world, His world.
Oh that we might have eyes to see

He loves you

May 10
To rest in His shadow

Whoever dwells in the shelter of the Most High will rest in the shadow of
the Almighty. I will say of the Lord, "He is my refuge and my fortress,
my God, in whom I trust." Psalm 91:1-2 NIV

Our secure place is in Him.
We are to dwell there, not just come and go as we choose but
live there. He is our secure shelter!
When we are there in this safe place we can rest.
There is always rest for the weary there, always.
His shadow covers us while we rest, secure in His shelter.
Shadows are often bigger than the thing that creates the shadow.
Shadows don't just appear, there is always some object that creates the
shadow.
On a hot day in Texas there is nothing nicer than to sit under the shadow
of a tree. You are protected from the intense heat of the sun.
Many times there is a gentle breeze created by the leaves of the trees.
It is a cool protected resting place.

Because you are my help, I sing in the shadow of your wings.
I cling to you; your right hand upholds me.
Psalm 63:7-8 NIV
Oh that we would dwell in this resting place!

May 11
He understands

I have loved you with an everlasting love;
I have drawn you with unfailing kindness.
Jeremiah 31:3 NIV

Jesus understands our hurt
He understands our pain
For you see He bore it all
Just for you and me

He knows what rejection feels like
For He was rejected by His own
He knows what physical pain feels like
For He was nailed to a cross
He knows what separation feels like
For he was separated from His Father
He knows what it feels like to not be loved
For the world hated Him
He knows what being alone feels like
For even His closest disciples fell asleep when He needed them the most
He knows what it feels like to be despised
For he had no honor even in His home town
He knows what it feels like to be misunderstood
For even his own mother and father did not understand him

He knows... He knows...He knows
And yet He loves you unconditionally
He always has, He always will

He loves you

May 12
Offer the fruit of our lips

Through him, then, let us offer up a sacrifice of praise to God continually,
that is, the fruit of lips which proclaim allegiance to his name. But don't
forget to be doing good and sharing,
for with such sacrifices God is well pleased.
Hebrews 13:15-16 WEB

The fruit of our lips
Is it good fruit
Or bad fruit
Does it build up or
Does it tear down

The good fruit is a sacrifice of praise to God
Lips that profess His name
That do good and share
Could it be that the fruit of our lips
Is not just what we say but what we do also?

Share the gentleness and kindness of Jesus

Build up

Restore

Make peace

This is what pleases God

He creates praise on our lips.

I have seen his ways, and will heal him:
I will lead him also, and restore comfort to him and to his mourners.
I create the fruit of the lips:
"Peace, peace, to him who is far off and to him who is near,"
says Yahweh; "and I will heal them."
Isaiah 57:18-19 WEB

May 13
Only God can see

Whatever you do, do it all for the glory of God.
1 Corinthians 10:31 NIV

"The most saintly souls are often those who have never distinguished themselves as authors or allowed any major accomplishment of theirs to become the topic of the world's conversation. No, they are usually those who have led a quiet inner life of holiness, having carried their sweet bouquets unseen, like a fresh lily in a secluded valley on the edge of a crystal stream."
(Streams in the Desert by Mrs. L. B. Cowman, November 12)

It may seem like no one sees.
But God sees.

It may seem like no one cares.
But God cares.

It may seem like no one hears.
But God hears.

He sees.

He cares.

He hears.

One day He will tell you all He has seen and heard.

Remember to look up He is there!

And whatever you do, whether in word or deed, do it all in the name of the Lord Jesus, giving thanks to God the Father through him.
Colossians 3:17 NIV

He loves you

May 14
To walk with God

After Methuselah's birth, Enoch walked with God for three hundred years,
and became the father of more sons and daughters. All the days of
Enoch were three hundred sixty-five years. Enoch walked with God,
and he was not found, for God took him.
Genesis 5:22-24 WEB

What happened the first 65 years of Enoch's life?
Why did he begin to walk with God in his 65th year?
There is no record of what Enoch did the first 65 years of his life.
What was recorded was that he did walk with God.

So it is for us, once we know Jesus, all that we've done, all of our sins are
washed away, never to be remembered or recorded.
God will remember all the years we walked with Him.
Then one day God will take us away too, to live with Him for all eternity.

It is never too late to walk with God.

Everything becomes new when you take that first step.

By faith, Enoch was taken away, so that he wouldn't see death, and he
was not found, because God translated him. For he has had testimony
given to him that before his translation he had been well pleasing to God.
Hebrews 11:5 WEB

He loves you

May 15
His gracious favor

He has delivered us from such a deadly peril, and he will deliver us again.
On him we have set our hope that he will continue to deliver us, as you
help us by your prayers. Then many will give thanks on our behalf for the
gracious favor granted us in answer to the prayers of many.
2 Corinthians 1:10-11 NIV

We will all go through "deadly perils". There will be times of great trials
but we need not ever lose hope.

Our assurance, our hope, our deliverer, our victory is in Him.
He will not fail us.
He will deliver us again and again and again
from every "deadly peril" that comes our way.
We can rest in that total assurance.

He who began a good work in you will complete it.

When others are going through these perils our job is to pray.
When we pray God hears.
And He will do the work.
We cannot save but we can pray.
Others will see this and give thanks

*Whether you are in the peril or praying for one who is,
God is working and has a plan.*

For deliverance
For assurance
For thanksgiving
We need each other. . . to pray, to encourage, to believe with us.
We will see His favor in our lives and in the lives of those we pray for.

He loves you

May 16
I have swept away your offenses

I have swept away your offenses like a cloud, your sins like the morning mist. Return to me, for I have redeemed you. Sing for joy, you heavens, for the Lord has done this; shout aloud, you earth beneath. Burst into song, you mountains, you forests and all your trees, for the Lord has redeemed Jacob, he displays his glory in Israel.
Isaiah 44:22-23 NIV

Just as the clouds move across the sky and disappear so have your sins. Just as the morning mist appears for a moment and then evaporates so have your sins.

You have been redeemed by the blood of the lamb
Sing!
Shout!
He has done amazing things for you!

God has done it
It is complete! It is finished!

You are new in Him.

Look at the clouds
Look at the mountains
Look at the trees
They are singing because you have been redeemed.

He loves you

He loves you

May 17
Then they remembered

Becoming terrified, they bowed their faces down to the earth. They said to them, "Why do you seek the living among the dead? He isn't here, but is risen. Remember what he told you when he was still in Galilee, saying that the Son of Man must be delivered up into the hands of sinful men, and be crucified, and the third day rise again?" They remembered his words, returned from the tomb, and told all these things to the eleven, and to all the rest. Now they were Mary Magdalene, Joanna, and Mary the mother of James. The other women with them told these things to the apostles. These words seemed to them to be nonsense, and they didn't believe them. But Peter got up and ran to the tomb. Stooping and looking in, he saw the strips of linen lying by themselves, and he departed to his home, wondering what had happened.
Luke 24:5 -12 WEB

Then they remembered His words . . .

There is a time that you will remember.
God will bring to memory what you need to know.
He will cause you to remember His words.

His words are the only words that will give life and hope and clarity to every situation in your life
You can trust Him. You need only to listen
He may have you share what you've heard
When you share, others may not believe or receive your words
"But they did not believe the women, because their words seemed like nonsense."
That is okay too because that is not your job to open their ears
That is God's. Your job is to be faithful to tell of what you have seen.
Speak with graciousness and without condemnation
There may be only one who receives what you say.
That is okay. "Peter, however, got up and ran to the tomb".
Be faithful to tell what you have seen.

May 18
If I have not love

If I can fathom all mysteries and all knowledge, and if I have a faith that
can move mountains, but have not love, I am nothing.
Corinthians 13:2

"Keep in mind that your aim in Bible reading is not to become a scholar or
to impress others with your knowledge of the Bible - a dreadful trap for
those aiming to be biblical. That aim will cultivate pride and lay a
foundation for the petty, quarrelsome spirit so regrettably common in
those outwardly identified as the most serious students of the Scriptures."
(Hearing God Dallas Willard Week 38 day 6)

If I have all knowledge
If I have all faith
If I have the biggest house or the most expensive car
If I have the highest degree
If I have the best children
If I memorize the whole Bible
If and more if's. . .
But I do not have love
I have nothing
What I do have no one will want

If we are to be Jesus to the lost world,

we must first have love!

If I speak in the tongues of men or of angels, but do not have love,
I am only a resounding gong or a clanging cymbal.
1 Corinthians 13:1 NIV

He loves you

May 19
Taste and see

Taste and see that the Lord is good; blessed is the one
who takes refuge in him. Psalm 34:8 NIV

The Lord is good.
Taste and see
You would think it would say look and see
Yet with tasting, it takes time for the flavors to soak in.
The taste buds do their work.
The brain sends its signal.
Then, only after chewing does the taste escape into the body.
It takes time to taste.
Take some time to taste His word. It is so rich and good.
You will love the flavor. It will nourish you in ways that you never thought
possible.
Taste and see that the Lord is good.

Like newborn babies, crave pure spiritual milk, so that by it you may grow
up in your salvation, now that you have tasted that the Lord is good.
1 Peter 2:2-3 NIV

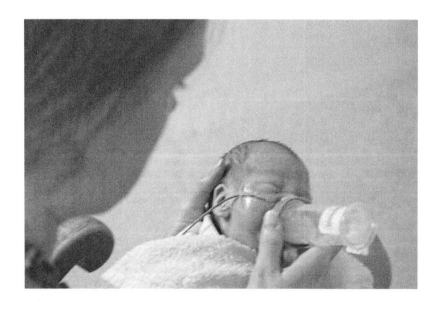

May 20
A sign to many

I have become a sign to many; you are my strong refuge.
My mouth is filled with your praise, declaring your splendor all day long.
Psalm 71:7-8 NIV

"Signs, Signs, Everywhere are signs"
An old popular song by the Five Man Electrical Band
The song was popular during the hippie movement of the sixties.

"Signs, signs, everywhere there's signs
Do this, don't do that, can't you read the sign"

Such confusion and judgment in the world
I wonder what kind of sign the world is seeing through us.
Is it a sign of hope and freedom and love and forgiveness?
Or is it judgment and law?

May our sign read:
Hope found here
Forgiveness found here
Freedom Lane
New life this way
Love everlasting
Judgment wrong way

May our signs be ONE WAY to Jesus!
May those that see our lives want to follow that one sign.
The sign that gives hope and forever love.
Take a moment and think about how the sign of your life would read.

He loves you

May 21
Knowledge

At that time shall Michael stand up, the great prince who stands for the children of your people; and there shall be a time of trouble, such as never was since there was a nation even to that same time: and at that time your people shall be delivered, everyone who shall be found written in the book. Many of those who sleep in the dust of the earth shall awake, some to everlasting life, and some to shame and everlasting contempt. Those who are wise shall shine as the brightness of the expanse; and those who turn many to righteousness as the stars forever and ever. But you, Daniel, shut up the words, and seal the book, even to the time of the end: many shall run back and forth, and knowledge shall be increased."
Daniel 12:1-4 WEB

Everyone whose name is written in the book will be delivered
Those who sleep in the dust of the earth will awake
Some to everlasting life
Others to shame and everlasting contempt

Those who are wise will shine like the brightness of the heavens
Those who lead many to righteousness will shine like the stars forever and ever

Until then many will go here and there to increase knowledge

Scientists recently landed a satellite, Rosetta, on a comet.
It had been traveling for over ten years.
The purpose of this robotic space probe was to land on this comet to find out more about the origins of our solar system!

"Until then many will go here and there to increase knowledge."
They have now gone over ten years and millions of miles in space to increase their knowledge.
All to find out what we already know...God is the creator of it all!

He loves you

May 22
Commit, trust, follow

Commit your way to the Lord; trust in him and he will do this.
He will make your righteous reward shine like the dawn,
your vindication like the noonday sun.
Psalm 37:5-6 NIV

Commit continuously
Walk by faith
Follow Him
Trust Him to guide you

He may lead you where you've never gone before.
He may lead you on a path where no one else is going.
He may lead you to the very edge, where it seems like you could fall.
He may lead you to a meadow where others are playing but He's said you are to "Be still".
He may lead you to a very dark place so you can be the one light in that darkness.
He may lead you to places you never thought you'd go.

But in all of these places He has gone before you, it is safe to follow Him.
He has a plan, a good plan for your life.
You can trust Him, your Abba Father.
He will show you incredible things on this journey that you never ever dreamed you'd see!

Daniel was left alone and he saw a great vision.
John the disciple stood alone, away from the crowd and he wrote Revelations.
Paul was left alone and he was forever changed.
Jesus was left alone and He saved the world!

"The man who dares to go where others hold back will find himself alone, but he will see the glory of God, and enter into the secrets of eternity."
Gordon Watt

He loves you

May 23
Do we give life?

Elisha died, and they buried him. Now the bands of the Moabites invaded
the land at the coming in of the year. As they were burying a man,
behold, they saw a band of raiders; and they threw the man into Elisha's
tomb. As soon as the man touched Elisha's bones,
he revived, and stood up on his feet.
2 Kings 13:20-21 WEB

When the dead man touched Elisha's bones...
The dead man came to life
And he stood up on his feet.

The man was dead but when he touched Elisha (this great man of God,
who was dead and buried), the dead man came to life!
There was power in Elisha's body, even when he was dead.
All the dead man did was touch the body of one who knew God, really
knew God...
Then life poured forth!
So much life that he didn't need to be helped up
He stood up on his feet.

What happens when the dead touch us?
Do we give forth life, with our words, with our touch?
We may not have the power to raise the dead but we do have the power
to give life through our words.
When you speak are others drawn to what you have to say?
Do they see Jesus in you?
Do they hear His words through you?
Do your words give hope, do they encourage?
We have this great power in us, may we use it for His kingdom.

He loves you

May 24
His refreshing springs

When she came, Caleb said, "What do you want?" She said, "Give me a blessing. Because you have set me in the land of the South, give me also springs of water." So he gave her the upper springs and the lower springs.
Joshua 15:18-19 WEB

"There are both "upper and lower springs" in life, and they are springs, not stagnant pools. They are the joys and blessings that flow from heaven above, through the hottest summer and through the most barren desert of sorrow and trials. But from the hills came the inexhaustible springs that cooled, refreshed, and fertilized all the land.
These springs flow through the low places, the difficult places, the desert places, the lonely places, and even the ordinary places of life. And no matter what our situation may be, these springs can always be found."
(Streams in the Desert by L. B. Cowman November 26)

"But from the hills came the inexhaustible springs that cooled, refreshed, and fertilized all the land.'

Springs that refreshed Springs that fertilized all the land

A source unseen, from springs deep underground
A source that we know not where it begins
A source you cannot see
But can be heard
Yet when it reaches the top of the ground it bursts forth
Through rocks and dirt
It has power to push whatever is in its way out of its way
Nothing can stop it
Nothing!

His refreshing springs

He loves you

May 25
To think His thoughts

Now I, Nebuchadnezzar, praise and exalt and glorify the King of heaven,
because everything he does is right and all his ways are just.
Daniel 4:37 NIV

*"He had so completely filled me with His breath, mind, and Spirit that I
would only think His thoughts and live His life. Within His life I had found
my own, but now it was eternally glorified. What would we poor humans
do without our God's nights and mornings!"*
George MacDonald

Oh to be filled with:
His breath
His mind
His Spirit
So that I would only
Live life by His breath
Think only His thoughts
Live only in His love
Then I will find my own
But it will be eternally glorified

He loves you

May 26
Just follow

But one who enters in by the door is the shepherd of the sheep. The gatekeeper opens the gate for him, and the sheep listen to his voice. He calls his own sheep by name, and leads them out. Whenever he brings out his own sheep, he goes before them, and the sheep follow him, for they know his voice.
John 10:2-4 WEB

The gatekeeper opens the gate.
The shepherd, Jesus, goes in first, He alone has the power to open the gate.
No one else could have done what He did.
He went in first to show us the way.
He knows each of His sheep.
He calls them each by their own name.
He knows your name. He calls you by name.
You are that important to Him.
Our job is to listen for His voice.
When we know His voice and hear it, we will follow Him.
The longer we follow Him the more we will want to follow Him.
The more we follow Him the more we will become like Him.
Look, do you see the gate?
Listen, do you hear His voice?

There is a children's song that I sang often with my Kindergarteners, "Mary Had a Little Lamb".
The words of this song reveal a great picture.
"Mary had a little lamb, little lamb, little lamb.
Mary had a little lamb, its fleece was white as snow.
And everywhere that Mary went the lamb was sure to go."
We are the lamb, Jesus is our shepherd.

Just follow Him

He loves you

May 27
He is faithful

For great is your love, higher than the heavens;
your faithfulness reaches to the skies.
Psalm 108:4 NIV

Have you ever wondered how high the heavens are?
We know when we fly in an airplane it looks like the sky goes on forever.
That's the way God's love is.

There is no limit, there is no end to His love.
We can never go higher than His faithfulness.
It reaches beyond the farthest star.
It goes deeper than the deepest ocean.

He loves you so.
In fact He loves you so much you will never totally
understand the depth of that love.
But you can rest in the assurance that His love will
never change for you.
He has always loved you. He will always love you!

He loves you

He loves you

May 28
The battle is His

"All those gathered here will know that it is not by sword or spear
that the Lord saves; for the battle is the Lord's,
and he will give all of you into our hands."
1 Samuel 17:47 NIV

This battle is not yours, but Gods.
He will fight for you.
You need only to be still.

He will guard your feet.
The wicked will be silenced.
It is not by your strength.
He will give you His strength.

Do not be afraid.
Do not be discouraged.
The battle is not yours, but God's.

He will give you victory over your enemies.
You will boast in your God.
You will praise His name forever.

He said: "Listen, King Jehoshaphat and all who live in Judah
and Jerusalem! This is what the Lord says to you:
'Do not be afraid or discouraged because of this vast army.
For the battle is not yours, but God's'."
2 Chronicles 20:15 NIV

He loves you

176

May 29
Enter His rest

For we who have believed do enter into that rest, even as he has said, "As I swore in my wrath, they will not enter into my rest"; although the works were finished from the foundation of the world. There remains therefore a Sabbath rest for the people of God. For he who has entered into his rest has himself also rested from his works, as God did from his. Let us therefore give diligence to enter into that rest, lest anyone fall after the same example of disobedience.
Hebrews 4:3, 9-11 WEB

His works have been finished since the creation of the world.
God rested from all His works.
It was finished on the sixth day.
Today, enter His rest.
A Sabbath-rest
A rest from your works
Just as God has
Enter into that rest

Father, show us what that rest looks like for us.

Rest from the worry, rest from the weariness,

rest from the anxiety, rest from the fear

Rest from the concerns of this world,

rest from the wonderings,

rest from the unknown

Total rest in you is what we want!

The Lord gave them rest on every side, just as he had sworn to their ancestors. Not one of their enemies withstood them; the Lord gave all their enemies into their hands.
Joshua 21:44 NIV

May 30
Get up, don't be afraid

While he was still speaking, behold, a bright cloud overshadowed them.
Behold, a voice came out of the cloud, saying, "This is my beloved Son, in
whom I am well pleased. Listen to him." When the disciples heard it, they
fell on their faces, and were very afraid. Jesus came and touched them
and said, "Get up, and don't be afraid." Lifting up their eyes,
they saw no one, except Jesus alone.
Matthew 17:5-8 WEB

Listen to Him
God is so pleased with His son.
They heard His words but they were afraid.
But Jesus came and touched them.
He spoke to them, "Get up. Don't be afraid."
They looked up because they trusted Him.
He was there for them.

He wants you to do the same.

Listen for Him
Look for Him
When you hear Him and you feel His touch, Get up!
Trust Him. He is there for you.
Don't be afraid

He has much to tell you!

He loves you

May 31
His wisdom and knowledge

My goal is that they may be encouraged in heart and united in love, so
that they may have the full riches of complete understanding, in order that
they may know the mystery of God, namely, Christ, in whom are hidden all
the treasures of wisdom and knowledge.
Colossians 2:2-3 NIV

Our world is filled with so many brilliant people.
Each one has a different kind of knowledge:
Knowledge about space and stars and planets
Knowledge about the human body and its genetics
Knowledge about every kind of machinery
Knowledge about construction and how things are built
Knowledge about numbers
Knowledge about physics
Knowledge about technology
Knowledge about history
And on and on and on.
These people all are working in jobs that I am sure I would not understand
even if they tried to explain them to me.
But if these very educated people don't know Jesus then we have
something they don't have.
In Bob Hamp's book,, "Lead Differently, Think Differently" he wrote about
the knowledge of the world. What the world has is knowledge, just
knowledge. What we as Christians have is more than that, much more.
We have wisdom, the wisdom that comes from God, the creator of the
universe, the creator of all life, the sustainer of all life, the one who knows
everything, the one who created all of these very knowledgeable people
who gave them the ability to learn.
We understand more than they do because we have the Holy Spirit living
within us.
We are such blessed children of God.

He loves you

June 1
God whistles

He lifts up a banner for the distant nations, he whistles for those at the
ends of the earth. Here they come, swiftly and speedily! Not one of them
grows tired or stumbles, not one slumbers or sleeps; not a belt is loosened
at the waist, not a sandal strap is broken.
Isaiah 5:26-27 NIV

What an amazing concept....He whistles, God whistles.

I've not heard God whistle but I would love to hear that sound.
I would imagine His whistle is:
Powerful and penetrating
Beautiful and melodic
Authoritative and compelling
Mystifying and unique

I would imagine His whistle commands.
He whistles for those at the ends of the earth and they hear. What
strength is behind that whistle!
A whistle powerful enough for people to hear from the ends of the earth!
That's a very long ways.
Our grandson's dad is from New Zealand. It takes 18 hours or more on an
airplane to get to New Zealand. It's over 7,000 miles from Texas to New
Zealand. Imagine the sound of a whistle that could be heard from that
distance!

They not only hear but they immediately come to Him.
They come swiftly and speedily.

I remember my husband telling me the story of when he was young, his
mom would just whistle in the summer evenings when it was time for him
to come home.

She would step out the door and whistle for him. He knew when he heard that whistle it was his mom. He knew the sound of her whistle and he knew what it meant. He knew it was time to go home.

I wonder if we heard God whistle if we would know it was Him.
I think we would!

May we always listen for Him
Whether He whistles or whispers or sings over us.

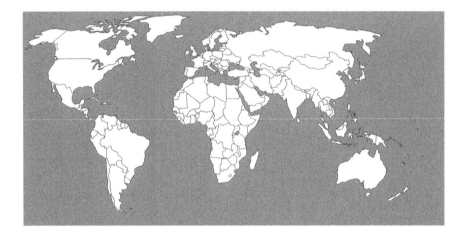

He loves you

June 2
For our good pleasure

When I consider your heavens, the work of your fingers, the moon and the
stars, which you have ordained; what is man, that you think of him?
What is the son of man, that you care for him?
For you have made him a little lower than God, and crowned him with
glory and honor. You make him ruler over the works of your hands.
You have put all things under his feet: All sheep and cattle, yes,
and the animals of the field,
The birds of the sky, the fish of the sea, and
whatever passes through the paths of the seas. Yahweh, our Lord,
how majestic is your name in all the earth!
Psalm 8:3-9 WEB

Miracles by Eric Metaxas is such a great book.
In his book he writes about the different parts of God's creation and how
each is such a miracle:
From the alignment of the earth in our solar system
To the distance from the sun
To the pull of gravity on earth
To the makeup of our bodies
To the sustaining of all of His creation
What is man that You are mindful of Him
Yet You created all of this for our good pleasure
Everything is so perfectly aligned
The flocks and herds
The animals of the wild
The birds in the sky
The fish in the sea
How majestic is Your name in all the earth...in all the universe
All of this He created for our good pleasure.

Do not be afraid, little flock, for your Father has been pleased
to give you the kingdom.
Luke 12:32 NIV

June 3
God is changing us

Therefore, since we have such a hope, we are very bold. We are not like
Moses, who would put a veil over his face to prevent the Israelites from
seeing the end of what was passing away.
2 Corinthians 3:12-13 NIV

This hope we have makes us very bold.
The old covenant, the law, makes their minds dull.
It creates a veil over their hearts.
They cannot see or hear the truth that sets them free.
Only Christ can take away that veil and cause them to see and hear Him.

The Lord is the Spirit.
Where the Spirit of the Lord is, there is freedom.
Now our faces are unveiled, uncovered.
We can see His glory.
He is transforming us into His image with ever-increasing glory.
We will reflect His glory.

It's such an astounding thought to think that we can reflect God's glory.
He allows us to see beyond what is humanly possible.
We begin to see through His eyes.
The world looks so different when we allow God to change us.

But whenever anyone turns to the Lord, the veil is taken away.
Now the Lord is the Spirit, and where the Spirit of the Lord is,
there is freedom. And we all, who with unveiled faces contemplate the
Lord's glory, are being transformed into his image with ever-increasing
glory, which comes from the Lord, who is the Spirit.
2 Corinthians 3:16-18 NIV

He loves you

June 4
Pray and expect

In the morning, Lord, you hear my voice; in the morning
I lay my requests before you and wait expectantly.
Psalm 5:3 NIV

I lay my requests before you and . . . I wait.
How many times do we pray and lay our requests before God and just wait.
We wait and we wait and we wait.
But we forget the rest of the verse.
We forget to expect.
We forget to wait in expectation.
Expectation - a strong belief that something will happen or be the case in the future; One's prospects of inheritance.

To expect something is to believe it will happen.

When you go to bed at night you expect to see the sun rise the next morning.
When you tell your child to do something you expect that they will do it. (I even expected my kindergarteners to do that for 25 years and they did! Most of the time!)
When someone becomes pregnant they expect to have a baby in nine months. (People used to say, "oh she's expecting", instead of she's pregnant.)
When you send your child to college you expect them to graduate in four years (or for some, like me, a little longer)!
When you expect, you wait in anticipation, never doubting it will happen.
Just as you never doubted the next sunrise or the birth of a baby or a college graduation.
Sometimes the wait may be short but sometimes the wait may be much longer.
But no matter how long it takes
God does hear and He wants us to be expectant of all He has for us.
His ways are always good. Always!

"Good, Good Father"
by Chris Tomlin
Oh, I've heard a thousand stories of what they think you're like
But I've heard the tender whisper of love in the dead of night
And you tell me that you're pleased and that I'm never alone

You're a Good, Good Father
It's who you are, it's who you are, it's who you are
And I'm loved by you
It's who I am, it's who I am, it's who I am

Oh, and I've seen many searching for answers far and wide
But I know we're all searching for answers only you provide
Cause you know just what we need before we say a word

Cause you are perfect in all of your ways
You are perfect in all of your ways
You are perfect in all of your ways to us

Oh, it's love so undeniable, I can hardly speak
Peace so unexplainable, I can hardly think
As you call me deeper still into love, love, love

You're a Good, Good Father
It's who you are, it's who you are, it's who you are
And I'm loved by you
It's who I am, it's who I am, it's who I am

June 5
An ornament to grace your neck

Happy is the man who finds wisdom,
the man who gets understanding.
By wisdom Yahweh founded the earth.
By understanding, he established the heavens.
By his knowledge, the depths were broken up,
and the skies drop down the dew.
Proverbs 3:3,19-20 WEB

In six days God created the world.
By His own wisdom He laid the earth's foundation
In those six days He created the heavens.
By His own understanding He set the heavens in place.
In these same six days He created the oceans and all that is in them.
By His own knowledge the waters were divided.
In these six days He made the skies and the clouds and the moisture in the clouds.
The clouds dropped the dew.

God says we are to:
Find wisdom
Then we will gain understanding
The knowledge of man is nothing without:
His wisdom and His understanding and His knowledge

Everything comes from God!
Every good thing!

An ornament to grace your neck!

My son, let them not depart from your eyes.
Keep sound wisdom and discretion:
so they will be life to your soul,
and grace for your neck.
Proverbs 3:21-22 WEB

June 6
To dwell

Whoever dwells in the shelter of the Most High will rest
in the shadow of the Almighty.
Psalm 91:1 NIV

Say of the Lord:
He is my refuge.
He is my fortress.
He is my God, the one in whom I trust.

He will save us.
He will cover us.
He will be faithful.
He will be our shield and rampart.
We will not fear.

He is our dwelling.
No harm will come near us.
No disaster will overtake us.
His angels will guard us because He will command them to.
His angels will lift us up in their hands.
He will rescue us.
He will protect us.
He will answer us when we call on Him.
He will be with us.
He will deliver us.
He will honor us.
He will give us long life.
He will satisfy us.
He will show us His salvation.

He longs for you to dwell in His shelter.
He wants to give you rest in Him.

June 7
Tenderness

Be kind to one another, tender-hearted, forgiving each other,
just as God in Christ also has forgiven you.
Ephesians 4:32

*"Tenderness of spirit cannot be borrowed or put on for special occasions;
it is emphatically supernatural, and must flow out incessantly from the
inner fountains of the life. Deep tenderness of spirit is the very soul and
marrow of the Christ life. What specific gravity is to the planet, what
beauty is to the rainbow, what perfume is to the rose, what marrow is to
the bone, what rhythm is to poetry, what the pulse is to the heart, what
harmony is to music, what heat is to the human body—all this, and much
more, is tenderness of spirit to religion. It is possible to be very religious,
and staunch, and persevering in all Christian duties; possible, even, to be
sanctified, to be a brave defender and preacher of holiness, to be
mathematically orthodox and blameless in outward life, and very zealous
in good works, and yet to be greatly lacking in tenderness of spirit—that
all-subduing, all-melting love, which is the very cream and quintessence of
Heaven, and which incessantly streamed out from the voice and eyes of
the blessed Jesus.*
I would that I could be
A wound-dresser
Of souls—
Reaching the aching heart,
The tortured mind,
Calming them as the night
Calms tired bodies
When he drops the mantle of sleep
Over the world.
As each cold, glittering star
So might I stand in mine,
But with the warmth of a smile
On my face,
And in my eyes
An image of the Soul Divine"
(L. B. E. Cowman. "Springs in the Valley." December 4)

God's sweetness and tenderness of nature. . .
It inundates the soul.
It saturates the manners, expressions, words and tones of the voice.
It mellows the will, softens the judgment, melts the affections, refines the manners, and molds the whole being after Jesus.
It can't be borrowed or even put on for special occasions.
It is supernatural.
It is the soul and marrow of the Christ life.
Tenderness is. . .
What gravity is to the planet
What color is to the rainbow
What oil is to the rose
What marrow is to the bone
What rhythm is to poetry
What the pulse is to the heart
What harmony is to music
Tenderness brings hope and love and compassion and understanding.
All melting love

This tenderness streamed from the voice and eyes of Jesus.

May it stream from you. Tenderness

June 8
Fan into flame the gift

For this reason I remind you to fan into flame the gift of God, which is in
you through the laying on of my hands. For the Spirit God gave us does
not make us timid, but gives us power, love and self-discipline.
2 Timothy 1:6-7 NIV

I've never been good at starting a fire but my husband is. He always
seemed to know just the right wood to gather, how to stack the wood and
the best kindling for the fire to catch. Once the flame caught, he would
use something to fan the flame. The more he fanned it the bigger the fire.
The more oxygen that the fire consumed the more it grew and spread.

So it is with the gift God has given each of us.
Our gifts need His oxygen, His life to grow.
Our breath alone will not spread the flame.
But once God breathes into us His life
we have the ability to do amazing things.

Let God fan into flame the gift which is in you.
The Spirit God gave us does not make us timid,
but rather gives us power, love and self-discipline.

Fan into flame the gift!

The Spirit you received does not make you slaves,
so that you live in fear again; rather, the Spirit you received
brought about your adoption to sonship.
And by him we cry, "Abba, Father."
Romans 8:15 NIV

There is no fear in Christ Jesus.
We will not be timid.
We will let You fan into flame the gift You have given us.

He loves you

June 9
God has all knowledge

Who can fathom the Spirit of the Lord, or instruct the Lord as his
counselor? Whom did the Lord consult to enlighten him, and who taught
him the right way? Who was it that taught him knowledge,
or showed him the path of understanding?
Isaiah 40:13-14 NIV

God needs no instructor.
He needs no counselor.
He does not need to be enlightened,
No one needs to teach Him the right way.
He has all knowledge.
He has all understanding.

He was before time.
He will remain forever God.

God is:
All knowing
All enlightened
All encompassing
All understanding

He will not change.
He cannot change.
He is God!

*He has all the answers you will ever need
for today and for all eternity.*

He loves you

June 10
The Hunger Games

Everyone who competes in the games goes into strict training.
They do it to get a crown that will not last,
but we do it to get a crown that will last forever.
1 Corinthians 9:25 NIV

There was a popular movie series called "The Hunger Games".
Different ones were chosen to represent their people.
The ones chosen were then put together and their goal was to be the last one "standing", the last one alive. They always fought to the finish. This was not their desire, they were required to do this by their ruler, the one who was over them. At the end of each race there would be victors but there was no joy just relief that they had survived. Each time they won, then, there was always another "race, fight" to the finish.

This is so like the world, satan promises if we will only do this then we will get this.
But it is all to no avail, you finish the fight only to find out that he has another fight for you. He is the greatest deceiver, there is never an end with him. There is never any peace with him.

Yet, the one who is over all gives you peace. He never requires you to fight in your own strength. He gives you His strength. He always will.

And He always wins!

He loves you

June 11
This is an easy thing

"But now bring me a musician." When the musician played, Yahweh's hand came on him. He said, "Yahweh says, 'Make this valley full of trenches.' For Yahweh says, 'You will not see wind, neither will you see rain, yet that valley will be filled with water, and you will drink, both you and your livestock and your other animals. This is an easy thing in Yahweh's sight. He will also deliver the Moabites into your hand."
2 Kings 3:15-18 WEB

This is an easy thing in the eyes of the Lord.
What seems impossible for us is never too hard for God.
In fact, when the Israelites asked for help God not only gave them more than they asked or needed, He also destroyed their enemy too!

What seems impossible to us is never

impossible with God

The impossible becomes possible.

The unbelievable becomes believable.

The lack becomes abundant.

The hopelessness becomes hopeful.

This is an easy thing in the eyes of the Lord!

In the morning, about the time of offering the sacrifice, behold, water came by the way of Edom, and the country was filled with water.
2 Kings 3:20 WEB

He loves you

June 12
What are you looking at

For our light and momentary troubles are achieving for us an eternal
glory that far outweighs them all. So we fix our eyes not on what is seen,
but on what is unseen, since what is seen is temporary,
but what is unseen is eternal.
2 Corinthians 4:17-18 NIV

What are you looking at?
What do you see?
Is what you see bringing you down?
Does it sometimes seem more than you can handle?
Then maybe just maybe you are looking at the wrong thing.
There is beauty all around you.

Ask God to let you see what He sees.
Ask Him to open the eyes of your heart.
Ask Him to show you eternal things.
Those things that will never fade away.

He will lift you up to see beyond the things of this world.
He will give you a new vision.
You will love what you see!
Once you see His way you won't ever want to go back.

He loves you

June 13
My peace be with you

Again Jesus said, "Peace be with you! As the Father has sent me, I am
sending you." And with that he breathed on them and said,
"Receive the Holy Spirit."
John 20:21-22 NIV

I can just see our Heavenly Father bending down to look in your eyes. He
is holding your face in His hands with a hand on your cheek very gently
touching you, speaking peace into your life, looking at you with such
loving, caring eyes. Even His touch brings peace. His look tells of His
love for you. His posture, bending over, shows His compassion to
you. As He speaks, His breath gives life

"Peace be with you. Peace I give you,
not as the world gives."
John 14:27

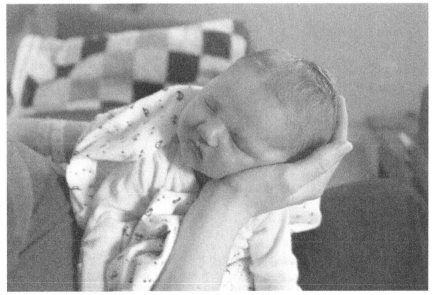

He loves you

June 14
His word heals

He sent out his word and healed them; he rescued them from the grave.
Psalm 107:20 NIV

He sent out His word.
He healed them.
He rescued them from the grave.
His word is powerful
Sharper than a two-edged sword
It has the power to:
Give life
Heal
Rescue
Love
Encourage
Give hope
His word is powerful!

It was in the beginning and will never pass away.
His word will remain forever!

Do you need to be healed?
Do you need to be rescued?

Search His word, look for your answers
to be met in Him.

Heal me, Lord, and I will be healed; save me and I will be saved,
for you are the one I praise.
Jeremiah 17:14 NIV

June 15
Grace in place of grace

Out of his fullness we have all received grace
in place of grace already given.
John 1:16 NIV

His body, the church, is the fullness of Christ.
He fills everything in every way.
This pleased God to have His fullness dwell in His son.
All that God is, lives in Jesus.
Now, because of what Christ did, we who know Him, are brought to this same fullness.
He rules over every power and every authority.
He gives this freely to us. It's His grace!
Grace in place of grace!
It does not get any better than this!

June 16
He sees your scars

The LORD binds up the bruises of His people
and heals the wounds He inflicted.
Isaiah 30:26 NIV

SCARS
*"When some friend has proved untrue—betrayed your simple trust; used
you for his selfish end, and trampled in the dust the Past, with all its
memories, and all its sacred ties, the light is blotted from the sky—for
something in you dies.*
*Bless your false and faithless friend, just smile and pass along—God must
be the judge of it: He knows the right and wrong. Life is short—don't
waste the hours by brooding on the past; His great laws are good and just;
Truth conquers at the last.*
*Red and deep our wounds may be—but after all the pain—God's own
finger touches us, and we are healed again...With faith restored, and trust
renewed—we look tow." ard the stars—the world will see the smiles we
have—but God will see the scars*
Patience Strong

He binds up your bruises.
He heals your wounds.

My younger sister and I were involved in a terrible car wreck when we
were both in high school. She was injured much more severely than
me. I had a broken ankle.
It was a bad break. I don't remember much pain right after the wreck
because I think I was in shock. And I was so concerned for my sister. She
was so badly injured. What I do remember about my pain was the next
day. They had placed a cast on my ankle sometime after the wreck. That
did not hurt. I do remember the terrible pain the next day. My ankle had
begun to swell and with the cast on it there was nowhere for the swelling
to go! It seemed at the time unbearable. I've always wondered if they put
the cast on too soon. Could they have let the swelling go down first,
before they put the cast on? I'm not a medical doctor so I don't
know. They did what they thought best. In the end my ankle healed fine.

Many years later I fell and broke the foot on the same leg that I had had my broken ankle. My husband and I were taking my 91-year-old dad out to eat. He used a walker and he didn't see a step down and he began to fall. My husband and I both tried to catch him but we all went down. It must have been a sight! I was the only one that was hurt, thankfully. I did have a bad break that required surgery to put in a plate and screws. Now a year later all I have left is a scar.

But each time I look at that scar I am reminded of the scars that cannot be seen by man. Scars like abuse and unkind words and emotional scars. Only God can see those scars and yet God says He can heal each of us from all the pain and hurt that caused these scars.

Sometimes the healing may take time.
Sometimes the healing may be painful.
Sometimes the healing may leave scars.
The world may not see your scars but God does.
But God is faithful He will heal you.

The moon will shine like the sun, and the sunlight will be seven times brighter, like the light of seven full days, when the Lord binds up the bruises of his people and heals the wounds he inflicted.
Isaiah 30:26 NIV

He loves you

June 17
A long life

"Because he loves me," says the LORD, "I will rescue him; I will protect him, for he acknowledges my name. He will call on me, and I will answer him; I will be with him in trouble, I will deliver him and honor him. With long life I will satisfy him and show him my salvation."
Psalm 91: 14-16

When our youngest child went away to college I had such mixed emotions. Happiness because he was healthy, just two years before he had had cancer. Excitement because he was going to further his education and start the next "adventure" of his life. Sadness because I knew I would miss him. Joy because I knew God had great plans for him Jacob very quickly made new friends. He even met his future wife there. One of those new friends was Michael. Michael loved to laugh, just like Jacob. Michael enjoyed life, just like Jacob. Michael loved to do crazy things, a little more than Jacob! But most importantly, Michael loved Jesus, just like Jacob.

Michael and Jacob became close friends. Michael would come to our house and Jacob would go to his house. We grew to love Michael like our own son. After Michael graduated from college he married his high school sweetheart, Brooke. They had not been married very long before Michael was diagnosed with a glioblastoma brain tumor. It was devastating. Through the four years that Michael lived I asked God daily to restore Michael to full health, to take away the cancer and to give him a long life. He had such a heart for Jesus. I remember the last time we saw Michael, just a couple of days before God took him home. He was still the sweet boy that we had grown to love but his body had suffered so very much. And yet at the very end he was able to say in sign language, "My heart is okay because He covered it." Brooke, his wife was a wonderful teacher to the deaf. She had taught Michael well. I remember crying out to God, asking, "But God I asked you for a long life for him". And God, in His very gentle voice spoke to me as only He can and He said, "I heard you. I gave Him life everlasting." And I could not argue with that. If you are questioning God about your prayers and wondering why they are not being answered in the way you think best, then maybe you are like me. You just need to trust Him. He does know what is best. His ways are so far above our ways.

For I am already being poured out like a drink offering. 2 Timothy 4:6

June 18
Encourage each other

And let us consider how we may spur one another on toward love and
good deeds, not giving up meeting together, as some are in the habit of
doing, but encouraging one another---and all the more
as you see the Day approaching.
Hebrews 10:24-25 NIV

Spur one another on to. . .
Love and good deeds
Meeting together
Encouraging one another
Even more now as the Day of Jesus' return approaches

Love speaks volumes.
Good deeds make others happy, the giver and the receiver.
Encouragement holds up a friend when they cannot stand alone.

Do these things and it will bring hope to someone who is hurting,
life to someone who feels like they can't go on and
joy to someone who only knows sadness.

As the world grows darker choose to be that light!

Let us hold unswervingly to the hope we profess,
for he who promised is faithful.
Hebrews 10:23 NIV

He loves you

June 19
Hidden treasures

I will give you hidden treasures, riches stored in secret places, so that you
may know that I am the Lord, the God of Israel,
who summons you by name.
Isaiah 45:3 NIV

I love looking for treasures.
I love secret places. I love hidden closets, secret rooms.
Now as I've grown older I see His word is so full of these hidden
treasures.
What fun it has been these past few years looking for these treasures.
You, Abba Father, have been so kind to reveal these hidden treasures to
me.

It seems that few find them.
It does take time to search but the hunt is so worth it.

His word is full of secret treasures.
He has so much He wants to show you
So much He wants to give you
These treasures are worth more than gold or silver
These treasures last forever

Take some time today to search for them
You won't be disappointed in what you will find!

He loves you

June 20
The peace of God

And the peace of God, which transcends all understanding,
will guard your hearts and your minds in Christ Jesus.
Philippians 4:7 NIV

The peace of God will guard your hearts and your minds in Jesus.
His perfect peace comes when we trust in Him.
He freely gives us His peace.

Who wouldn't want this peace?
It's free.
It guards our hearts.
It guards our minds.
It is perfect.
All we have to do is trust in Him.

Life is so difficult at times.
You may have financial difficulties.
You may have cancer or some other disease.
You may struggle with depression.
You may have recently lost a child.
You may have been rejected by your spouse.
You may have lost all hope.
God wants you to hear this.
He wants to whisper so gently to you that in all of this,
He can give you peace.
The peace He gives goes beyond all our understanding.
This peace, His peace, is so powerful and good that it can and will guard
not only our minds but our hearts too, in Jesus.
Ask Him for it, He will freely give to you.

You will keep in perfect peace those whose minds are steadfast,
because they trust in you.
Isaiah 26:3 NIV

He loves you

June 21
Just knock

"I tell you, keep asking, and it will be given you. Keep seeking, and you will find. Keep knocking, and it will be opened to you. For everyone who asks receives. He who seeks finds. To him who knocks it will be opened. "Which of you fathers, if your son asks for bread, will give him a stone? Or if he asks for a fish, he won't give him a snake instead of a fish, will he? Or if he asks for an egg, he won't give him a scorpion, will he? If you then, being evil, know how to give good gifts to your children, how much more will your heavenly Father give the Holy Spirit to those who ask him?"
Luke 11:9-13 WEB

I have four little grandsons. I love them each so much.
When they come to our house to visit I anxiously await their arrival. I am usually at the door before they even knock but occasionally they beat me to the door. There is never a shadow of a doubt about me opening the door for them.
It never enters my mind to not 'open the door'.
It never enters their mind that their Mamae would not 'open the door' for them.
I am always waiting with open arms.
Just as my love for my grandchildren is unwavering
So is God's love for you.

His words to you are. . .
Ask and it will be given
Seek and you will find
Knock and the door will be opened

If you ask me you will receive
If you seek me you will find me,
If you knock I will open the door.
God only gives good gifts. But you have to ask!

He is waiting to hear your voice. Just knock!

June 22
Finish your work

I have brought you glory on earth by finishing the work you gave me to do.
John 17:4 NIV

Jesus said to the Father, "I have brought you glory by finishing the work you gave me to do".

We can bring God glory by finishing the work that He has given us to do.

This work is not as the world says work is.
This work is often not as the church says work is.
This work is what the Spirit says to do.

That alone brings Him glory.

In order to know the work He has for us

we must be able to recognize His voice.

When you recognize His voice then

you can hear His voice.

When you hear His voice you will know

what work you are to do.

And now, Father, glorify me in your presence with the glory
I had with you before the world began.
John 17:5 NIV

He loves you

June 23
Holiness

Make every effort to live in peace with everyone and to be holy;
without holiness no one will see the Lord.
Hebrews 12:14 NIV

"Some of my views on holiness, as I once wrote them, are as follows:
Holiness appears to me to have a sweet, calm, pleasant, charming, and
serene nature, all of which brings an inexpressible purity, radiance,
peacefulness, and overwhelming joy to the soul. In other words, holiness
makes the soul like a field or garden of God, with every kind of pleasant
fruit and flower, and each one delightful and undisturbed, enjoying a sweet
calm and the gentle and refreshing rays of the sun." Jonathan Edward

We are to be holy.
When we live in this holiness our eyes are opened to see the Lord.

Holiness is: Sweet, Calm, Pleasant, Charming, Serene
Holiness brings an inexpressible:
Purity, Radiance, Peacefulness, Overwhelming Joy
Holiness produces a fragrant and pleasant garden in the soul.
Others will be attracted to this garden. It is pleasant to look at. It is
calming to the senses. It is peaceful to the soul. It causes overwhelming
joy.

*The greatest thing about holiness is that we don't have
to work it up. We surrender to God and He does all of
this in us. He is faithful and He will do it.*

May the God of peace himself sanctify you completely. May your whole
spirit, soul, and body be preserved blameless at the coming of our Lord
Jesus Christ. He who calls you is faithful, who will also do it.
1 Thessalonians 5:23-24 WEB

He loves you

June 24
Everything is under His feet

And God placed all things under his feet and appointed him to be head
over everything for the church, which is his body, the fullness of him
who fills everything in every way.
Ephesians 1:22-23 NIV

God placed everything under His feet.
Not just some things, everything. . .
death, illness, depression, insecurity, hopelessness, anxiety,
everything was placed under His feet.

He appointed Jesus to be head over everything for the church, his body.
This body is to be the fullness of Him, Jesus.
This body who fills everything in every way.

This body, that's us as believers, are to be "Him here".
We are to fill everything in every way.
How are we filling everything?
Are we filling it with good things, things that are full of the fruits
of the spirit?
Things like love, peace, patience, kindness, gentleness, self-control,
compassion, hope, joy
with no trace of hypocrisy or partiality.

If we are, then we are fulfilling this word.
We are then being the fullness of Him, Jesus,
the one who gave it all for us.

He loves you

June 25
He holds all things together

He is before all things, and in him all things hold together.
Colossians 1:17 NIV

He was before all things.
He holds everything together.
Everything!

Miracles is a book by Eric Metaxas. The first part of the book explains in great detail what a miracle creation is. From the creation of the world and everything in it to the creation of the universe and everything in it to the creation of the millions of galaxies and all they contain.
Not only is all of creation such an amazing miracle, the fact that all of these things stay together and stay perfectly aligned are incredible miracles, too.

This scripture so confirms all that was written in this book.

God was before all of this, before He created any of this.
He is the one that holds all of this, all things, together.

What an amazing God we serve.
And yet He created all of this and holds all of this together and He still knows how many hairs are on your head. He knows when you arise and He knows when you sleep. He hems you in both behind and before. He loves you so!

And even the very hairs of your head are all numbered.
Matthew 10:30 NIV

You hem me in behind and before, and you lay your hand upon me.
Psalm 139:5 NIV

He loves you

June 26
Call back

This will result in your being witnesses to them.
Luke 21:13 NIV

Have you ever climbed a mountain? When our children were young we would take our vacations and go to the mountains in New Mexico. We loved these mountains. Each time we went we would hike a mountain or two.   When our children were young it was much work but it wasn't long before they could out walk me! My husband would lead us and he was always so kind to encourage me along the way. He would 'call back', "Just a little bit more and we will rest" or "just a little bit more and we will be at the top". His words always helped me to go on! The view from the top was always worth the climb! 'Call back' so that others will be encouraged to not give up. Bear testimony, tell others of God's faithfulness. There is such a 'great cloud of witnesses' watching and waiting to hear your report.

And so you will bear testimony to me. But make up your mind not to worry beforehand how you will defend yourselves. For I will give you words and wisdom that none of your adversaries will be able to resist or contradict.
Luke 21:13-15 NIV

June 27
He knew discrimination

Then one of the Twelve---the one called Judas Iscariot---went to the chief priests and asked, "What are you willing to give me if I deliver him over to you?" So they counted out for him thirty pieces of silver. From then on Judas watched for an opportunity to hand him over.
Matthew 26:14-16 NIV

Our country cries of discrimination! African Americans, Native Americans, Hispanics, whites.... It goes on and on.

But the one that suffered true discrimination was Jesus.
He was sold for thirty pieces of silver.
He was rejected.
He was despised.
He was misunderstood.
He was without honor in His own home town.
He was beaten.
He was nailed to a cross.
He was not even able to raise himself up to breathe.

Yet He blamed no one!
He simply prayed, "Father, forgive them for they know not what they do".

May we look to Him, the Son of God, the creator of all life, to show us how we are to love.

When Judas, who had betrayed him, saw that Jesus was condemned, he was seized with remorse and returned the thirty pieces of silver to the chief priests and the elders. "I have sinned," he said, "for I have betrayed innocent blood."
Matthew 27:3-4 NIV

He loves you

June 28
I am not alone

Jesus replied, "A time is coming and in fact has come when you will be scattered, each to your own home. You will leave me all alone.
Yet I am not alone, for my Father is with me."
John 16:32 NIV

"There are no birds that live in as much solitude as eagles, for they never fly in flocks. Rarely can even two eagles be seen together. And a life that is dedicated to God knows divine fellowship, no matter how many human friendships have had to be forfeited along the way.
God knows how to change our circumstances in order to isolate us. And once we yield to Him and He takes us through an experience of isolation, we are no longer dependent upon those around us, although we still love them as much as before. Then we realize that He has done a new work within us and that the wings of our soul have learned to soar in loftier air."
(Streams in the Desert by L. B. Cowman December 20)

Yet in our solitude, we are never ever alone. God is always there, always.

He is faithful to never, ever leave our side. If we turn to the right or to the left He is there.

If we make our bed in the depths or on the far side of the sea He is there. There is not a place you can go that He is not there.

He is always with you. You are never alone!

And you can soar with Him, on wings of eagles!

Whether you turn to the right or to the left, your ears will hear a voice behind you, saying, "This is the way; walk in it."
Isaiah 30:21 NIV

He loves you

June 29
He makes me strong

And the God of all grace, who called you to his eternal glory in Christ,
after you have suffered a little while, will himself restore you
and make you strong, firm and steadfast.
To him be the power for ever and ever. Amen.
I Peter 5:10-11

He arms you with strength.
He keeps your way secure.
He gives you eternal encouragement and good hope.
He encourages your heart.
He strengthens you in every good deed and word.
He makes you strong.

It is God who arms me with strength and

keeps my way secure.

Psalm 18:32 NIV

May our Lord Jesus Christ himself and God our Father, who loved us and
by his grace gave us eternal encouragement and good hope, encourage
your hearts and strengthen you in every good deed and word.
2 Thessalonians 2:16-17 NIV

He loves you

June 30
He understands

Then there were two robbers crucified with him, one on his right hand and
one on the left. Those who passed by blasphemed him, wagging their
heads, and saying, "You who destroy the temple,
and build it in three days, save yourself!
If you are the Son of God, come down from the cross!"
Matthew 27:38-40 WEB

Jesus understands every hurt you've ever felt.
He knows how it feels to be insulted,
He knows how it feels to be ridiculed,
He knows how it feels to be made fun of.
He knows how it feels to have your leaders, those in authority, those who
rule over you, to mock you.
He knows how it feels to have others use your words and twist them out of
context, and use them to say something you never meant.
He knows how it feels to be misunderstood.
He knows how it feels when those close to you desert you.
He knows how it feels to be left alone.
He knows and He understands your pain.

Likewise the chief priests also mocking, with the scribes, the
Pharisees, and the elders, said, "He saved others, but he can't save
himself. If he is the King of Israel, let him come down from the cross now,
and we will believe in him. He trusts in God. Let God deliver him now, if he
wants him; for he said, 'I am the Son of God.'" The robbers also who were
crucified with him cast on him the same reproach.
Matthew 27:41-44 WEB

He loves you

July 1
Go. . . I will be with you

Judges 6:14-18 The Message
But GOD faced him directly: "Go in this strength that is yours. Save Israel
from Midian. Haven't I just sent you?" Gideon said to him, "Me, my
master? How and with what could I ever save Israel? Look at me. My
clan's the weakest in Manasseh and I'm the runt of the litter." GOD said to
him, "I'll be with you. Believe me, you'll defeat Midian as one man."
Gideon said, "If you're serious about this, do me a favor: Give me a sign to
back up what you're telling me. Don't leave until I come back and bring
you my gift." He said, "I'll wait till you get back."
Judges 6:14-18 The Message

Gideon felt small and very insignificant, yet when God looked at Gideon
He saw something completely different.
So often that's the way we are. We look at ourselves and say,
we aren't good enough, we aren't worthy, we don't deserve it and on and
on.
But God looks at us through His eyes.
His eyes love unconditionally

The Lord turned to him.

The Lord spoke to him.

The Lord listened to him.

The Lord answered him.

The Lord waited on him.

He will do the same for you.
Let Him show you what He sees.

He loves you

July 2
A gentle tongue

Through patience a ruler can be persuaded,
and a gentle tongue can break a bone.
Proverbs 25:15 NIV

Through patience:
A gentle tongue can break a bone.
There is much power in a gentle tongue.
Words softly spoken can do amazing things.
They can lift someone up.
They can bring conviction.
They can give life and hope.
They can break down walls.
They can open doors that have long been closed.
They can reveal love.
They can change a heart.

A soothing tongue is a tree of life,
but a perverse tongue crushes the spirit.
Proverbs 15:4 NIV

From the mouth of the righteous comes the fruit of wisdom,
but a perverse tongue will be silenced.
Proverbs 10:31

He loves you

July 3
Strengthen my hands

They were all trying to frighten us, thinking, "Their hands will get too weak
for the work, and it will not be completed." But I prayed,
"Now strengthen my hands."
Nehemiah 6:9 NIV

Now strengthen my hands!
The world tries to frighten us.
The world tells us we are too weak.
The world tells us we will never complete the work.

Yet God says I am with you.
I will uphold you with my righteous right hand.
I will never leave you or forsake you.
I will strengthen you.
You can do all things through me.
Trust me!
I will strengthen your hands!

Whatever He's told you to do, do it!
He has strengthened your hands.

When all our enemies heard about this, all the surrounding nations were
afraid and lost their self-confidence, because they realized that this work
had been done with the help of our God.
Nehemiah 6:16

July 4
They asked. . . He heard

He spread out a cloud as a covering, and a fire to give light at night.
They asked, and he brought them quail; he fed them well with the bread of
heaven. He opened the rock, and water gushed out;
it flowed like a river in the desert.
Psalm 105:39-41 NIV

They asked. . . He heard.
He spread out a cloud as a covering.
He made a fire to give light at night.

They asked....He heard
He brought, He fed well.
He opened...water gushed out, it flowed.

They asked . . . He heard
He covered them by day.
He gave light by night.

They asked... He heard.
He fed them well, not just with ordinary food but with the bread of heaven.
He opened the rock, water, unending, abundant water gushed out
So much so that it was like a river in the desert.

He hears our cries.
He knows before we ask what we need.
He always gives in abundance.
He provides in miraculous ways.
His supply is unending, it will never run dry.

He loves you

July 5
Open our eyes

The seventh time the servant reported, "A cloud as small as a man's hand
is rising from the sea." So Elijah said, "Go and tell Ahab, 'Hitch up your
chariot and go down before the rain stops you.'"
1 Kings 18:44 NIV

There had been no rain for three years yet Elijah believed God.
He knew if He asked God, God would do it.
The drought had been very bad but Elijah knew His God.
He knew God would hear his prayer and He would send the rain.
Yet when he sent his servant to look, the servant saw nothing each time
he looked. Elijah had him look six times and still he saw nothing.

But on the seventh time he saw a cloud the size of a man's hand rising
from the sea. A cloud that small was all Elijah needed. He knew God was
sending the rain, not just a few drops of rain but abundant rain!

If you are waiting on God to answer your need, never give up.
It may look impossible. The world may even say it is impossible
but God says otherwise. Look for His signs. He will show them to you.

Watch for God's faint beginnings!

Open our eyes that we might see!

He loves you

July 6
You are my hiding place

You are my hiding place; you will protect me from trouble
and surround me with songs of deliverance.
Psalm 32:7 NIV

He is your hiding place.
He will protect you from trouble.
He will surround you with songs of deliverance.

His hiding place for you is your safe shelter.
It will be your shade from the heat of the day.
It will be your refuge from the storm and the rain.

His voice is tender. When He speaks to you it is sweet.
His presence always dwells within your shelter.

This hiding place is just for you
because He delights in you.
You have no reason to fear.
You can dwell in this place with Him forever.

He brought me out into a spacious place; he rescued me
because he delighted in me.
Psalm 18:19 NIV

He loves you

July 7
The Lord bless you

The Lord said to Moses, "Tell Aaron and his sons, 'This is how you are to
bless the Israelites. Say to them: "The Lord bless you and keep you;
the Lord make his face shine on you and be gracious to you;
the Lord turn his face toward you and give you peace. "
Numbers 6:22-26 NIV

What great words to pray over someone or to bless someone.
May He do all of these things for you.
May you sense His presence in every moment of everyday.

May The Lord bless you.

May The Lord keep you.

May The Lord make His face to shine on you.

May The Lord be gracious to you.

May The Lord turn His face toward you.

May The Lord give you peace.

Peace I leave with you; my peace I give you. I do not give to you as the
world gives. Do not let your hearts be troubled and do not be afraid.
John 14:27 NIV

He loves you

July 8
He walks along with us

As they talked and discussed these things with each other,
Jesus himself came up and walked along with them;
but they were kept from recognizing him.
Luke 24:15-16 NIV

I heard a tragic story on the news a few years ago. A small plane had gone down and all aboard the plane were killed except one little girl. Her dad was the pilot and her mom and nine-year-old sister were killed, along with her cousin. The plane crashed into some dense woods. The little girl some how crawled out of the wreckage and found her mother and father were dead. She was bleeding and had some broken bones and only had one sock on yet she some how managed to walk through overgrown dense wooded areas down a twelve foot ravine to where she saw a house. She very lightly knocked on the door and a man opened the door. She began to explain to him what had happened...that she had been in a plane crash and that her parents were asleep or dead! The man knew what to do and he called 911! What incredible strength this precious little seven-year-old girl displayed! Yet in the midst of total disaster she found strength to find help. I can't help but think, really know, that Jesus was there right beside her. Maybe He actually picked her up and carried her and sat her on the doorstep of the kind man. I can see a picture in my mind of the little girl surrounded by angels, going before her, beside her and behind her protecting her from the darkness...
with Jesus carrying her in His arms.

What a picture for God's children to see...
In our darkest hour He is there
In our lost state He has a path marked out for us
In our alone time He is right beside us
In our fear He is our protector
In our dazed confusion He holds us
He goes before us!
He walks along with us!

He loves you

July 9
His face is shining on you

Let your face shine on your servant; save me in your unfailing love.
Psalm 31:16 NIV

"Have you ever watched a child who loves her father but the father's face is continually directed away from that child - not "shining" upon her? Have you been in that place yourself? Did you experience your father's or mother's turning away from you in anger and withdrawal - when their faces did not shine on you but instead scowled at you or ignored you? Communication was cut off. You were agonized by it until you learned to harden your heart against it. In a similar way a certain communication is absolutely necessary to our having the kind of confidence and peace appropriate to a child of God. Without real communication from God, our view of the world is impersonal, however glorious we may find God's creation. There is all the difference in the world between having a general view that this is our Father's world (or even that God has arranged for our eternal redemption) and having confidence, based in experience, that the Father's face is turned toward us, shining upon us, and that the Father is speaking to us individually.
("Hearing God" week 46 day 2 by Dallas Willard)

This has been true in my life, especially as a child and then as a teenager. I don't remember seeing or feeling my father's face shining on me.

But now I know my Abba Father is with me. His face is shining on me. Even when I do not sense it and the enemy tries to tell me it's not true...even then His face is still shining on me. He has saved me and He will continue to save me. He has a good plan for me. He is turned toward me. He is speaking to me. He loves me with an everlasting love.

As you pray the words above may you begin to believe it, really believe that He loves you.

That His face is shining on you. That He is holding you so near.

That His love for you is deeper than the deepest ocean, higher than the highest star. That His love will never, ever, ever fail you. That He gave His most precious possession, His son, just for you. May you sense all of this, His pleasure with you and His forever love for you.

When I smiled at them, they scarcely believed it;

the light of my face.

Job 29:24 NIV

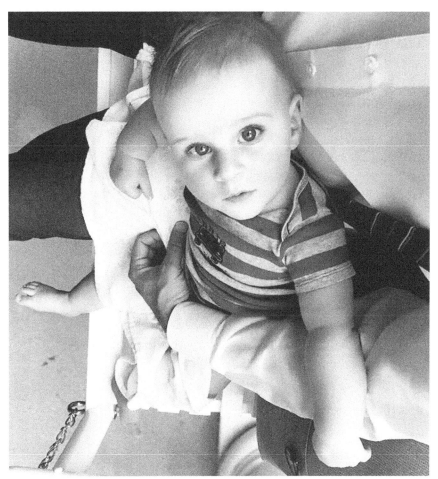

He loves you

July 10
Living water will flow from us

Whoever believes in me, as Scripture has said, rivers of living water
will flow from within them.
John 7:38 NIV

Rivers will flow
Not just one river but many rivers
Not trickle but flow, it will gush forth
Not from the outside but from the inside

It will be something God does within you.
It won't be something you can make up or create on your own.
It will be a natural flowing, just as rivers burst forth from hidden springs
under ground.
So shall God do that in those that believe in Him.

May it be so in your life.
May His living water spring forth from within you.
May it splash on others and as it splashes may they see Jesus in you.
May what they see in your life give them a thirst for this same living water.
May they be drawn to the source of all life, Jesus.
All because you let the rivers of living water flow through you.

But whoever drinks the water I give them will never thirst.
Indeed, the water I give them will become in them
a spring of water welling up to eternal life.
John 4:14 NIV

He loves you

July 11
They were prepared

Now the priests who carried the ark remained standing in the middle of the Jordan until everything the Lord had commanded Joshua was done by the people, just as Moses had directed Joshua. The people hurried over, and as soon as all of them had crossed, the ark of the Lord and the priests came to the other side while the people watched. The men of Reuben, Gad and the half-tribe of Manasseh crossed over, ready for battle, in front of the Israelites, as Moses had directed them. About forty thousand armed for battle crossed over before the Lord to the plains of Jericho for war.
Joshua 4:10-13 NIV

They crossed over ready for battle.
Ready for battle, armed for battle.

God miraculously parted the waters of the Jordan River for all the people to cross over to safety.
Yet there were those that were ready for battle, they were so prepared that they were armed for battle. Even as they crossed over, walking on dry ground through the Jordan River bed, they were prepared for what lay ahead. They were ready to fight the enemy if need be.

So must we be ready for battle. We must be armed for this battle.
Those that were armed crossed over first. They crossed over before the Lord to the plains for war. They knew their job. They were willing to go first, through the river to war.

They not only had to trust God that they could walk through on dry ground but that He would go before them and give them the strength they would need for this battle that lay ahead.

They were prepared!

Put on the full armor of God, so that you can take your stand against the devil's schemes.

Ephesians 6:11

July 12
Fill our hearts with joy

Command those who are rich in this present world not to be arrogant nor to put their hope in wealth, which is so uncertain, but to put their hope in God, who richly provides us with everything for our enjoyment.
1 Timothy 6:17 NIV

God richly provides us with everything for our enjoyment.

Enjoyment - rain from heaven, crops in their season, abundant food, fills our hearts with joy

Help us to grasp enjoyment!
Rain from heaven, teach us how to drink your rain
Fill our hearts with joy

Father, teach us to enjoy, to be still, to dwell with You.

May we see you in everything as we begin

on our path of enjoyment.

As we enjoy seeing the butterfly spread its wings and fly.
As we enjoy looking at the blue jay resting on the branch.
As we enjoy examining the flowers with all their symmetrical beauty.
As we enjoy life, our life, the life You have given us.

He loves you

He loves you

July 13
He listens

The man answered, Now that is remarkable! You don't know where he comes from, yet he opened my eyes. We know that God does not listen to sinners. He listens to the godly person who does his will. Nobody has ever heard of opening the eyes of a man born blind.
John 9:30-32 NIV

He listens
He listens
He listens

He not only listens, He hears.
Many will not know where He comes from.
Less will have their eyes opened.
But those few that do have their eyes opened will see, really see Him.

Then they will speak and He will listen.
When He listens He in turn will speak to them.
They will want to do His will because He has so graciously opened their eyes.

They can see, really see Him.
They are forever changed!
Whatever you are going through He listens to you.
He hears your heart's cry.
You will be forever changed.

As He passed by, He saw a man blind from birth.
When He had said this, He spat on the ground, and made clay of the spittle, and applied the clay to his eyes, and said to him, "Go, wash in the pool of Siloam" (So he went away and washed, and came *back* seeing.
John 9:1.6-7

July 14
He looks at the heart

When they arrived, Samuel saw Eliab and thought, "Surely the Lord's anointed stands here before the Lord." But the Lord said to Samuel, "Do not consider his appearance or his height, for I have rejected him. The Lord does not look at the things people look at. People look at the outward appearance, but the Lord looks at the heart."
1 Samuel 16:6-7 NIV

The Lord said, "Do not consider his appearance or his height".
The Lord does not look at the things people look at.
People look at the outward appearance, but the Lord looks at the heart.

God looks at the heart.
He doesn't see the diamonds or the fancy houses or the fast cars.
He sees the heart.

What do we see?
We so often look at ones appearance or what they have or own.
But God says "Look again, look past all of that, I want you to look at his heart!"

When others look at our hearts, what do they see?
May they see hope and joy and peace and love.
May they see a reflection of Jesus.

As water reflects the face, so one's life reflects the heart.
Proverbs 27:19

He loves you

July 15
Joy

You make known to me the path of life; you will fill me with joy in your presence, with eternal pleasures at your right hand.
Psalm 16:11 NIV

Joy
I look up and I see my table before me. My chair has been pulled out.
I am reminded of what that means. It's an invitation to come and sit for a while. Before me on the table are things that represent what I like to do.
I love to create, to make things. I love to give these things away.
I love to see the response of someone when I give them something I have created. There is nothing that brings me more joy than to know that I have refreshed the hearts of the saints.

My chair is pulled out... It is bidding me to come...To create... To make...
To give joy to another.

That's just the way Jesus is...
He has pulled out a chair for you
Come sit in it
He has everything ready for you...to give you joy!

"Your greatest door to success lies directly in front of the gifts you have. The key to unlock the door is only found in using those gifts."
(a quote from Dreams and Mysteries)

Light shines on the righteous and joy on the upright in heart.
Psalm 97:11 NIV

He loves you

He loves you

July 16
The Sound of marching

"As soon as you hear the sound of marching in the tops of the poplar trees, move out to battle, because that will mean God has gone out in front of you to strike the Philistine army." So David did as God commanded him, and they struck down the Philistine army, all the way from Gibeon to Gezer.
1 Chronicles 14:15-16 NIV

Before the enemy attacked David knew about it.
But first David prayed and asked God what he should do.
God spoke and David obeyed. David defeated his enemy by God's power.
The enemy attacked again.
David sought the Lord. God answered again.
This time God revealed a different strategy or plan.
"As soon as you hear the sound of marching in the tops of the poplar trees, move out to battle, because that will mean God has gone out in front of you."
So David did as God commanded him.

In order for David to defeat his enemy. . .
He had to pray first
Listen to what God said
Obey His words
He had to listen again for "the sound of marching in the tops of the poplar trees", then move out to battle.
That will mean God has gone out before you.

The victory comes only when we pray, then obey and listen again.

"King David's conversational interactions with God are well documented in the Bible. In the text above, when David "inquired of God," God gave him de- tailed instructions for battle. It occurred just as God said. In this and other biblical passages, God supplies specific information. These are not the impressions, impulses or feelings, which are so commonly thought to be what God uses to communicate with us, but clear and detailed cognitive content concerning what is the situation, what is to be done and

what will happen. David was not left to wonder if he should do this or that. He was simply told. David did not have to speculate about the meaning of "the sound of marching in the tops of the balsam trees"; he was told its meaning."
("Hearing God" week 47 day 2 by Dallas Willard)

My family and I have vacationed in the mountains of New Mexico for many years. Now that our children are married and have families of their own my husband and I still go to these same mountains. We now take the time to just sit and listen. One of my favorite sights is the aspen trees gently moving in the wind. They do it ever so quietly and as the light catches the leaves they actually began to sparkle. It is a beautiful sight to see. I do wonder what the sounds of marching in the tops of these trees would sound like!

He loves you

July 17
Be assured

I will rejoice in doing them good and will assuredly plant them
in this land with all my heart and soul.
Jeremiah 32:41 NIV

To Assure. . .
1. To declare earnestly, state with confidence
2. To cause to know surely
3. To pledge or promise, guarantee
4. To make (a future event) sure
5. To secure or confirm, render safe or stable
6. To give confidence, encourage

You are to be assured of this. . .
God goes ahead of you.
He will destroy your enemy as He has promised.
God will protect you.
God has perfect knowledge of you and He is with you.
God gives rain in season and regular harvest.
He meets all your needs.
God speaks truth.
He rejoices in doing good for you.
He has a certain place for you.
He sees and knows all.
God has made Jesus both Lord and Messiah.
God cannot lie. He speaks only truth.
God wants you to stand firm in His will, mature and fully assured.

Be assured, He sees and He knows.

Be assured that my words are not false; one who has
perfect knowledge is with you.
Job 36:4 NIV

He loves you

July 18
God's voice

For prophecy never had its origin in the human will, but prophets, though human, spoke from God as they were carried along by the Holy Spirit.
2 Peter 1:21 NIV

"With very little exception, the form in which "men and women [were] moved by the Holy Spirit [and] spoke from God" - we call this inspiration - was nothing more than thoughts and perceptions of the distinctive character that these people had come, through experience, to recognize as the voice of God in their own souls. The thoughts and perceptions were still their thoughts and perceptions. It could not be otherwise. But the thoughts and perceptions bore within themselves the unmistakable stamp of divine quality, spirit, intent and origination. Peter would have known and experienced this process and seems to have thought it important to us."
(Hearing God week 47 day 4 by Dallas Willard)

This light, His light, shines within us. It turns our darkness into His light. God will reveal Himself to you. He will speak to you. When you hear His voice it will be like the dawning of a new day. He will shed light on your path. It will be like the sun as it breaks forth in the morning, so shall the power of His word be to you.

We also have the prophetic message as something completely reliable, and you will do well to pay attention to it, as to a light shining in a dark place, until the day dawns and the morning star rises in your hearts. Above all, you must understand that no prophecy of Scripture came about by the prophet's own interpretation of things.
2 Peter 1:19-20 NIV

He loves you

July 19
I have loved you with an everlasting love

The Lord appeared to us in the past, saying: "I have loved you with an everlasting love; I have drawn you with unfailing kindness.
Jeremiah 31:3 NIV

We got our golden retriever when our son was young, probably around eight years old. Our son named him Austin. Austin loved our son. He loved to be with him. He loved it when he petted him. He loved it when he played with him. He just loved him. Then one day everything changed. Our son was diagnosed with an inoperable brain tumor. He had to begin very intense chemo. Our son could no longer play with Austin. He had to lie on the couch most of the day. He did not have the energy to play. But the amazing thing is our golden retriever seemed to sense something was wrong. So when our son lay on the couch Austin lay on the floor right beside him and he always placed his paw on the couch beside Jacob. He never left his side. He was such a faithful friend.

Sometimes God uses the things of this world to remind us of His abiding love for us, His love that will never ever leave us or forsake us.

He loves you

He loves you

July 20
Get wisdom

Do not forsake wisdom, and she will protect you; love her, and she will
watch over you. The beginning of wisdom is this: Get wisdom. Though it
cost all you have, get understanding. Cherish her, and she will exalt you;
embrace her, and she will honor you. She will give you a garland to grace
your head and present you with a glorious crown.
Proverbs 4:6-9 NIV

Get wisdom
Get understanding
Cherish her
She will exalt you
Embrace her
She will honor you

She will be a garland to grace your head

And present you with a glorious crown

How many will receive this garland to grace their head?
How many will have this glorious crown?

We may be surprised at who receives these.
It may be the very lowly, meek and quiet.
It may be the ones you've never heard of.
The ones that took the time to be still and know.
The ones who took the time to listen, really listen.
We may never know their names.
We may not even know what they did.
But God knows.
He will one day place on them a glorious crown.
May we desire to get wisdom.
May we cherish understanding.
May we embrace them.
They will bring life to you and those that surround you.

July 21
A sacrifice of praise

May my prayer be set before you like incense; may the lifting up
of my hands be like the evening sacrifice.
Psalm 141:2 NIV

May our prayer be set before you like incense.
May the lifting of our hands be like the evening sacrifice.

Incense is . . .
Fragrant to the nose
Used to block other smells
Used to calm, to relax, to kill germs
Pleasing to the senses

Evening sacrifice is . . .
Given at the close of the day
An offering
Focusing attention on one purpose

May our prayer be pleasing to your senses,

a fragrant aroma to you.

As we lift our hands, may it be an offering to you

Abba Father.

May it be a sacrifice of praise.

May our focus be entirely on you, the giver of all life.

Another angel came and stood at the altar, holding a golden censer; and
much incense was given to him, so that he might add it to the prayers of
all the saints on the golden altar which was before the throne. And the
smoke of the incense, with the prayers of the saints, went up before God
out of the angel's hand.
Revelation 8:3-4

July 22
God's pattern

Do not conform to the pattern of this world, but be transformed by the
renewing of your mind. Then you will be able to test and approve what
God's will is---his good, pleasing and perfect will.
Romans 12:2 NIV

The pattern of this world. . .
Patterns are everywhere.
Defining patterns can sometimes be difficult.
We have patterns in our solar system.
We have patterns in our world.
We have patterns on our city streets.
We have patterns on our houses.
We have patterns on our clothes.
We have patterns in our DNA.
Patterns are everywhere.

So often we live our lives by a pattern.
Maybe it's a pattern you saw in your mom or dad.
A pattern of fear or worry or anxiety.
Maybe it's a pattern of anger and hurt and abuse.

Whatever the pattern God wants to give you a new pattern,
A pattern of love and peace and comfort.
A pattern of kindness and tenderness and acceptance,
He can do it.
He wants to renew your mind, create a new pattern there.
Then you will see him, you will really hear him.
You will know His good and pleasing and perfect pattern for your life.

Look around you for the beautiful patterns God has created.
Look intensely at them. He will begin to renew your mind through these
patterns He has created for your pleasure.

He loves you

He loves you

July 23
Guard my mouth

Set a guard over my mouth, Lord; keep watch over the door of my lips.
Psalm 141:3 NIV

How often do we speak without thinking?
How often do words come out that we wish we could take back?

Do unto others as you would have them do unto you.
How would that make you feel if they did or said that to you?
It is such a good reminder to just be still.

Guard our mouths Father.
We live in a hurting world.
Our words need to be words of hope and life
not condemnation and judgment.
Teach us to be still.

For this people's heart has become calloused; they hardly hear with their
ears, and they have closed their eyes. Otherwise they might see with their
eyes, hear with their ears, understand with their hearts and turn,
and I would heal them.
Matthew 13:15 NIV

*Oh that we might see with our eyes and hear with our
ears and understand with our hearts!*

He loves you

July 24
Drink from this cup

There came a woman of Samaria to draw water. Jesus said to her, "Give
Me a drink." Therefore the Samaritan woman said to Him, "How is it that
You, being a Jew, ask me for a drink since I am a Samaritan woman?"
(For Jews have no dealings with Samaritans.) Jesus answered and said to
her, "If you knew the gift of God, and who it is who says to you, 'Give Me a
drink,' you would have asked Him,
and He would have given you living water."
John 4:7-10 NIV

Jews did not use the dishes the Samaritans used.

I remember a story told years ago by a great man of God, Leonard
Ravenhill. He came to our church when we lived in east Texas. He told a
story of a woman who lived in England, where he was from. This woman
was very poor and had very little and what she did have was very dirty. It
was tea time and she wanted to offer him tea. He said when he looked
into the cup and saw how unclean it was, he did not want to drink from the
cup. At that moment God said to him, "I have done this just for you and
for the world. I drank from the cup that contained the sins of the world. I
did it just for you." Mr. Ravenhill said he then drank from the cup.

Many times God asks us to do things that we might think are beneath us
or might be humbling to us or might even be difficult for us. Do it
anyway! God has a plan. He will use your obedience to shed the light of
His son to a darkened and dirty world.

He went away a second time and prayed, "My Father, if it is not possible
for this cup to be taken away unless I drink it, may your will be done."
Matthew 26:42 NIV

He loves you

July 25
Whatever you did

"The King will reply, 'Truly I tell you, whatever you did for one of the least of these brothers and sisters of mine, you did for me."
Matthew 25:40 NIV

Whatever you did
Whatever you did for one
Whatever you did for one of the least
Whatever you did for one of the least of these brothers and sisters
Whatever you did for one of the least of these brothers and sisters of mine
Whatever you did, you did for me

Whatever you did for one of the least

Who are the least?
Is it the one that always screams, I am right
Is it the one begging on the street corner
Is it the one that always talks, but never listens
Is it the gay guy or girl
Is it your unkind boss
Is it the child that has no home
Is it the politician on the news

I must become less, He must become more.

Whatever I do, I will do it unto Him

He loves you

July 26
Remember His words

He is not here; he has risen!
"Remember how he told you, while he was still with you in Galilee:
'The Son of Man must be delivered over to the hands of sinners,
be crucified and on the third day be raised again.' "
Then they remembered his words.
Luke 24:6-8 NIV

Remember how He told you...
Then they remembered His words.

Sometimes our job is to just remind others of what God has said.
Sometimes our job is to just be a reminder of Jesus to the world.

Then they will remember. . .
By our words
By our deeds
By our smiles
By our acts of kindness
By our touch
By our love

He loves you

July 27
Stand at the crossroads and look

This is what the Lord says: "Stand at the crossroads and look; ask for the
ancient paths, ask where the good way is, and walk in it, and you will find
rest for your souls. But you said, 'We will not walk in it.'
I appointed watchmen over you and said, 'Listen to the sound of the
trumpet!' But you said, 'We will not listen.'
Jeremiah 6:16-17 NIV

You have a choice of which way to go.
Do you follow the path God says is right
or do you follow the path that you think is right.
It is your choice.
He will not make you go down His path.
He is such a kind and gentle God He will never push you.
He stands and waits at the open door for you.

His path is right.
His way is good.
He goes before you.
He gives you rest.
He will teach you the right way.
He will bless your way.
Go to Him if you are weary and burdened
He will give you rest.
Learn from Him.
He is gentle and humble.
His yoke is easy and His burden is light.
You will find rest.

"Come to me, all you who are weary and burdened, and I will give you
rest. Take my yoke upon you and learn from me, for I am gentle and
humble in heart, and you will find rest for your souls. For my yoke is easy
and my burden is light."
Matthew 11:28-30 NIV

He loves you

July 28
Immediately Jesus reached out

But when he saw the wind, he was afraid and, beginning to sink, cried out, "Lord, save me!" Immediately Jesus reached out his hand and caught him. "You of little faith," he said, "why did you doubt?"
Matthew 14:30-31

How many times have I been here?

I look around and fear overtakes me.
I hear the words your three-month-old baby has pneumonia
I hear the words your daughter has diabetes
I hear the words your daughter has a brain cyst
I hear the words your son has a malignant brain tumor
I hear the words your husband may have had a stroke
I hear the words they have not honored their words
I hear the words you have breast cancer.
I hear the words your grandbaby was born last night, he weighs only 2 pounds 5 ounces
I hear the words . . . and fear overtakes me
I cry out, "Lord save me!"

Then immediately Jesus reaches out his hand and catches me. I know I am not alone. He will uphold me with His righteous right hand! When the storm finally passes I think, "Why did I ever doubt?" He is always faithful!

When you are fearful
When you think you can't stand anymore
When all hope is lost,

You will feel His hand reaching out for you.

His hand is strong.

He will catch you,

He will hold you.

He will not let you fall.

July 29
Heart cheer

Suddenly an angel of the Lord appeared and a light shone in the cell.
He struck Peter on the side and woke him up.
"Quick, get up!" he said, and the chains fell off Peter's wrists.
Acts 12:7 NIV

"Dear reader, is this an hour of distress with you? Then ask for peculiar help. Jesus is the Angel of the Covenant, and if His presence be now earnestly sought it will not be denied. What that presence brings is heart cheer." CHARLES H. SPURGEON

Father, would you send your angels to cheer us on?
We do ask for 'peculiar help'.
May Jesus' presence shine on our lives.
May the chains be forever broken.
Never to be seen again.
Set us free from all that so easily entangles us.

We so desperately need your heart cheer.

The same night when Herod was about to bring him out, Peter was sleeping between two soldiers, bound with two chains.
Guards in front of the door kept the prison. And behold, an angel of the Lord stood by him, and a light shone in the cell. He struck Peter on the side, and woke him up, saying, "Stand up quickly!" His chains fell off his hands. The angel said to him, "Get dressed and put on your sandals."
He did so. He said to him, "Put on your cloak and follow me." And he went out and followed him. He didn't know that what was being done by the angel was real, but thought he saw a vision. When they were past the first and the second guard, they came to the iron gate that leads into the city, which opened to them by itself. They went out, and went down one street, and immediately the angel departed from him.
When Peter had come to himself, he said, "Now I truly know that the Lord has sent out his angel and delivered me out of the hand of Herod, and from everything the Jewish people were expecting."
Acts 12:6-11 WEB

July 30
Run to Him

The power of the Lord came on Elijah and, tucking his cloak into his belt,
he ran ahead of Ahab all the way to Jezreel.
1 Kings 18:46 NIV

We took our three grandchildren to church with us. Because it was raining
my husband let us out at the door. I was holding Austin (who was one)
and James and Rivers (both were two) were walking beside me and they
were holding hands.

As soon as we entered the building James took off running! Which meant
Rivers did too since they were here holding hands! I yelled and yelled at
James to stop, but to no avail! I must have said his name 10 times and he
just kept running! My hands were full and I could not catch him. It was as
if he was so caught up in the moment he could not hear my voice. Finally
he turned around and looked at me and came back.
I was a little frustrated.

Then later in church I remember thinking I am tired and I'm having a hard
time concentrating on you Father. But as He always does, He whispered
very gently to me.
I want you to run to me just like James and Rivers did! I want you to run
in freedom. I don't want you to listen to others that are calling for you to
stop! I want you to run like the wind!

I want you to feel my pleasure! I'm waiting with open arms.

I'm so thankful for the way God uses children to teach us of His love for
us.

Run, child, run!

He loves you

July 31
Go out and stand

The Lord said, "Go out and stand on the mountain in the presence
of the Lord, for the Lord is about to pass by."
1 Kings 19:11 NIV

Elijah was hiding in a cave. He was afraid. He was scared. He chose to
hide because of his fears. God saw him and he knew why he was
afraid. Yet God said "Go out and stand. Don't hide anymore I am about
to pass by and I want to see you. I not only want to see you, I want to talk
to you. I have a very specific word for you but you must come out".

I believe God is saying the same thing to us today. "Come out and stand,
I know you are afraid. I see you. But I need you to come out so I can give
you the word I have just for you."
It takes courage to come out. It takes courage to stand on the mountain
for all to see.
But He will give you that courage. He will give you the strength to stand.
Your only job is to go out!

Years ago I read a children's book called, The Travels of Monarch
X. Every year I reread it to my kindergarten classes. It's a true story
based on the life of a monarch butterfly. A scientist in Canada wanted to
find out how far monarch butterflies actually migrated. He tagged
monarchs with tiny numbers and he put his phone number on the tag so
that if anyone found one of these butterflies they could call him.
They began their flight in Canada. Monarch X was found by a little boy in
Mexico. The scientist was notified and he discovered that the monarch
had flown over 2,000 miles! He had flown through much on his long
journey, high winds and lakes and mountains and valleys yet he
persevered. He never gave up until he reached his destination.
Yet a monarch butterfly is so very tiny. His wingspan is only 3.7 to 4.1
inches. His weight is a mere .0095 to .026 ounces and they only live 6 to
8 months.

Our strength is not our own. We will soar on wings as eagles!

But we must take the first step. We must "Go out"!

August 1
To touch the water's edge

So when the people broke camp to cross the Jordan, the priests
carrying the ark of the covenant went ahead of them.
Joshua 3:14 NIV

The ones carrying God's word went first.
The priests carrying the ark of the covenant went first.
The waters were at their highest, at flood stage.
Yet... As soon as their feet touched the waters edge...
The water stopped flowing!
It piled up in a heap a great distance away.
The water from upstream and downstream was completely cut off.
Those carrying His word walked out on dry ground into the middle of the
river.
They stood there until everyone had crossed over.

Sometimes you might have to go first.

You might be the only one to carry His word.

You might have to be the watchman

while others cross over.

If God calls you to do that He will create the miracle

for your "feet to touch the waters edge"!

And to stand in victory!

Now the Jordan is at flood stage all during harvest. Yet as soon as the
priests who carried the ark reached the Jordan and their feet touched the
water's edge, the water from upstream stopped flowing. It
piled up in a heap a great distance away, at a town called Adam
in the vicinity of Zarethan, while the water flowing down to the Sea of the
Arabah (that is, the Dead Sea) was completely cut off. So the people
crossed over opposite Jericho. The priests who carried the ark
of the covenant of the Lord stopped in the middle of the Jordan
and stood on dry ground, while all Israel passed by
until the whole nation had completed the crossing on dry ground.
Joshua 3:15-17

August 2
That we might rely on God

Indeed, we felt we had received the sentence of death. But this happened
that we might not rely on ourselves but on God, who raises the dead.
2 Corinthians 1:9 NIV

This happened that we might rely on God.
That we might rely on God
Not on ourselves, but on God

He can be trusted. You can rely on Him. There never was nor will there
ever be one so faithful as Him. His love never waivers. He is
constant. He is bigger than any obstacle you have to pass through. He
will take you through the deep waters.

Others may never know all you are going through but He does. He sees it
all, He sees your past, He sees your present, He sees your future. He is
there! "Streams of life, heavenly grace and spiritual power" will flow
through your life into others that you minister to.

Trust Him, He will never leave you

"Give me the love that leads the way,
The faith that nothing can dismay,
The hope no disappointments tire,
The passion that will burn like fire"
Amy Wilson Carmichael

He loves you

August 3
Teach your children

The evening meal was in progress, and the devil had already prompted
Judas, the son of Simon Iscariot, to betray Jesus.
John 13:2 NIV

Mary, Martha and Lazarus were all at supper at Simon, the leper's house.
Simon, the leper, had already been healed by Jesus. He no longer had
leprosy. (Lepers were not allowed to mingle with those who were not
infected. So Simon had to have been healed by this time.)
All the disciples, including Judas Iscariot, were at the supper. Judas was
the treasurer and kept the bag that contained all the money that had been
donated to Jesus and His disciples to give to the poor.
He was the one that stole from the bag of money.
What happened to Judas Iscariot?
Did he not see Jesus heal his own father of leprosy?
Did his father not talk about what Jesus had done for him?
Why did Judas turn away from the truth?
What made his heart hard?
Teach your children. Talk about Jesus when you walk
When you arise. When you lie down
Speak His name.

Therefore you shall lay up these my words in your heart and in your soul.
You shall bind them for a sign on your hand, and they shall be for frontlets
between your eyes. You shall teach them to your children, talking of them,
when you sit in your house, and when you walk by the way, and when you
lie down, and when you rise up. You shall write them on the door posts of
your house, and on your gates; that your days may be multiplied, and the
days of your children, in the land which Yahweh swore to your fathers to
give them, as the days of the heavens above the earth.
Deuteronomy 11:18-21 WEB

Fix these words in your heart
Tie them as symbols on your hands
Bind them on your foreheads
Teach them to your children

Talk about them when you sit at home
When you walk along the road
When you lie down
When you get up
Write them on the doorframes of your houses and on your gates

Teach your children

He loves you

August 4
Use your talent

Those He predestined, He also called; and those He called,
He also justified; and those He justified, He also glorified.
Romans 8:30 NIV

*Beth Moore wrote in one of her books, "All of us who are believers in
Christ have a calling. I am convinced God assigns our callings for a host
of reasons, many of which serve a purpose in us, not just in those we will
serve. God is the master of multitasking. God knew that what He called
me to do would force me to deal with the deeply embedded thorns of my
past. Therefore, our callings can be at stake if we are not willing to allow
Him to deal with our insecurities."*
(Moore, Beth. "Believing God Day by Day." April 21)

*"It is said that Gainsborough, the artist, longed also to be a musician. He
bought musical instruments of many kinds and tried to play them. He once
heard a great violinist bringing ravishing music from his instrument.
Gainsborough was charmed and thrown into transports of admiration. He
bought the violin on which the master played so marvelously. He thought
that if he had the wonderful instrument that he could play, too. But he
soon learned that the music was not in the violin, but was in the master
who played it. Gainsborough is one of the most famous artists of the
1700's. One of his most famous paintings is "The Blue Boy".*
(L.B.E.Cowman. "Springs in the Valley." April 21)

Be who He created you to be.

What if Gainsborough had never picked up the brush and used
the talents God had given him?

He loves you

August 5
It takes time

And He shall bring it to pass.
Psalm 37:5

"Often we fail to give God an opportunity to work, not realizing that it takes time for Him to answer prayer. It takes time for God to color a rose or to grow a great oak tree. And it takes time for Him to make bread from wheat fields. He takes the soil, then grinds and softens it. He enriches it and wets it with rain showers and with dew. Then He brings the warmth of life to the small blade of grass, later grows the stalk and the amber grain, and finally provides bread for the hungry."
(L.B.E. Cowman, "Streams in the Desert", April 18)

It takes time. His timing is not our timing.
We have to wait on His time.
When we wait on Him to answer our prayers, the end result will be so much bigger and better than we thought possible.

He loves you

August 6
Jesus took him by the hand

But Jesus took him by the hand
and lifted him to his feet,
and he stood up.
Mark 9:27 NIV

Jesus took him by the hand.
And lifted him up.
And he stood.

Jesus reached out his hand.
Jesus lifted him up.
He stood.
It was Jesus' strength that helped him to stand.
It was Jesus' strength that lifted him up.
It was not his own, but Jesus'.

He stood up.
Never to be lame again.
Never!
He stood!

So he said to me, "This is the word of the Lord to Zerubbabel: 'Not by
might nor by power, but by my Spirit,' says the Lord Almighty.
Zechariah 4:6 NIV

He loves you

August 7
Everything is possible

Jesus said to him, "If you can believe,
all things are possible for him who believes."
Immediately the father of the child cried out with tears,
"I believe. Help my unbelief!"
Mark 9:23-24 WEB

Everything is possible
For healing for your child
For your finances to be turned around
For favor for you at work
For restoration of your marriage or your loved one's marriage
For protection for your children
For your children to follow Jesus
For a baby for your barren child or friend
For healing for your health issues
For salvation for your husband or wife

Everything is possible!

For most certainly I tell you, whoever may tell this mountain,
'Be taken up and cast into the sea,' and doesn't doubt in his heart,
but believes that what he says is happening;
he shall have whatever he says. Therefore I tell you,
all things whatever you pray and ask for, believe
that you have received them, and you shall have them.
Mark 11:23-24 WEB

He loves you

August 8
He reveals Himself

"I revealed myself to those who did not ask for me; I was found by those
who did not seek me. To a nation that did not call on my name,
I said, 'Here am I, here am I.'
Isaiah 65:1 NIV

God is so gracious that He reveals Himself
To those who do not even ask for Him.
To those who did not even seek Him
Even the nations that do not call on Him, He extends His hand.
Such mercy!
Such grace!

He so patiently waits to reveal Himself to all people.
He is not hiding, He is here.
He is so gracious, waiting, waiting, waiting to say,
"Here I am, here I am!"

Playing hide and seek with young children is such fun.
They hide but they are so excited to be found that they can't contain that
excitement.
They laugh, they giggle, they talk, they whisper, they move.
They are easily seen and easily found.
That's the way it is with God.
So many think He has hidden or He is far away.
In reality He is right here, waiting to be found, hoping you will see Him,
trying to contain His excitement over you!

Isaiah is very bold, and says, "I was found by those who didn't seek me.
I was revealed to those who didn't ask for me."
But as to Israel he says, "All day long I stretched out my hands
to a disobedient and contrary people."
Romans 10:20-21 WEB

August 9
He has shown kindness

Yet he has not left himself without testimony: He has shown kindness by
giving you rain from heaven and crops in their seasons;
he provides you with plenty of food and fills your hearts with joy.
Acts 14:17 NIV

This is His testimony to us.
Showing kindness by giving rain from heaven
Giving crops in their seasons
Providing you with plenty of food
Filling your hearts with joy

Have you felt His kindness?
Have you tasted His food?
Have you known His joy?

He did all of this so you might know Him!

If you could paint your testimony,
What He has given you
What He shown you
What He has spoken to you
What He has done for you
What would it look like?
I believe it would be a beautiful picture!

Look around you
You will see Him
He has shown such kindness

He loves you

August 10
He is able

And God will generously provide all you need. Then you will always have everything you need and plenty left over to share with others.
2 Corinthians 9:8 Living Translation

And God is able to give you an overflowing measure of all good gifts, that all your wants of every kind may be supplied at all times, and you may give of your abundance to every good work.
To bless abundantly. . .

Look at a sunset
Have you ever seen two sunsets look the same?
Each one is unique and beautiful.
He never gives sparingly on the sunsets.
He placed billions of stars in the universe,
All for our good pleasure.
He created hundreds of unique flowers,
All for our good pleasure.

2 Corinthians 9:8-11 MSG
God can pour on the blessings in astonishing ways so that you're ready for anything and everything, more than just ready to do what needs to be done. As one psalmist puts it, He throws caution to the winds, giving to the needy in reckless abandon. His right-living, right-giving ways never run out, never wear out. This most generous God who gives seed to the farmer that becomes bread for your meals is more than extravagant with you. He gives you something you can then give away, which grows into full-formed lives, robust in God, wealthy in every way, so that you can be generous in every way, producing with us great praise to God.
2 Corinthians 9:8-11 MSG

He lavishes His good gifts on us.

August 11
Who do you believe

At Iconium Paul and Barnabas went as usual into the Jewish synagogue. There they spoke so effectively that a great number of Jews and Greeks believed. But the Jews who refused to believe stirred up the other Gentiles and poisoned their minds against the brothers. The people of the city were divided; some sided with the Jews, others with the apostles. Then some Jews came from Antioch and Iconium and won the crowd over. They stoned Paul and dragged him outside the city, thinking he was dead.
Acts 14:1-2,4,19 NIV

They spoke effectively. Some believed. Those who refused to believe caused dissension. The people were divided. Others came who did not believe. They turned the crowd towards evil. They stoned the one God sent.

There will always be people who do not believe the truth.
They will try to cause confusion and division.
Stand on what you know to be true!

Be careful who you listen to
When I was young we sang this children's song in church.
"Oh be careful little eyes what you see
For the Father up above is looking down in love
Oh be careful little ears what you hear
For the Father up above is looking down in love

We could add a verse to this that says
Oh be careful little feet where you walk!
Listen for His voice
Look through His eyes. Walk where He leads

But there they are, overwhelmed with dread,
for God is present in the company of the righteous.
You evildoers frustrate the plans of the poor,
but the Lord is their refuge.
Psalm 14:5-6 NIV

August 12
God led them

When Pharaoh had let the people go, God didn't lead them by the way of
the land of the Philistines, although that was near; for God said, "Lest
perhaps the people change their minds when they see war, and they
return to Egypt"; but God led the people around by the way of the
wilderness by the Red Sea; and the children of Israel
went up armed out of the land of Egypt.
Exodus 13:17-18 WEB

How many times does it seem like the road is too long
or too difficult or too indirect?
Often, it seems. Yet, how many times has God spared us of greater hurt
and difficulty by directing us in a "round about" way. A way that seems
much too long!

God in His infinite wisdom sees the whole picture and He knows what He
is protecting us from. He knows we aren't ready for the battle that lies on
the shortest route.

He knows we might become discouraged and give up. He knows that we
might even "turn around" and go back the way we came.

He never wants that for us. He wants us to continue down the path He
has for us. This path may not be for anyone else but He planned it just for
you, for your good.

You can trust him.

Let God lead.

He loves you

August 13
The watchmen

The angel of the LORD encamps round around those
that fear him, and he delivers them.
Psalm 34:7

*"A wonderful story is told by a Moravian missionary in connection with
angelic protection. An American missionary and his wife bravely went to
their station, where, twenty years before, two missionaries had been killed
and eaten by the natives. They said as they took up their work it seemed
as if often they were surrounded not only by the hostile natives, but by the
very powers of darkness. These latter were so real, that night after night
they were forced to get up and strengthen their hearts by reading the
Word of God. Again, they would pray.*
*One day a man came and said, "I would like to see your watchmen close
at hand." The missionary replied: "I have no watchmen; I have only a
cook and a little herd boy. What watchmen do you mean? The man asked
permission to look through the missionaries' home. Every corner of the
house was carefully searched, and the man came out of the house greatly
disappointed. Then the missionary asked the man to tell him about the
watchmen to whom he referred. Here is the man's answer.*
*When you and your wife came here we determined to kill you as we did
the missionaries twenty years ago. Night after night we came to carry out
our intentions, but there always stood around your house a double row of
watchmen with glittering weapons, and we dared not come near. At last
we hired a professional assassin, who said he feared neither God nor
devil. Last night he came close to your house—we followed at a distance
brandishing his spear. There stood the shining watchmen, and the killer
fled in terror. So we have given up our purpose to kill you, but tell me, who
are the watchmen?" The missionary opened the Word of God and read:
The angel of the LORD encamps round about them that fear him, and
delivers them."*
(L.B.E.Cowman, "Springs in the Valley."February10)

He encamps around us. He delivers us. He keeps us secure.
You may not be able to see His protection but you can know by faith it is
there.

August 14
The power of your words

From the fruit of their lips people are filled with good things,
and the work of their hands brings them reward.
Proverbs 12:14 NIV

Your words can build up or tear down.
They can encourage for a lifetime or
they can destroy for a lifetime.
Your words can bring healing and hope or
they can bring desolation and destruction.
Choose your words carefully
Be careful who you listen to.

God's words bring life and hope!
Listen to Him

God has a work for you to do with your hands.
If you seek Him He will show you what it is.
It may be something you've never done before but
He will reveal to you what it is.
Whatever it is it will be rewarding to you and to others.

He loves you

August 15
A single cluster of grapes

They came to the valley of Eshcol, and cut down from there a branch
with one cluster of grapes, and they bore it on a staff between two.
They also brought some of the pomegranates and figs.
That place was called the valley of Eshcol, because of the cluster
which the children of Israel cut down from there.
They returned from spying out the land at the end of forty days.
Numbers 13:23-25 WEB

They cut off a branch bearing a single cluster of grapes!
Two of them carried it on a pole between them.

A single cluster of grapes!
It was so big it took two men to carry it on a pole!
A single cluster of grapes!

Sometimes when God tells you to go explore you may discover huge
treasures! What you find may be much bigger than anything you've seen
or experienced before. The treasures you find may be hard to explain to
others. There may even be those who do not believe you. Explore
anyway! The hunt is worth what God has for you. Don't hesitate to bring
it back. You may even have to ask for help to carry your newfound
treasures!

A single cluster of grapes!

He loves you

He loves you

August 16
I have seen your tears

"Go and tell Hezekiah, 'This is what the Lord, the God of your father
David, says: I have heard your prayer and seen your tears;
I will add fifteen years to your life.
Isaiah 38:5 NIV

How many tears have you shed?
We shed tears of joy.
We shed tears of sadness.
We shed tears of laughter.

Our tears are most often associated with sorrow.
Sorrow comes in many forms. . .
The death of a loved one
The sickness of a child
The divorce of a daughter
The near fatal accident of a friend
The loss of a job
The end of a dream
There are a million different reasons for our tears.

Yet God says He has seen our every tear.
He even has a record of them.
He's even felt our tears!
He remembers our tears.
He knows your heart.
He knows what makes you happy,
He knows what makes you sad.
He longs to comfort you.
The world may forget your tears but He will never.

As she stood behind him at his feet weeping, she began to wet his feet
with her tears. Then she wiped them with her hair, kissed them and
poured perfume on them.
Luke 7:38 NIV

August 17
He used His hand to cover

Then the Lord said, "There is a place near me where you may stand on a
rock. When my glory passes by, I will put you in a cleft in the rock and
cover you with my hand until I have passed by. Then I will remove my
hand and you will see my back; but my face must not be seen."
Exodus 33:21-23 NIV

My presence will go with you. I will give you rest.
I will do the very thing you have asked because I am pleased with you.
And I know you by name.

How very gracious of God to show us His glory and to also protect us from
it. God put His hand on Moses' face to protect him. His goodness is more
than we can withstand.
It is overpowering! It is beyond our ability to look upon!

God revealed Himself and yet used his own hand to protect him.
Thank you for your graciousness to us in not revealing to us more of you
than we can handle.

Yet His presence, this presence, will go with you,
This presence, His presence, will give you rest.

He said, "My presence will go with you, and I will give you rest."
He said to him, "If your presence doesn't go with me, don't carry us up
from here. For how would people know that I have found favor
in your sight, I and your people? Isn't it that you go with us,
so that we are separated, I and your people, from all the people
who are on the surface of the earth?" Yahweh said to Moses,
"I will do this thing also that you have spoken; for you have found favor
in my sight, and I know you by name." He said, "Please show me
your glory." He said, "I will make all my goodness pass before you,
and will proclaim Yahweh's name before you.
Exodus 33:14-19 WEB

August 18
He heals the brokenhearted

He heals the brokenhearted and binds up their wounds. He determines
the number of stars and calls them each by name.
Psalms 147:3-4 NIV

There is a famous picture painted by one of the greatest European
artists. It is called "The Consoler". It is a picture of a bedroom in a small
cottage. On the bed sits a beautiful little baby. He has in his hand a toy
soldier that he is holding close to his body. He doesn't seem to sense
anything around him. On the wall behind him is a picture of a soldier, the
baby's father. Beside the bed, on her knees, with her head in her hands,
is the widow of the soldier. She is dressed in black and crying her heart
out. It's one of the saddest pictures. The widow with a broken heart, the
baby never to know his dad. But the beautiful part of the picture is the one
who is learning over her. It's Jesus with His beautiful face. He is laying
His hand on her shoulder. "The Consoler". No one can console like
Jesus.

Brooke, my friend lost her husband, Michael, to a malignant brain tumor. (I
wrote about them earlier in my book.) He was only 26! They had been
married a very short time when Michael was diagnosed with the worst
type of brain cancer. The life expectancy is less than a year with this
particular cancer. Yet Michael lived four years, all while sweet Brooke was
caring for him. In his last year of his life Brooke got pregnant. Michael
was not supposed to be able to father a child. He had had so much
chemo and so many steroids that it wasn't physically possible. But with
God all things are possible. Michael died when their precious baby boy,
Titus, was only three months old! Brooke had been strong for so long and
now she had to be strong for their son. She was such a gracious woman.
She endured three years of being a widow and a single mom. But in the
fourth year God brought an amazing man into her life! God knew about
Bryan all along and He had a plan. That plan had been unfolding for the
last year. And now they are married and have a baby together. And yet
God knew about this from the foundation of the world.

What an incredible story this is! Thank you Father for your plans which are always so good! You do heal the broken hearted. You do bind up their wounds, You do call the stars by name.

From a broken heart
To the stars!

He loves you

August 19
How majestic is your name

When I consider your heavens, the work of your fingers,
the moon and the stars, which you have ordained;
what is man, that you think of him?
What is the son of man, that you care for him?
For you have made him a little lower than God,
and crowned him with glory and honor.
You make him ruler over the works of your hands.
You have put all things under his feet:
All sheep and cattle,
yes, and the animals of the field,
The birds of the sky, the fish of the sea,
and whatever passes through the paths of the seas.
Yahweh, our Lord,
how majestic is your name in all the earth!
Psalm 8:3-9 WEB

I watched a video and I was astounded to see how big some stars are and how many stars there are!
The largest known star makes the earth look like a tiny black dot, barely visible.
The diameter of the star is about 2.800.000.000 km.
If you were in an airplane flying the surface of this star at 900 km/h it would take 1100 years to circle it one time. Yet this giant star is only a tiny dot among several hundred billion stars forming our galaxy.
And there are a hundred billion galaxies out there!!

God says, what is man that you are mindful of him?
He has crowned us with glory and honor!

He loves you

August 20
The sun stood still

On the day the Lord gave the Amorites over to Israel, Joshua said to the
Lord in the presence of Israel: "Sun, stand still over Gibeon, and you,
moon, over the Valley of Aijalon. " So the sun stood still, and the moon
stopped, till the nation avenged itself on its enemies,. The sun stopped in
the middle of the sky and delayed going down about a full day. There has
never been a day like it before or since, a day when the Lord listened to a
human being. Surely the Lord was fighting for Israel!
Joshua 10:12-14 NIV

God actually made the sun stand still and the moon stop.
There has never been a day like it before or since,
a day when the Lord listened to a human being.
Surely the Lord was fighting for Israel!

The sun actually stood still!
If God can make the sun stand still so that the Israelites could fight their
battle against their enemies and win, then He can help you too.

He can give you strength you didn't know you had.

He can give you provision you knew not of.

He can stop your enemy in their tracks.

He can move heaven and earth to give you the victory.

He can and He will, you need only ask.

He loves you

He loves you

August 21
Light from darkness

The god of this age has blinded the minds of unbelievers, so that they
cannot see the light of the gospel that displays the glory of Christ, who is
the image of God. For God, who said, "Let light shine out of darkness,"
made his light shine in our hearts to give us the light of the knowledge of
God's glory displayed in the face of Christ.
2 Corinthians 4:4,6 NIV

Their eyes have been blinded, they cannot see the light
that displays Jesus.
The ISIS cannot see, the Muslim cannot see, the atheist cannot see.

There is such darkness, so much blindness in our world today.
Yet God said, Let there be light!
That's God's desire that all men would see the light of His glory.

May His light penetrate the darkness.
May His light shine through you and me.
May others be drawn to God because of His light
that shines through us.
May the darkness be forever expelled.

He loves you

August 22
At night His song is with me

By day the Lord directs his love, at night his song is with me,
a prayer to the God of my life.
Psalm 42:8 NIV

By day He directs you, at night His song is with you.

We hear music everywhere, on the TV, on the computer, on our phone.
We hear it when we go to restaurants and concerts and baseball games.
We hear all kinds of music but the kind of music God wants us to hear at night is His music.
Songs that tell of His goodness and faithfulness and kindness
Some of my favorite songs are sung by Bethel music.
This is a quote from their website.

"The core of Bethel Music is to capture God's heart through worship, declaring who He is and who we are in Him. Our desire is for every album we produce to be saturated with the presence of God and draw people deeper into worship of Him."

I believe that happens, I believe God's heart is captured, when I listen to their music.   At night their songs are in my heart. I sense His presence throughout the night as I sleep.

"We will not be shaken!
I will not be shaken
Though the battle rages on!
We will not be shaken!
I will not be shaken!"

Listen for His song, His words, they will give you peace as you sleep.

August 23
An aroma pleasing to God

Offer it as an aroma pleasing to the Lord.
Numbers 15:7 NIV

Five times these nine words are used in this chapter.
God said they were to bring their drink and food offerings to the Lord and they were to be. . .An aroma pleasing to the Lord.
I wonder if our offerings bring an aroma pleasing to the Lord.

What does God smell when we lift our gifts to Him?
Is it like the sweet smell of a gardenia?
Or the smell of a fragrant rose?

Could it be that each offering we give Him produces a different smell?
Maybe each smell reminds Him of our hearts.
The act of giving that we do for Him.

May our offerings bring an amazing aroma
that pleases you, our Lord and our God.

He loves you

He loves you

August 24
Through His eyes

Jesus went about all the cities and the villages, teaching in their synagogues, and preaching the Good News of the Kingdom, and healing every disease and every sickness among the people. But when he saw the multitudes, he was moved with compassion for them, because they were harassed and scattered, like sheep without a shepherd.
Matthew 9:35-36 WEB

Healing every disease and sickness
Having compassion on them
Because they were harassed and helpless
The harvest is plentiful
The workers are few

When Jesus looked at the crowd:
He saw their need
He knew immediately what they needed
He didn't delay in giving them what they needed
He healed completely
He gave wholeness and freedom
He gave all of this because He had compassion!

When He looks at you He knows exactly what you need

Oh that when we look at others we might see as He sees

That we might have this same compassion for others

Then he said to his disciples, "The harvest indeed is plentiful, but the laborers are few. Pray therefore that the Lord of the harvest will send out laborers into his harvest."
Matthew 9:37-38 WEB

He loves you

August 25
Roll away the stone

Jesus therefore, again groaning in himself, came to the tomb. Now it was a cave, and a stone lay against it. Jesus said, "Take away the stone." Martha, the sister of him who was dead, said to him, "Lord, by this time there is a stench, for he has been dead four days." Jesus said to her, "Didn't I tell you that if you believed, you would see God's glory?" So they took away the stone from the place where the dead man was lying. Jesus lifted up his eyes, and said, "Father, I thank you that you listened to me. I know that you always listen to me, but because of the multitude that stands around I said this, that they may believe that you sent me." When he had said this, he cried with a loud voice, "Lazarus, come out!" He who was dead came out, bound hand and foot with wrappings, and his face was wrapped around with a cloth.
John 11:38-44 WEB

Jesus said to them, "Free him, and let him go. Take away the stone,". So they took away the stone. Lazarus, who was once dead, came forth!

The people took away the stone!
Jesus gave new life, but the people took away the stone.
There are times in our lives that God says "Take away the stone"!
It may be through the encouraging word you speak
It may be by the prayer you pray
It may be by the hug you give
It may be by the phone call you make
It may be by the text you send
It may be by the meal you prepare
It may bc by the visit you make

But whatever it is God has a reason for it.
You may very well be the one person that can "Take away the stone"
so that new life from Jesus can come forth!

Take the time to roll away the stone!

283

August 26
For Him

There came a woman having an alabaster box of ointment of spikenard
very precious; and she brake the box, and poured it on his head.
Mark 4:3 NIV

For him . . .
Whatever you do, do it for Him
Whether you clean
Whether you write
Whether you cook
Whether you rock babies
Whether you teach
Whether you nurse
Whether you preach
Whether you drive
Whether you build
Whether you design
Whether you doctor

Whatever you do, do it for Him
He sees!

The fragrance you produce will fill "your house".
All who enter "your house" will smell it and
be drawn to Him!

And the house was filled with the odor of the ointment.
John 12:3 NIV

He loves you

August 27
Put your hope in God

Why, my soul, are you downcast? Why so disturbed within me? Put your
hope in God, for I will yet praise him, my Savior and my God.
Psalm 42:5 NIV

David understood our loss of hope.
He understood our pain.
He wrote about it often in the Psalms.
In fact he wrote the exact same verse twice in this chapter.
He knew, just as we know,
Our only hope is in God.
He alone is the one who rescues.
He alone is the one who lifts us up.

Out of the miry pit
He sets our feet on a rock, a solid rock
That cannot be shaken
That cannot be moved
We will yet praise Him, our savior and our God.
You will get through this difficult time.
You will again praise Him.

Why, my soul, are you downcast? Why so disturbed within me?
Put your hope in God, for I will yet praise him, my Savior and my God.
Psalm 42:11

He loves you

August 28
Reach out and touch

Because we wanted to come to you—indeed, I, Paul, once and again—
but Satan hindered us. For what is our hope, or joy, or crown of rejoicing?
Isn't it even you, before our Lord Jesus at his coming?
For you are our glory and our joy.
1 Thessalonians 2:18-20 WEB

What is our hope?
What is our joy?
What is the crown in which we will glory in His presence?
It is people!

People are our glory as we stand before Him.
People are our joy as we stand before Him.

How many people's lives have you touched?

People need you.
They need the Jesus in you.
Reach out and touch.
You have much to offer!

He loves you

August 29
Your conversation, full of grace

Let your conversation be always full of grace, seasoned with salt,
so that you may know how to answer everyone.
Colossians 4:6 NIV

Full of grace
Kindness, gentleness, meekness, self-control

Seasoned with salt
Salt adds flavor
It keeps food from being bland and tasteless
It preserves, it keeps it from spoiling or going bad.

When you speak, listen to Jesus first.
He will tell you what to speak.
Let your words be full of mercy.
And be tasteful and kind.
Offer encouragement but speak in truth.

Others will respect you and they will want to hear your words.

Be known as the man or woman of "grace"

He loves you

August 30
Then He blessed Joseph

Then he blessed Joseph and said, "May the God before whom my fathers
Abraham and Isaac walked faithfully, the God who has been my shepherd
all my life to this day, may He bless these boys."
Genesis 48:15 NIV

Then he blessed them...
The blessings of a father are so important.
Many people never experience that.
I never felt like I did.
My relationship with my father was at times not a close one.
Because of this I did not see my Heavenly Father in the right way.
I only saw God as a very demanding father,
Not one of grace and mercy.

Oh how I have learned how wrong I was.
I see my Heavenly Father is such a new way now.
He is so gentle and kind.
And loves to show me mercy.
He speaks so tenderly to me.
He loves me so.

There was an incredible man of God named John Paul Jackson.
His countenance so reflected Jesus.
When he taught he drew men unto Jesus.
He talked of a father's blessing once.
He said if you had not received that yourself he wanted to speak one over
you.
I listened to this blessing and I received it!
The words were truth and life.
They gave hope and promise.

God called this man of God home.
He spoke Jesus over my life and I will never forget him!

He loves you

August 31
When things change

Then the angel of God, who had been traveling in front of Israel's army, withdrew and went behind them. The pillar of cloud also moved from in front and stood behind them, coming between the armies of Egypt and Israel. Throughout the night the cloud brought darkness to the one side and light to the other side; so neither went near the other all night long.
Exodus 14:19-20 NIV

The angel had been traveling in front of them.
Then the angel withdrew.
To go behind them.

The pillar of cloud had been moving in front of them.
The cloud moved.
It stood behind them.

It must have seemed for a moment that God had left.
That their protection had been withdrawn.
That it was different, it did not look the same.

Yet God knew what His people needed.
He knew that things would look different to them.
God knew where their protection was needed most.
He came between them and their enemies.
The cloud from God brought darkness to the enemy
And light to them.
They were completely protected by God.

He will do the same for you.
He will hem you in.
He will be your front guard.
He will be your rear guard.
He will be your light.
You will see the victory in Him.

He loves you

September 1
Just take his hand

He came to Bethsaida. They brought a blind man to him, and begged him
to touch him. He took hold of the blind man by the hand, and brought him
out of the village. When he had spit on his eyes, and laid his hands on
him, he asked him if he saw anything. He looked up, and said, "I see men;
for I see them like trees walking." Then again he laid his hands on his
eyes. He looked intently, and was restored, and saw everyone clearly.
He sent him away to his house, saying,
"Don't enter into the village, nor tell anyone in the village."
Mark 8:22-26 WEB

Sometimes we may need to physically take "the blind" to Jesus.
We may need to "beg" or intercede for them.

If we are faithful to do these things
Bring "the blind" to Him
And intercede for them.
God will touch them.
They will be healed of their blindness.
And they will see, really see for the first time.

Jesus will take them by the hand and lead them.
Our job is to get them there.

He loves you

September 2
You are His treasured possession

*For you are a people holy to the Lord your God. The Lord your God has
chosen you out of all the peoples on the face of the earth
to be his people, his treasured possession.*
Deuteronomy 7:6 NIV

You are His treasured possession.
He loves you so.
He would do anything for you.
He would even give His only son, Jesus, just for you
If you had been the only person alive He still would have given Jesus just
for you.
That's how deep His love is for you.

He chose you before the foundation of the world to be His.
He chose you.
Don't ever let that truth leave your thoughts.
He chose you.
You are His.

You are His treasured possession.

September 3
He saw Jesus

John 1:36-39 WEB
And he looked at Jesus as he walked, and said, "Behold, the Lamb of
God!" The two disciples heard him speak, and they followed Jesus.
Jesus turned, and saw them following, and said to them, "What are you
looking for?" They said to him, "Rabbi" (which is to say, being interpreted,
Teacher), "where are you staying?" He said to them,
"Come, and see." They came and saw where he was staying,
and they stayed with him that day. It was about the tenth hour.
John 1:36-39 WEB

He recognized Jesus.
He knew him well enough to pick him out of the crowd.
He knew him because he had spent time with Jesus.
He had talked to Jesus.
He didn't just call him by name,
He knew who He was, "the lamb of God"!
When John spoke boldly about who Jesus was
they began to follow Jesus.
We must know who Jesus is, who He really is, before others will want to
follow Him.
When they do begin to follow Him
Jesus will know.

Jesus turned around because he knew they were following Him.
Just like the lady that touched the hem of His garment, He knew!

He knows you.

He wants you.

He sees you.

He loves you

September 4
One look from Jesus

One of the two who heard John, and followed him, was Andrew, Simon
Peter's brother. He first found his own brother, Simon, and said to him,
"We have found the Messiah!" He brought him to Jesus. Jesus looked at
him, and said, "You are Simon the son of Jonah. You shall be called
Cephas" (which is by interpretation, Peter).
John 1:40-42 WEB

When you hear Jesus, really hear Him,
You will want to tell others about Him.
"The first thing Andrew did was to find his brother and tell him."
Not only tell them but bring them to Him. Jesus will know them.

One look from Jesus and you will know who you are!
He will call you by name, by the name He knows you as.
Simon, immediately became Cephas or Peter, which means rock.
(Cephas is Aramaic, Peter is Greek, both mean rock)

And I tell you that you are Peter, and on this rock I will build my church,
and the gates of Hades will not overcome it. I will give you the keys of the
kingdom of heaven; whatever you bind on earth will be bound in heaven,
and whatever you loose on earth will be loosed in heaven."
Matthew 16:18-19 NIV

All that Peter was to become was spoken to him when Jesus changed his
name. You are Peter! On this rock, I will build my church. I will give you
the keys to the kingdom of heaven.

Whatever you bind on earth will be bound in heaven.
Whatever you lose on earth will be loosed in heaven.
Peter, the one who denied Jesus three times.
When Jesus spoke Peter's name He already knew that one day Peter
would deny him before men. But Jesus knew Peter's heart and He knew
the plans He had for him.

September 5
He knows you

The woman said to him, "Sir, give me this water, so that I don't get
thirsty." Jesus said to her, "Go, call your husband, and come here." The
woman answered, "I have no husband." Jesus said to her, "You said well,
'I have no husband,' for you have had five husbands; and he whom you
now have is not your husband. This you have said truly."
John 4:15-18 WEB

Jesus chose to sit down at this well.
He knew this woman would be coming to draw water.
He knew who she was.
He knew who He was.
He knew where she had come from.
He knew where she was going.
He knew what she needed.
He offered her life.

He did not condemn her.
He merely told her who she was.
She wanted what He had.

He knows you.
He knows what you need.
He has what you need.
He is waiting to offer it to you.
He will not make you take it.
He knows you.

He loves you

September 6
Like a spring

The Lord will guide you always; he will satisfy your needs in a sun-scorched land and will strengthen your frame. You will be like a well-watered garden, like a spring whose waters never fail.
Isaiah 58:11 NIV

You will be like a spring whose waters never fail
The water that comes from the spring never fails.
Many who are thirsty will want this same water you have.
They will see through your life that the water is refreshing and satisfying to the soul.

Drink from it often so that you will be refreshed.
Share this spring water with those that God brings into your life.

God will then produce this spring in their lives.

But whoever drinks the water I give them will never thirst.
Indeed, the water I give them will become in them
a spring of water welling up to eternal life."
John 4:14 NIV

He loves you

September 7
You are a child of God

For as many as are led by the Spirit of God, these are children of God.
For you didn't receive the spirit of bondage again to fear, but you received
the Spirit of adoption, by whom we cry, "Abba Father!"   The Spirit himself
testifies with our spirit that we are children of God.
Romans 8:14-16 WEB

The papers for your adoption were signed on the cross.
Everything was fulfilled for your adoption by His blood.
You never have to live in fear again.
You will never ever be abandoned.

God has your name written on the palm of His hand.
His scars represent what He did just for you.
It is guaranteed!
Nothing can change that, nothing!

Now follow Him.
He will never lead you astray.
He is your Abba Father forever.

I love this song by Bethel Music – "No Longer Slaves".
Let the words sink into your heart as you read them.
He has chosen you. He wants to rescue you.

He loves you

No Longer Slaves

"You unravel me, with a melody
You surround me with a song
Of deliverance, from my enemies
Till all my fears are gone
I'm no longer a slave to fear
I am a child of God
From my Mother's womb
You have chosen me
Love has called my name
I've been born again, into your family
Your blood flows through my veins
You split the sea, so I could walk right
through it
All my fears were drowned in perfect love
You rescued me, so I could
stand and sing
I am a child of God"
Bethel Music
(Brian Johnson, Jonathan David Helser,
Joe Case)

September 8
We are God's handiwork, to do good works

For we are God's handiwork, created in Christ Jesus to do good works,
which God prepared in advance for us to do.
Ephesians 2:10 NIV

Look at the works of His hands
The sky
The ocean
The mountain
The tree
The flower
The blade of grass
He created it all
Yet in all of His amazing creation it wasn't enough
God wanted companions.
He wanted a family.
He wanted us.

So by His hand He created us.
We are His handiwork!
The works of His hands
So if He created us
And we are the works of His hands
And He created us to do good works
This same God that made us has given us the ability to create too
To do good works

If He made us and He planned in advance
the good works we are to do then
We will find our joy and our purpose in life (both for
this life and for our eternal life) when we begin
to do these good works.

September 9
Come to the waters and drink

"Come, everyone who thirsts, to the waters!
Come, he who has no money, buy, and eat!
Yes, come, buy wine and milk without money and without price.
Why do you spend money for that which is not bread,
and your labor for that which doesn't satisfy?
Listen diligently to me, and eat that which is good,
and let your soul delight itself in richness."
Isaiah 55:1-2 WEB

Come

Drink

Eat

Listen

Delight

It's really pretty simple.
Come to Jesus
Drink and eat what He offers
Listen to Him
It is a guarantee. You will delight in the richest of fare
In the things that matter, in the things that satisfy, in the things that last.

Come to the waters.

He knows everything about you and still

He says, "Come, I have water just for you"

Come and drink!

Blessed are those who hunger and thirst after righteousness,
for they shall be filled.
Matthew 5:6 WEB

September 10
The power of the tongue

The soothing tongue is a tree of life,
but a perverse tongue crushes the spirit.
Proverbs 15:4 NIV

With our tongues we can destroy. We can do such harm it can last for
generations. Yet God made our tongues to speak life.
This life can last for generations
I remember when I was just out of college and I was working at the early
childhood center on campus. I was co-teaching kindergarten behind a
two-way glass. This was so that the students studying early childhood
could observe and learn. I remember this little girl becoming so angry that
she spit in my face! I don't remember ever being so humiliated! I could
only smile at her and try to reason with her. (We were not allowed to use
any form of discipline.) I knew others were watching so I had to remain
calm! I later learned this little girl came from a very difficult home life. She
used her tongue not to speak but to express her anger.

As a child there were those who spoke to me with very hurtful words. It
has taken me years to get over the pain inflicted by this tongue. But now I
have been set free and I hear the words my Heavenly Father speaks over
me and I realize how much I am loved.

I have chosen to speak life over my own precious children and
grandchildren. The tongue can be used to heal, encourage, give hope and
show love. It is a choice, use it wisely.

When my son was going through chemo I remember his nurse telling us
about a teenage boy getting an infection in his tongue. He got the
infection from a piercing in his tongue. The infection got so bad that they
had to cut half of his tongue off. The infection continued to spread and the
sadly the boy eventually lost his life.

The tongue may seem like a small part of our body but

if not kept clean it can destroy the whole body!

He loves you

September 11
He lives to intercede for you

Therefore he is able to save completely those who come to God through
him, because he always lives to intercede for them.
Hebrews 7:25 NIV

Jesus lives to intercede for you
What an incredible thought!
He not only died for you
And arose for you
And lives for you
But He also lives to intercede for you

"To intercede is to plead on another's behalf
To act as a mediator in a dispute"

He is pleading on your behalf.
He is your mediator.

He sees you through His Father's eyes.
He longs to help you.
He knows your purpose and your potential.
Therefore He is able to completely save you.
He never grows tired or weary.
He will always be there for you
Interceding for you
Speaking kind words to the Father about you.
He loves you so.

He will never ever stop interceding for you.

Who then is the one who condemns? No one. Christ Jesus who died---
more than that, who was raised to life---is at the right hand of God
and is also interceding for us.
Romans 8:34 NIV

September 12
Let light shine out of darkness

For God, who said, "Let light shine out of darkness," made his light shine
in our hearts to give us the light of the knowledge of God's glory
displayed in the face of Christ.
2 Corinthians 4:6 NIV

God said, "Let light shine out of darkness!"
He is light.
Without Him there is only darkness.
His light brings His glory
We see this light in Jesus.
When we come to Him He puts that light in us
Others will see this light
Our world so needs this light, His light.

I remember when I was a little girl going on a trip to Carlsbad Caverns in
New Mexico. I had never been in a cave before. I remember walking for
what seemed like miles and miles!
There were lights along our path. I saw the stalagmites and the
stalactites.

It was beautiful. Then the guides had us all stop. They said they were
going to turn out the lights so we could see how dark it really was. The
lights went out and I saw for the first time what total darkness really
was. You could see nothing, not even your hand in front of your face.

Our world is in this same darkness. Without the light of Jesus there is no
direction, there is no real hope, there is no real joy, and there is no real
life! The world cannot see where it is going!

He loves you

May we be the light of Jesus to a darkened world
Father, Shine your light through us

He loves you

September 13
God intended it for good

But Joseph said to them, "Don't be afraid. Am I in the place of God? You
intended to harm me, but God intended it for good to accomplish what is
now being done, the saving of many lives. So then, don't be afraid.
I will provide for you and your children. "
And he reassured them and spoke kindly to them.
Genesis 50:19-21 NIV

Joseph's life is one of my favorite stories in the Bible.

Beaten and dumped into a pit by his brothers
Sold into slavery, rescued by a king
Accused wrongly, sentenced to prison
Served others even in prison
Released and found favor with the king
Placed second in command under the king
Rescued his whole family from famine
Forgave his brothers

His life is an amazing picture of God's. . .
Protection even when we find ourselves in the pit
Rescuing us when it looks like all hope is lost
Protecting us even when we are wrongly accused
Using us even when we are at our lowest point
Placing His favor on us so that others will see
Using us to rescue others who don't even know they need rescuing
Teaching us how to forgive those who have hurt us so badly
Using all things for our good

*It may seem that Satan is trying to use your
circumstances for evil but God will always use them
for good! Always!*

He loves you

September 14
Nothing can separate you from the love of God

Nor height, nor depth, nor any other created thing, will be able to separate
us from the love of God, which is in Christ Jesus our Lord.
Romans 8:39 WEB

It has been recorded that Mount Everest is the tallest mountain in the
world. It stands at over 29,000 feet above sea level.
Man has been to the top.

The lowest point in the world that man has seen is through The
Challenger Deep at over 35,000 feet.

Yet neither this height of over 29,000 feet or this depth of over 35,000 feet
can separate us from the love of God.
The most amazing thing is God created this mountain and this ocean too.
It is all a part of His incredible creation. But no matter where we go or
what we do, nothing can separate us from His love.

Where could I go from your Spirit?
Or where could I flee from your presence?
If I ascend up into heaven, you are there.
If I make my bed in Sheol,[a] behold, you are there!
If I take the wings of the dawn,
and settle in the uttermost parts of the sea;
Even there your hand will lead me,
and your right hand will hold me.
Psalm 139:7-10 WEB.

He is with you.

He is for you.

Nothing can separate you from His love!

He loves you

September 15
If you know me

Jesus answered, "I am the way and the truth and the life.
No one comes to the Father except through me.
If you really know me, you will know my Father as well.
From now on, you do know him and have seen him."
John 14:6-7 NIV

"If you really know me," those are the words of Jesus.
If we really know Him we will know His Father as well.

For years I knew Jesus but I didn't really know His Father.
The Father I knew scared me.
I knew Him as a father who laid out rules for me to follow.
I knew Him as a father who I must perform for to be accepted.
I knew him as a father who was demanding.
I knew him as a father who did not show grace.
I could not get past these views of an earthly father.

Yet now I do really know my Abba Father!
He is a father who accepts me just as I am.
He is a father who never demands.
He is a father who always, always shows me grace.
He is a father who loves me unconditionally.
He is a father, who speaks gently to me,
words of hope and love.
I am so very thankful that He has revealed himself to me.
I am forever changed!
He longs for you to hear Him too.
Be oh so still and listen.
You will begin to know Him in ways you never thought possible.

He loves you

September 16
We must feel

Carry each other's burdens, and in this way you will fulfill the law of Christ.
Galatians 6:2 NIV

"We can never heal the needs we do not feel."
Excerpt From: L. B. E. Cowman. "Springs in the Valley." March 25

So often people say, "I feel your pain".
Those words are so easily said.
What does it feel like to take on someone else's pain?
Jesus knows. He really knows!

It seems the older I get the more God is allowing me to feel other's pain.
But the most pain I've ever felt is when my own children or grandchildren are hurting.
The pain runs so deep.
When they hurt, I hurt.

To feel others pain:
It takes time.
It hurts, really hurts.
It isn't easy.
It requires prayer.
It sometimes lasts a long time.
It has far reaching consequences.
Only when we get to heaven will we truly know the effects of our "hurting" for others.

The prayer of a righteous man is powerful
and effective.
James 5:16

He loves you

September 17
God will meet your need

Then Yahweh's word came to him, saying, "Go away from here, turn eastward, and hide yourself by the brook Cherith, that is before the Jordan. You shall drink from the brook. I have commanded the ravens to feed you there." So he went and did according to Yahweh's word; for he went and lived by the brook Cherith that is before the Jordan. The ravens brought him bread and meat in the morning, and bread and meat in the evening; and he drank from the brook.
Kings 17:2-6 WEB

The word from God came first.
God told the ravens to give Elijah food.
God spoke to the ravens and they did what He said.
He spoke to the birds!
The birds listened and obeyed!

The ravens brought Elijah bread and meat in the morning and in the evening.
Elijah believed God and God used the ravens to meet his needs!
What a great reminder that God can use anything,
even what may seem impossible to us, to meet our needs!

God spoke to the ravens!

Consider the ravens: they don't sow, they don't reap, they have no warehouse or barn, and God feeds them.
How much more valuable are you than birds!
Luke 12:24 WEB

Even the ravens know who supplies their food.
If God provides for the ravens and their young then
how much more will He provide for you, His own child.

He loves you

September 18
He reached out his hand

But the dove could find nowhere to perch because there was water over all the surface of the earth; so it returned to Noah in the ark. He reached out his hand and took the dove and brought it back to himself in the ark.
Genesis 8:9 NIV

The dove could find no place to land.
Water was everywhere, the dove needed dry land.
The dove knew where he would be safe.
He knew Noah. He trusted Noah.
Noah had taken the dove in and fed him for many days.
The dove flew back to the one safe place he knew, to Noah and his ark.

Noah reached out his hand and took the dove back into the ark.

What a perfect picture of what God does for us.
When we feel like. . .
There is no safe place to go
All our hopes are dashed
We are at the end of all our resources
No one sees or cares

Then Jesus reaches out His hand and says "Come to me"!
His hand is secure.
He will take you to safety.
He will bring you to Himself.

You can relax in His embrace.

His hand is secure.

He loves you

September 19
God is love

God is love. Whoever lives in love lives in God, and God in Him.
1 John 4:16

You cannot know God and not love.
You cannot know love if you don't know God.

God's love is made complete in our lives through Jesus.
Once you know Him, really know Him, you will know love.

He loved first.
He is love.

He longs to show you His love.

I grew up during the hippie movement. A popular sign was the "peace"
sign. Another popular thing was "free love". I remember seeing clips from
Woodstock (one of the biggest concerts ever) and people were running
around half clothed and pretending to show "love". The problem was they
didn't really know what love is, they did not know the agape love of
Jesus. They knew a "feel good" love.

Yet out of the movement so many met Jesus and their lives were forever
changed. Keith Green was one of those. Oh how he loved God. He and
his wife, Melody, wrote some of the most amazing songs of worship.

Keith met Jesus and Jesus' love broke through!

In 1982, Keith met Jesus, His Redeemer, face to face! He was only 28!

He loves you

Your Love Broke Through
by Keith Green

"Like a foolish dreamer, trying to build a highway to the sky
All my hopes would come tumbling down,
and I never knew just why
Until today, when you pulled away the clouds that hung like
curtains on my eyes
Well I've been blind all these wasted years and I thought
I was so wise
But then you took me by surprise

Like waking up from the longest dream, how real it seemed
Until your love broke through
I've been lost in a fantasy, that blinded me
Until your love broke through

All my life I've been searching for that crazy missing part
And with one touch, you just rolled away the stone
that held my heart
And now I see that the answer was as easy, as just asking you in
And I am so sure I could never doubt your gentle touch again
It's like the power of the wind

Like waking up from the longest dream, how real it seemed
Until your love broke through
I've been lost in a fantasy, that blinded me
Until your love, until your love, broke through"

September 20
Take every thought captive

We demolish arguments and every pretension that sets itself up against
the knowledge of God, and we take captive every thought
to make it obedient to Christ.
2 Corinthians 10:5 NIV

"Every second we get a sting from some fiery shaft, some imagination,
some memory, some foreboding, some fear, some care, and God lets us
get them in order that they may be destroyed and we so armed against
them that they can never hurt us anymore. The only way to be armed
against them is to refuse them and the source from which they come.
Have you given your thoughts to God? Have you learned the meaning of
that cry of David, "I hate thoughts, but thy law do I love"?" A. B. Simpson
L. B. E. Cowman. "Springs in the Valley." March 27

They swarmed around me like bees, but they were consumed as
quickly as burning thorns; in the name of the Lord
I cut them down. Psalm 118:12 NIV

I've never been surrounded by bees but I have been by mosquitoes! They
were everywhere! Every step I took more swarmed out of the grass. I
was in Canada and I had never seen anything like it! It was really more
annoying than harmful. But because of the numerous amount of these
insects they consumed my thoughts. My one goal was to escape from
them.
That's the way our thoughts are. I went through a very dark depression
when I was younger. I felt as if I were in a deep dark hole and there was
no escape. All my thoughts were negative. I could not get past them. My
only escape was to sleep. It was one of the most difficult times of my life.
It was so very bad that I wanted to take my own life!
Yet I now know none of this was from God, I had let my own thoughts
consume me. The thoughts I had were desperate and without hope. I
had to allow God to "reprogram" my mind. I had to learn what it meant to
let Him take every thought captive. He did that over a period of time, I
learned the power of His word! It saved my life!

September 21
He longs to remake you

When the vessel that he made of the clay was marred in the hand of the
potter, he made it again another vessel, as seemed good to the potter to
make it. Then Yahweh's word came to me, saying,
House of Israel, can't I do with you as this potter? says Yahweh. Behold,
as the clay in the potter's hand, so are you in my hand, house of Israel.
Jeremiah 18:4-6 WEB

We often see ourselves as failures. We look at our past and even our
present and say "There is no hope. I am a failure. All is lost!" We hear
these words played over and over in our head like a broken record. But
there is hope, these words, these things spoken in the dark are all lies of
the enemy. He only has one goal and that is to destroy you.
But the lies can be stopped.

The truth is what God sees and what He says about you.
He sees someone who has been broken and defeated.
He longs to rise to show you His compassion,
He wants to whisper in your heart how much He loves you.
He wants to reshape you into a new creation.
His creation that now has direction and hope and meaning.

He's waiting to rescue you.

To remake you.

To show you His way.

"For I know the plans I have for you," declares the Lord, "plans to prosper
you and not to harm you, plans to give you hope and a future. Then you
will call on me and come and pray to me, and I will listen to you. You will
seek me and find me when you seek me with all your heart."
Jeremiah 29:11-13 NIV

He loves you

September 22
One day

"This is the covenant I will make with them after that time, says the
Lord. I will put my laws in their hearts,
and I will write them on their minds."
Hebrews 10:16 NIV

One day:
There will be no more battle with bad thoughts.
There will be no more battle with depression.
There will be no more battle with anxiety.
There will be no more battle with doubt.
There will be no more battle with fear.
There will be no more battle with the lies of the enemy.

One day God will write upon our minds, His laws, His thoughts.
All the old way of thinking will be gone,
Our minds will be totally set free,
To only hear His voice.
There will be no more voice of the enemy.
There will be no more voice from self, the old nature.

We will only hear His voice!

What a day that will be .... For all eternity!

This is the covenant I will establish with the people of Israel after that
time, declares the Lord. I will put my laws in their minds and write them on
their hearts. I will be their God, and they will be my people. No longer will
they teach their neighbor, or say to one another, 'Know the Lord,' because
they will all know me, from the least of them to the greatest.
Hebrews 8:10-11 NIV

He loves you

September 23
Face your fears

So do not throw away your confidence; it will be richly rewarded. You
need to persevere so that when you have done the will of God,
you will receive what he has promised.
Hebrews 10:35-36 NIV

Face your fears
Never give up
Pursue your dream

One of my very favorite movies is, "The Man from Snowy River".
I love the way in which Jim, the main character, pursues his dream.
He has one great fear, the black horse, which caused his beloved father's
death.
He overcomes that fear. So much so that what he once feared, the black
horse, is later used to save his life! Many, many obstacles stand in his
way but he never gives up!

So should we never give up.
God sees what you are doing.
He knows what you are striving for.
He will help you accomplish your dream, as long as it aligns with His word.
He can never go against what is true.
He will help you. He may even have to carry you.
But you can be assured of this, whatever stands in your way He will
remove it so that you can become all that He created you to be.

All, Nothing less!

He loves you

September 24
He is your Father

A father to the fatherless, a defender of widows, is God in his holy dwelling. God sets the lonely in families, he leads out the prisoners with singing; but the rebellious live in a sun-scorched land.

Psalm 68:5-6 NIV

I love the movie, Les Miserables.

Colette is a little girl whose mother has died. Terrible people, who pretend to care for her, are raising her but they really don't care about her or even love her. Collette has lived with no love from a father or a mother.

Jean Valjean sees this and feels her pain. He now knows his calling in life is to be her father, He says, "She needs a father. I will be her father."

God has always known.

There was no beginning for God.

There will be no end for God.

He has always known He wanted to be your Father.

There is no end to this desire.

He longs to carry you as only a loving, caring Father can.

His arms are so secure. They are open for you!

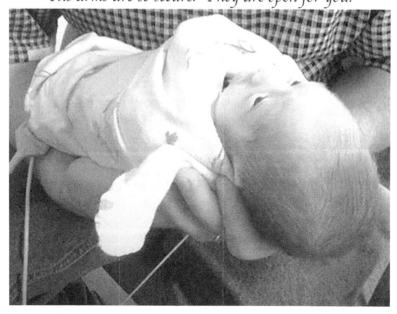

September 25
He forgives

Bear with each other and forgive one another
if any of you has a grievance against someone.
Forgive as the Lord forgave you.
Colossians 3:13

"Who is this man?
What sort of devil is he
To have me caught in a trap
And chose to let me go free?
It was his hour at last
To put a seal on my fate
Wipe out the past
And wash me clean off the slate!

How can I now allow this man
To hold dominion over me?
This desperate man that I have hunted
He gave me my life. He gave me freedom.
I should have perished by his hand
It was his right
It was my right to die as well
Instead I live.. but live in hell"

The world does not understand this kind of love.
These are words from the movie Les Miserables.
Inspector Javert was played by Russell Crowe. He could not understand
why Jean Valjean, played by Hugh Jackman, could forgive him. In the
end Inspector Javert took his own life.

*Forgiveness is so very hard. But it is so freeing if we
allow God to do it in our lives.*

September 26
I know every bird by name

For every animal of the forest is mine, and the cattle on a thousand hills.
I know every bird in the mountains, and the insects in the fields are mine.
Psalm 50:10-11 NIV

Every animal of the forest is His.
He created each one.
All the cattle on a thousand hills are His.
He created each one.
He knows every bird in the mountains.
He created each one.
He knows every insect in the field.
He created each one.
What an amazing thought . . . He knows every bird!
I wonder how many birds there are in the world.
According to Wikipedia there are over 10,000 different species of birds.
Some of these species have over 3 billion in them.
That's an incredible amount of birds!
Yet God knows them all!
If He knows them all and cares for them
How much more does He know and care for you.

September 27
Sometimes our strength is in fewer numbers

The Lord said to Gideon, "You have too many men. I cannot deliver
Midian into their hands, or Israel would boast against me,
'My own strength has saved me.' ""
Judges 7:2 NIV

Sometimes it may seem there are few walking with you.
Sometimes it may seem there are too few warriors to fight the battle.
Sometimes God has to reduce the number in order for the battle to be
won.

God knows our hearts.
He knows how easily we can get swallowed up in our own pride

So....
He calls only those He knows that will walk
He calls only those He knows that will fight

He wants to walk with you
He wants to fight for you
He wants to show you His power

When you become less, He becomes more.
The battle is His, you need only listen
and follow His lead!

He must become greater; I must become less.
John 3:30 NIV

He loves you

September 28
Jesus finished His work

I have brought you glory on earth by finishing the work you gave me to do. And now, Father, glorify me in your presence with the glory I had with you before the world began.
John 17:4-5 NIV

The cross that Jesus hung on was made of wood
This wood came from a tree
This tree came from the land
This land that God spoke into existence
God made this tree and said it was good
Yet because God is all knowing
He knew when He created this tree it would one day be used to form a cross
A cross that would hold His son, Jesus
A cross that would become the most popular symbol ever known
A cross that would represent death and agony and pain and drops of blood
A cross for Christians that would represent not only death but life!
Eternal life
Freedom from sin
Hope for tomorrow

God said, "Let the earth yield grass, herbs yielding seeds, and fruit trees bearing fruit after their kind, with their seeds in it, on the earth"; and it was so. The earth yielded grass, herbs yielding seed after their kind, and trees bearing fruit, with their seeds in it, after their kind; and God saw that it was good. There was evening and there was morning, a third day.
Genesis 1:11-13 WEB

Jesus finished His work on the cross for you and for me. It is finished! Now and for all eternity!

He loves you

September 29
In the right place

A certain man from Cyrene, Simon, the father of Alexander and Rufus,
was passing by on his way in from the country,
and they forced him to carry the cross.
Mark 15:21 NIV

Simon:
A man from Cyrene
The father of Alexander and Rufus
Passing by
Coming from the country
Seized by the Roman soldiers
Forced to carry Jesus' cross

What started out for Simon as just a regular day, coming in from the
country . . .
Changed His life forever!
He was the one in just the right place at just the right time to carry the
cross for Jesus.
He was the one to walk beside Jesus to Golgotha.
He was the one to hear Jesus speak just to him.
He was the one to see and hear and touch Jesus.
He was the one to feel Jesus' pain as His drops of blood fell to the ground.

Before the foundation of the world God knew this day and He chose
Simon of Cyrene to be a witness to all of this.
God knew it would forever change Simon of Cyrene!

He knows where we are.
He puts us in our time and place.
He places those in our path for a reason.
He meets us and we are forever changed!

All it takes is one encounter
to change our destiny forever!

September 30
You are fearfully and wonderfully made

For you created my inmost being; you knit me together in my mother's womb. I praise you because I am fearfully and wonderfully made; your works are wonderful, I know that full well.
Psalm 139:13-14 NIV

"Sea Biscuit" is a movie about a horse.
Sea Biscuit, the horse, was abused for years by his trainer, and then one day a man becomes interested in the horse and takes him as his own. The horse eventually becomes free to be what God made him to be!
A Horse!

"He just needs to learn how to be a horse again," is a quote from the new owner. When the horse was born the owner and trainer 'expected' him to do certain things. When the horse would not, the trainers tried to make him by hitting him and using different forms of punishment. When this did not work they gave up on him and decided he was of no use.

How many people are raised just like this, often even those in our churches. When a child is born parents often have their own expectations for their child. They do everything they can to make this child be what they think he or she should be. Sometimes they give too much, sometimes they abuse, sometimes they say hurtful words... All in the hopes that this child will "look and be like they think he should".

Yet, all the while, this child is being destroyed inside. Their hope begins to give way. Their dreams are shattered. Many times they just give up! Yet, God in His infinite wisdom, sees this and He reaches down from on high and says,
"Just be my child! I created you. I formed you.
I love you and I have a plan for you. Believe in me.
You can trust me. I long to be your Father!"

You just need to learn how to be a child again,
a child of the King!

October 1
Just let go

He replied, "Blessed rather are those who hear the word of God
and obey it."
Luke 11:28 NIV

Blessed are those who hear and obey.
As I've grown older I've grown more in love with His word.
God has made it come alive to me.
He's used it to give me direction when I didn't know where to go.
He's used it to raise my head up when I didn't think I could.
He's used it to give me hope when it seemed all hope was lost.
He's used it to give me understanding in difficult circumstances.
He's used it to shed light on my path.
He's used it to bless me and reveal His love to me.

And as I've grown more in Him, He's used it to give me words to
encourage others. Most of the time when I share His word with others it is
received and when it is received God uses it for good in their lives. "His
word will not return void but will accomplish what He sent it for." I have
had times when I shared words with a friend that God had laid upon my
heart for them. I wanted them to know the hurtful thoughts they had were
not from God. But instead of receiving the words, they just rolled their
eyes at me and said, "I know! I know!" They did not want to hear what I
had to say nor did they receive the words. I left very hurt and
discouraged. And confused.
Why would they not want to hear that God loved them just the way they
are and that they are doing a good job? Why would they not want to know
that the enemy longs to kill, steal and destroy us and if he can do that
through our own thoughts he will.

I realized just today that sometimes people don't want to give up their
"worries"! For some it is easier to continue in their own ways and in their
own thought patterns than to let God change them.
Please be the one that hears and receives and obeys for you will be
forever changed and blessed!

October 2
Creation waits in expectation

For the creation waits in eager expectation for the children of God to be revealed. For the creation was subjected to frustration, not by its own choice, but by the will of the one who subjected it, in hope that the creation itself will be liberated from its bondage to decay and brought into the freedom and glory of the children of God.
Romans 8:19-21 NIV

One day all of creation will be liberated from its bondage and decay.
It will be brought into freedom and glory.
Creation now groans as it waits.

Creation is amazing now.
What will it look like when it is set free from its bondage and decay?
What will all of creation look like when it's brought into freedom and glory?
Will the rose bush no longer have thorns?
Will the butterfly no longer live only two weeks?
Will the apple no longer decay?
Will the wind no longer form a tornado?
Will the hurricane no longer form over the ocean?
I can only imagine!

What will we look like when we are set free from our own bondage and decay?
What will we look like when we are brought into total freedom and glory?
Will we never have a bad thought again?
Will we never shed a tear of sorrow?
Will we never feel alone?
Will our hair never turn gray?
Will we never break a bone?

We can only imagine!

He loves you

October 3
He laid the earth's foundation

By wisdom the Lord laid the earth's foundations, by understanding he set
the heavens in place; by his knowledge the watery depths were divided,
and the clouds let drop the dew.
Proverbs 3:19-20 NIV

By wisdom He laid the earth's foundations.
I don't know a lot about science but I do understand enough to know what
an amazing miracle all of creation is!

God did all of this by His own wisdom!
He set the heavens in place by His own understanding.
He divided the oceans and the lakes and the rivers and the streams and
formed dew to drop from the clouds by His own knowledge.

If His wisdom and His understanding and His knowledge can do all of this,
then He can take care of us!

He can make a way where it seems there is no way.
He can provide when it seems provision is impossible.
He can change a person's heart when they've lost all hope.
He can do the impossible when nothing seems possible!

May we rest in His wisdom and His understanding
and His knowledge.

He loves you

October 4
Love is

There is a way which seems right to a man but the end there of is death.
Proverbs 14:12 KJV

This picture is of two of my grandsons at a restaurant. They were enthralled by this barking 'not real' dog. No matter how many times I told them both, "it's not real", they still couldn't grasp that. He moved and he barked, how could he not be real! They were worried about him and wanted to pet him and even wanted to rescue him. The only way I could get them to leave the 'not real' dog alone was to distract them with something else.

This made me think about how so many are confused in our world. They are constantly looking for something that is real. Something they can latch on to, something that they can hold on to, something that will give them meaning and purpose. But the thing that so many hold on to is not real. In fact it can be very harmful to them. It can give them false hope. It can lead them down the wrong path. It can and eventually will destroy them. I was reminded of the words to this song by John Lennon, of The Beatles.

Love (September, 1970)
"Love is feeling, feeling love
Love is wanting to be loved
Love is touch, touch is love
Love is reaching, reaching love
Love is asking to be loved
Love is you, you and me
Love is knowing we can be
Love is free, free is love
Love is living, living love
Love is needing to be loved""

As I read about his life I realized what a very sad and confused person he was. I don't think he ever knew real love, the kind of love that a Heavenly Father gives. When I think about him, I am reminded once again that Jesus died for John too, in all of his hurt and heartache and rebellion. Jesus gave it all for him but I don't think John ever knew that. "In March 1966, during an interview John Lennon remarked, 'Christianity will go. It will vanish and shrink ... We're more popular than Jesus now—I don't know which will go first, rock and roll or Christianity.'" The world is full of 'John Lennon's'. We don't know what makes someone be the way they are. We don't know what they've gone through. We don't know where they've come from. We don't know their story. But we do know our story. We do know our hope. We do know our future. If you know Jesus, be Jesus. The world is full of hurting and confused people. Share His love!

October 5
Eat what is good

Why spend money on what is not bread, and you labor on what does not
satisfy? Listen, listen to me, and eat what is good,
and you will delight in the richest of fare.
Isaiah 55:2 NIV

Eat what is good
And you will delight in the richest of fare!

We strife and we strife for things
For better houses
For bigger cars
For healthier food
For more prestigious jobs

Yet God in all His wisdom says, "Eat what is good!"
He offers us His word.
His word satisfies.

He promises us if we will eat we will delight in the richest of fare!

Fare - "a journey for which a price is paid".

Our journey will be rich on this earth (and forever) as we walk with Jesus.
He promises to bless what we sow. He promises to bless our land.

He wants us to delight in Him.

He will also send you rain for the seed you sow in the ground, and the
food that comes from the land will be rich and plentiful.
In that day your cattle will graze in broad meadows.
Isaiah 30:23 NIV

He loves you

October 6
Go tell Peter

"Don't be alarmed," he said. "You are looking for Jesus the Nazarene, who was crucified. He has risen! He is not here. See the place where they laid him. But go, tell his disciples and Peter, 'He is going ahead of you into Galilee. There you will see him, just as he told you.' "
Mark 16:6-7 NIV

What amazing words, just three words!
These three words speak of such forgiveness and compassion!
Peter, the one who denied he ever knew Jesus, not once but three times.
Yet, God in all of His mercy spoke Peter's name.
He didn't call out the other disciples by name, just Peter's.
He wanted Peter to know He was alive.
He wanted Peter to know He had come back.
He wanted Peter to know He loved him, nothing had changed.

Jesus knew what Peter was going to say before he said it.
He knew Peter would deny Him.
Jesus in His infinite mercy knew He would need to say Peter's name.
He knew how Peter felt.
He wanted to encourage Peter.

Jesus knows where we have failed Him.
He knows our pain.
But still He calls us out.

Out of the crowd He calls!
Such love, such forgiveness, such hope!

He loves you

October 7
My ways are not your ways

"For my thoughts are not your thoughts, and your ways are not my ways,"
says Yahweh. "For as the heavens are higher than the earth, so are my
ways higher than your ways, and my thoughts than your thoughts.
For as the rain comes down and the snow from the sky, and doesn't return
there, but waters the earth, and makes it grow and bud, and gives seed to
the sower and bread to the eater; so is my word that goes out of my
mouth: it will not return to me void, but it will accomplish that which I
please, and it will prosper in the thing I sent it to do. For you shall go out
with joy, and be led out with peace. The mountains and the hills will break
out before you into singing; and all the trees of the fields will clap their
hands. Instead of the thorn the cypress tree will come up; and instead of
the brier the myrtle tree will come up: and it will make a name for Yahweh,
for an everlasting sign that will not be cut off."
Isaiah 55:8-13 WEB

You, Father, speak in such kind and gentle ways,
You are ever before us. You know our thoughts.
Your thoughts are not our thoughts.
Your ways are so much higher than our ways.
Your thoughts are so much higher than our thoughts.
Just as You Father send the rain and the snow to water the earth and to
make life bud and flourish, so that this new life will produce seeds and
these seeds will produce food.
Your word that goes out never, ever returns empty. It will accomplish
what you desire it to. And will achieve the purpose you sent it for.
Because of this we are not consumed. We will go out with joy. You will
lead us out with peace. There will be music surrounding us. We will clap
our hands to you. All the things that satan meant for evil You Abba Father
will use for good, "Where there was once briers there will now be roses."
This will be our sign for us and for all of our children and for all of our
grandchildren and for all of our future generations!
My daughter recently sent me a video of my sweet grandson saying
'Jesus'. God used it to remind me all of the above is true!
If He can breathe life into a tiny two pound baby (that we did not know if
he would even live or breathe on his own) and then give him the ability to
speak your name, Jesus, then nothing is impossible with you!

*"From thy brier, dear heart, shall blow
a rose for others."*
L. B. E. Cowman. "Springs in the Valley." April 11

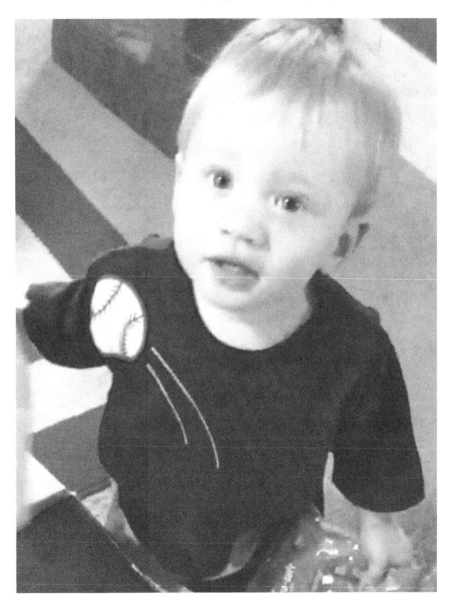

He loves you

October 8
God's word is not chained

But God's word is not chained.
2 Timothy 2:9 NIV

There is nothing that can hold God's word back.
Nothing!
No man
No mayor
No governor
No president
No father
No mother

No one can keep God's word chained.
It will do whatever God intended it to do.

It will bind up the brokenhearted.
It will set the captives free.
It will give sight to the blind.
It will shine light in the darkest place.
It will speak through all of creation.
It will not be held back.
It has no chains.

Hebrews 4:12 NIV
For the word of God is alive and active. Sharper than any double-edged sword, it penetrates even to dividing soul and spirit, joints and marrow; it judges the thoughts and attitudes of the heart.
Hebrews 4:12 NIV

He loves you

October 9
Look up

For his anger lasts only a moment, but his favor lasts a lifetime; weeping
may stay for the night, but rejoicing comes in the morning.
Psalm 30:5 NIV

"Pilgrim, look up! The road is dusty; the journey is long. Look up! Look up
in the early morning when the sun comes peeping over the horizon out of
the shadows of the night. Look up in the noontide when the resting-spot is
still afar in the distance. Look up when you see the evening star. Look up!"
(L. B. E. Cowman. "Springs in the Valley." April 15)

How many times God has whispered these two words to me, "Look up".
When I seem to be at my lowest point He reminds me, Look up!
Look up when there seems no way through the loss, the pain, and the
hurt.

Look up when no one stands around you.

Look up when there are no apparent answers.

Look up!

He is there!

He sees you.

He knows you.

He loves you.

The sun will come up tomorrow.

It always has, it always will.

Though the fig tree does not bud and there are no grapes on the vines,
though the olive crop fails and the fields produce no food, though there
are no sheep in the pen and no cattle in the stalls, yet I will rejoice in the
Lord, I will be joyful in God my Savior.
Habakkuk 3:17-18 NIV

October 10
He makes my feet secure

The Sovereign Lord is my strength; he makes my feet like the feet
of a deer, he enables me to tread on the heights.
Habakkuk 3:19 NIV

He makes us do what seems, in our minds, impossible.
We think we were never meant to walk so nimbly, like a deer.
Have you ever seen a deer walk on the side of a mountain or leap so
effortlessly over a fence?
It is incredible to watch their agility and their gracefulness and their
beauty.

We never think of ourselves as being able to do these things. Yet God
says He has made our feet like the feet of a deer. He gives us strength
not our own. He gives us grace beyond what is humanly possible. He
even bestows beauty on us as we undertake these impossible feats.

It is His strength that enables us to do all of this.

Not only can we walk on these heights,
we can also stand on them!
Be still and know that He is God.

He makes my feet like the feet of a deer;
he causes me to stand on the heights.
Psalm 18:33 NIV

He loves you

October 11
His supply is limitless

He took him outside and said, "Look up at the sky and count the stars
if indeed you can count them." Then he said to him,
"So shall your offspring be."
Genesis 15:5 NIV

"We are profoundly impressed with the unlimited resources of the God of the Bible. He never does anything small. When He makes an ocean He makes it so deep that no man can fathom it. When He makes a mountain He makes it so large that no one can measure or weigh it. When He makes flowers, He scatters multiplied millions of them where there is no one to admire them but Himself. When He makes grace, He makes it without sides or bottom and leaves the top off. Instead of giving salvation with a medicine dropper, He pours it forth like a river.

Whatever blessing is in our cup it is sure to run over. With Him the calf is always the fatted calf; the robe is always the best robe; the joy is unspeakable; the peace passes understanding; the grace is so abundant that the recipient has all-sufficiency for all things, and abounds to every good work."
(L.B.E.Cowman, "Springs in the Valley." April 18)

He scatters flowers where no one can see them but Himself!
Whatever blessing is in our cup it is sure to run over.
The fatted calf
The coat of many colors
Grace that knows no bounds
Peace that passes all understanding
Joy that never ceases
Grace that has no limits
All for you!

He loves you

October 12
He exercises kindness

"But let the one who boasts boast about this: that they have the
understanding to know me, that I am the Lord, who exercises kindness,
justice and righteousness on earth,
for in these I delight," declares the Lord.
Jeremiah 9:24 NIV

God exercises kindness
God exercises justice
God exercises righteousness
He does all of this while we are here on this earth.

These are what He delights in!

He is so loving that these three things are what He is all about.
He cannot be anything but kind and just and righteous.
He longs to show us His kindness.
He wants justice to reign.
He is righteousness!

He is all of this and so much more.
We have all of this inside of us because
He sent His Holy Spirit to live within us
To reveal to others through us His kindness
To show to others His justice and
To be to others His righteousness.

He loves you

October 13
He gives good gifts

If you then, though you are evil, know how to give good gifts
to your children, how much more will your Father in heaven
give the Holy Spirit to those who ask him!"
Luke 11:13 NIV

I remember one Christmas many years ago when we gave computers to each of our three children. I was so excited, I could hardly contain my excitement. I could not wait for them to see their gifts. They'd never had their own computer. They had no idea how we were about to bless them. At that time they were very extravagant gifts for us to give. They were thrilled when they saw their gifts.

That's the way God is. He loves to give His children extravagant gifts
Gifts that we have no idea that He wants to give
Gifts beyond our wildest dreams.
Gifts that far exceed all our desires.
Gifts that are good for us and bless us.
Gifts that reveal His love for us, His children.

"So I say to you: Ask and it will be given to you; seek and you will find;
knock and the door will be opened to you.
For everyone who asks receives; the one who seeks finds;
and to the one who knocks, the door will be opened.
Luke 11:9-10 NIV

He loves you

October 14
I will wait until you return

"Please do not go away until I come back and bring my offering and set it
before you." And the Lord said, "I will wait until you return."
Judges 6:18 NIV

Gideon spoke these words. He talked to God face to face. In fact he
requested of God a favor. God listened to Gideon's request. God not
only listened He granted Gideon his request. Gideon asked God, the Lord
of the universe, to wait on him. And the amazing thing is God, the Lord of
the universe, did not say, "I'm too busy, No, I can't wait, I have more
important things to do". Rather God said, "I will wait until you return".

Such a kind God

Such a patient God

Such an understanding God

Such a loving God

He listens and He responds to your request.

He waits for you.

The Lord turned to him and said, "Go in the strength you have and save
Israel out of Midian's hand. Am I not sending you?" "Pardon me, my lord,"
Gideon replied, "but how can I save Israel? My clan is the weakest in
Manasseh, and I am the least in my family." The Lord answered, "I will be
with you , and you will strike down all the Midianites, leaving none alive."
Gideon replied, "If now I have found favor in your eyes, give me a sign
that it is really you talking to me."
Judges 6:14-17 NIV

He loves you

October 15
How God sees you

Now Jephthah the Gileadite was a mighty man of valor, and he was the
son of a prostitute. Gilead became the father of Jephthah. Gilead's wife
bore him sons. When his wife's sons grew up, they drove Jephthah out,
and said to him, "You will not inherit in our father's house,
for you are the son of another woman."
Judges 11:1-2 WEB

God sees us through His eyes.
The world sees us through their eyes.
What a difference there is!

Jephthah's mother was a prostitute.
His brothers condemned him and drove him away.
Yet God saw him as a "mighty warrior"!
The same words God used to describe Gideon.

When the world looks at you and says you are nothing
Remember they are only looking through their eyes.

God sees you as mighty.
He has a great purpose for your life.
Ask Him to reveal to you how He sees you.
You will be amazed by His response!
Then wait to see His plan unfold for you.
It will be beyond anything you could have ever imagined.

What more shall I say? For the time would fail me if I told of Gideon,
Barak, Samson, Jephthah, David, Samuel, and the prophets; who,
through faith subdued kingdoms, worked out righteousness, obtained
promises, stopped the mouths of lions, quenched the power of
fire, escaped the edge of the sword, from weakness were made strong,
grew mighty in war, and caused foreign armies to flee.
Hebrews 11:32-34 WEB

October 16
Bless your family

Praise be to the Lord, the God of Israel, from everlasting to everlasting.
Then all the people said "Amen" and "Praise the Lord."
Then all the people left, each for their own home,
and David returned home to bless his family.
1 Chronicles 16:36, 43 NIV

After worshiping with the body of believers my heart is always full.
God says after we've worshipped to go home and bless our families.
That's what David did.

David was a man after God's own heart.

It is so good for us to join together with other believers.
In fact it's so good God says,
"Do not forsake the assembling of the body."
He doesn't say it to try to rule over you.
He doesn't say it as law.
He says it because He knows how it encourages you and blesses Him.
True worship with the body of Christ is like a "good medicine".
It does your heart good.

A cheerful heart is good medicine,
but a crushed spirit dries up the bones.
Proverbs 17:22 NIV

He loves you

October 17
The waters saw you

The waters saw you, God, the waters saw you and writhed;
the very depths were convulsed.
Psalm 77:16 NIV

The waters saw you.
The waters saw God.

What an incredible statement,
The waters saw!
The waters saw God and writhed.
The waters convulsed.

If God has the ability to make "the waters see"
then He can perform whatever miracle it is you need!
Nothing is beyond His grasp.
Nothing is beyond His control.

The waters saw God and moved.
The waters made a dry path for God's people.
He can do the same for you!

Then Moses stretched out his hand over the sea, and all that night the
Lord drove the sea back with a strong east wind and turned it into dry
land. The waters were divided, and the Israelites went through the sea on
dry ground, with a wall of water on their right and on their left.
Exodus 14:21-22 NIV

He loves you

October 18
We come into your house

But I, by your great love, can come into your house; in reverence
I bow down toward your holy temple.
Psalm 5:7 NIV

When I was a little girl we used to do this little finger play:
Here is the church, (lace fingers together so they are inside your palms
and close hands)
Here is the steeple, (point index finger up)
Open the doors, (unfold your hands)
And see all the people. (wiggle your fingers around)

As a child I thought the only place you could be with God was at church.
And I really wasn't sure He was there.

As I've begun to understand Him, I now realize He goes with me
everywhere.
If I "make my bed in the depths He is there".
If I "go to the far side of the sea He is there".
He "never leaves me or forsakes me".

He loves for His church to assemble to worship Him
But even more He longs for us to individually "bow
down" and be with Him.
Just Him, no one else, no distractions, just Him.
You can do this. He will reveal His great love to you!

He loves you

We Bow Low
by Tim Sheppard
by Gateway Worship

"We bow low, we bow low
Faces down to the ground in Your presence Lord
With our tears we wash Your feet
We bow low, we bow low
Falling on our knees
We bow low, we bow low
To the King of Kings

We bow low, we bow low
Faces down to the ground in Your presence Lord
With our tears we wash Your feet
We bow low, we bow low
Falling on our knees
We bow low, we bow low
To the King of Kings

Holy, Holy, Holy, Holy, Holy, Holy
Holy are You Lord forevermore"

He loves you

October 19
His touch

When I saw him, I fell at his feet as though dead. Then he placed his right hand on me and said: "Do not be afraid. I am the First and the Last. I am the Living One; I was dead, and now look, I am alive for ever and ever! And I hold the keys of death and Hades.
Revelation 1:17-18 NIV

When John saw Jesus he was so afraid he fell facedown as though he were dead.
Then, Jesus touched him and spoke to him.

Jesus' touch can bring calm to the most raging storms.
Jesus' voice can bring peace when it seems there is no peace to be found.

Jesus knows what we need.
His touch
His words

Jesus said to John, "Now look!"

He wants us to gaze upon Him...
To see and know He is alive forevermore

He is all we need!

He loves you

October 20
They are radiant

Those who look to him are radiant; their faces
are never covered with shame.
Psalm 34:5 NIV

"Of all the lights you carry in your face
Joy will reach the farthest out to sea."
H.W. Beecher

When we look to him we are radiant.
There is no shame.

Where are you looking?
Where is your focus?
Where is your gaze?

It must be on Him.
He alone brings light.
He alone brings joy.
He alone keeps you pure.

His light makes your face radiant!

When Moses came down from Mount Sinai
with the two tablets of the covenant law in his hands,
he was not aware that his face was radiant
because he had spoken with the Lord.
Exodus 34:29 NIV

He loves you

October 21
The sunlight will come

And the God of all grace, who called you to his eternal glory in Christ,
after you have suffered a little while, will himself restore you
and make you strong, firm and steadfast.
1 Peter 5:10 NIV

"We cannot know Thy stillness until it is broken. There is no music in the silence until we have heard the roar of battle! We cannot see Thy beauty until it is shaded." LEAVES FOR QUIET HOURS

"After the shadows, the sunlight will come."
(L. B. E. Cowman. "Springs in the Valley." May 3)

"After the shadows, the sunlight will come."

It may seem God is not in the shadows but I can assure you He is there.
He sees you. He knows you. He can make a way where there seems to
be no way.
He can and will walk you through the darkness.
When you come out of the darkness you will never see the sun in the
same way again.
Your eyes will be forever changed. You will be forever changed.
You will be restored.
You will be strong again.
You will hear the music of life again!

He loves you

October 22
Not a word

Now Jesus stood before the governor: and the governor asked him,
saying, "Are you the King of the Jews?" Jesus said to him, "So you say."
When he was accused by the chief priests and elders, he answered
nothing. Then Pilate said to him, "Don't you hear how many things they
testify against you?" He gave him no answer, not even one word,
so that the governor marveled greatly.
Matthew 27:11-14 WEB

Jesus only reply to His accusers was to say, "You have said so".
He stood before the governor, the chief priests and the elders.
Jesus made no reply, not to a single charge!

No reply, how often I have felt the need to defend myself,
to defend my cause...
Yet Jesus did neither.

Witness in love, not a word!
Like the dew you will be blessed.
When dew falls it makes no sound.
You cannot know when it falls by listening for it.
In the same way our stillness, our utter quietness,
displays to the world God's splendor.

Not a word!
You will be quietly blessed!
Allow God to display His splendor through you

He loves you

October 23
So faithful

Love and faithfulness meet together; righteousness and peace
kiss each other.
Faithfulness springs forth from the earth,
and righteousness looks down from heaven.
Psalm 85:10-11 NIV

We have one kind of flower in our yard that always comes back year after
year after year.   It's our gerbera daisies.
We started with two to three very small gerbera daisy plants and now we
have several flowerbeds full of them. From the first year we planted them
they have been faithful to come back year after year after year. It matters
not what kind of winter we have they still come back. We don't even
fertilize them.
Still they are faithful! Their blooms are beautiful. They are like the
rainbow and bloom in many beautiful colors.
Just as my daisies are faithful to spring forth every year from the earth so
is my God.

He is always with me.

He is always faithful.

He always goes before me.

He even puts a covering over my head.

His right hand is always there for me.

He leads me down His path.

Surely your goodness and love will follow me all the days of my life, and I
will dwell in the house of the Lord forever.
Psalm 23:6 NIV

So faithful!

He loves you

October 24
The work of His hands

Then all your people will be righteous and they will possess the land
forever. They are the shoot I have planted, the work of my hands,
for the display of my splendor.
Isaiah 60:21 NIV

I've always had a desire to create things. When I was in college I did
macramé and quilling. I even sewed on my grandmother's treadle sewing
machine. It gave me much pleasure to make something with my
hands. Then I got married and had three children in five years so my
handiwork became my children. Now our children are grown and gone
and have children of their own. Once again I have time to create with my
hands.

It is an incredible thought to think that we are the works of God's
hands! We are the display of His splendor. An amazing thought! I know
the joy I get when I create and I know how much more joy I get from my
children, the gifts He has created and given to me.

If I feel this way about what I make and what He's made and given to me,
how much more joy God must find in His handiwork, that's us!

We are pleasing to our Abba Father.
He does smile when He looks at us,
the work of His hands.

He loves you

October 25
He gives life to the dead

He is our father in the sight of God, in whom he believed---the God who
gives life to the dead and calls into being things that were not.
Romans 4:17 NIV

The God who gives life to the dead
And calls into being things that were not

I had a dream. In my dream there were many people, mostly young
people that needed organ transplants. There was testing being done to
see what organs were needed.
Most needed heart transplants. Once it was confirmed what was needed,
the hearts were immediately made available. I remember being amazed
that the organs were immediately available! I did not know where they
came from, just that the people in need received them immediately!
They were all immediately made whole.

What a great picture of what God does to each of us when we come to
know Jesus.
He does give us a "new heart", His heart, and we are immediately given
"new life".
We are no longer dead but alive in Him!

He calls into being things that were not!
You were once dead
Now you are alive forevermore!

He loves you

October 26
Inhale, exhale

All Scripture is God-breathed and is useful for teaching, rebuking,
correcting and training in righteousness.
2 Timothy 3:16 NIV

This is a quote from Beth Moore's book, Believing God Day by Day.
"We can read the Scripture for hours, but if we don't receive it by faith,
it doesn't abide in us, bringing its vitality, energy, and effectiveness. We
may be encouraged by it, but we are neither empowered nor changed.
But if we do receive it by faith— thereby accepting it into our belief
system—we might think of the practice like inhaling a breath of faith, like
receiving spiritual CPR. Then when we choose to speak what we believe,
we might think of ourselves as exhaling that same breath into speech,
speaking it over our specific circumstances."
(Moore, Beth. "Believing God Day by Day.") May 10

My job is to inhale His word by faith.
Then when I exhale that same word becomes speech and accomplishes
what it was sent out for.
It's the power in His breath spoken through His word that causes change.

In this same way He breathed life daily into my little micro preemie
grandson.

His word when breathed in and exhaled out
becomes powerful and effective
It will accomplish what it was sent out for. . .
To give life to you, to give life to the world.

He loves you

October 27
He will teach you

But the Advocate, the Holy Spirit, whom the Father will send in my name,
will teach you all things and will remind you of everything
I have said to you.
John 14:26 NIV

The Holy Spirit is within you.
He goes with you.
He speaks to you.
He guides you.
He teaches you.
He reminds you of God's love.

He is forever for you.

Dr. Holly Ordway is a college professor who was once an atheist. She gives an account of how difficult and fearful it was for her to begin to change her beliefs and to become a Christian. "It is a hard thing to look at the truth when it runs contrary to what you've always believed. The experience is like pulling back the curtains in a dimly lit room and looking out the window to see what's really inside. When your eyes are used to artificial light, the bright sunlight is almost blinding; your eyes may sting and even water at the brightness, and the temptation is to turn away to the more comfortable dimness."

But eventually she knew she could not turn away from the light, God's truth. It drew her in. She knew and believed that the New Testament was true. She believed in the resurrection of Jesus. She knew and she was changed.

When you meet Jesus, really meet him,
you are forever changed!

He loves you

October 28
Singing in the storm

All the lands are at rest and at peace; they break into singing.
Isaiah 14:7 NIV

The bird sang and sang and sang all while the skies rumbled and roared and streaked with lightning. How could the little bird be singing? I was nervous and yet this little creature that was so much smaller than me and was out in the weather continued to sing! This little bird that God created was at peace in the midst of a bad storm. I realized I needed to learn from this one so close to God. He realized what the rain meant. It was for his good, for life and nourishment. It would satisfy his thirsty body.
He was not afraid.

Oh that I would be like a bird, trusting and singing through the storm!

The birds of the sky rest by the waters,
they sing among the branches.
Psalm 104:12

Oh that we might sing through the storm!

He loves you

October 29
Lead a quiet life

Make it your ambition to lead a quiet life: You should mind your own
business and work with your hands, just as we told you,
so that your daily life may win the respect of outsiders and
so that you will not be dependent on anybody.
1 Thessalonian 4:11 NIV

Our world today is driven by go go go and do do do
Yet God says "Lead a quiet life".

His words are to:
Mind your own business and
Work with your hands

This is the key to contentment and happiness.
Then you will gain the respect of others.
You won't be dependent on anyone.

When you go about your work, do it not for recognition by anyone.
But for your Heavenly Father. He sees and knows what you do.
Strive to please His heart and in so doing others will see your good works.

The words to an old song were:
"Slow down you move to fast, you've got to make the morning last."

I would say you've got to make the moment last.
You will never have this moment again.
Enjoy the moment
Lead a quiet life
The reward is so much better!

For it is God who works in you to will and to act
in order to fulfill his good purpose.
Philippians 2:13 NIV

He loves you

October 30
Hold firmly to the word of life

Do everything without grumbling or arguing, so that you may become blameless and pure, "children of God without fault in a warped and crooked generation." Then you will shine among them like stars in the sky   Philippians 2:14-15 NIV

Hold firmly to the word of life, then you will shine like the stars in the sky.
Don't let go
Don't waver
Move forward
Walk the path He has for you
Believe His word
Stand firm
Remember to look up
He is with you
He is for you
His ways are good
You can trust His plan for your life
Then you will shine like the stars in the sky.

Hold firmly

October 31
Do it all for the glory of God

So whether you eat or drink or whatever you do,
do it all for the glory of God.
1 Corinthians 10:31 NIV

"Our aim in such a life is to identify all that we are and all that we do with God's purposes in creating us and our world. Thus we learn how to do all things to the glory of God (1 Corinthians 10:31, Colossians 3:17). That is, we come to think and act in all things so that God's goodness, greatness and beauty will be as obvious as possible - not just to ourselves but also to all those around us."
(Hearing God by Dallas Willard week 52 day 6)

Whatever you do . . .
Whether you eat
Whether you drink
Whatever you do
Whether in word
Whether in deed
Do it all in the name of the Lord
Always giving thanks to God

Let our words
Let our actions
Let our eating
Let our drinking
All be pleasing to you

May You be lifted up in all we do!

And whatever you do, whether in word or deed, do it all in the name of the
Lord Jesus, giving thanks to God the Father through him.
Colossians 3:17 NIV

He loves you

November 1
In the secret places

In the secret places of the stairs, let me see thy countenance,
let me hear thy voice; for sweet is thy voice.
Song of Songs 2:14 KJV

I often dream about stairs and stairways. Sometimes I am walking up the stairs and sometimes I am walking down. There have been stairs in multi-level houses. There have been stairs outside on cliffs. There have been stairs that wind. There have been stairs that have no sides. There have been stairs that are not level and not stable. There have been stairs that seem to drop off on one side. Many, many different kinds of stairs. In my dreams I am walking on these stairs usually alone and I am afraid I can't do this. But in every dream even though I am afraid I can't, I find I can. Jacob (in Genesis) had a dream in which there were stairs and angels were ascending and descending on the stairs.

In life we have many different kinds of "stairs". Sometimes our path seems too difficult and yet God says He is there with us on all of these different kinds of "stairs". The path may be steep and there may be secret places on the stairs, yet He is there. He wants us to go there with Him!

"In the hush of breathless and holy silence
The clearest vision of the glory of the face of Christ
Hear the melody of the divine voice
As He tells us the story of His love
He reveals His visions to us
Alone with God to know His sweetness"
(Springs in the Valley, L.B.E. Cowman, May 29)

He whispers oh so gently

Take the time to meet with Him.

He has much to tell you!

And there stood no man with him, while Joseph made himself known.
Genesis 45:1

November 2
God's abundant, miraculous provision

But Jehoshaphat asked, "Is there no prophet of the Lord here, through whom we may inquire of the Lord?" An officer of the king of Israel answered, "Elisha son of Shaphat is here. He used to pour water on the hands of Elijah." Jehoshaphat said, "The word of the Lord is with him."
2 Kings 3:11-12 NIV

Elisha used to pour water on the hands of Elijah.
Jehoshaphat knew the word of the Lord was with him.
Elisha only listened and helped because he had respect for Jehoshaphat. Jehoshaphat's character, his "walk" was seen by many, including Elisha. His testimony went before him and Elisha knew what God he served.

The hand of the Lord came upon Elisha.
God told Elisha what he was about to do, the impossible. God filled the valley with water, not from rain or wind. He met their needs and even the needs of their animals in a supernatural way, a way that only God could do. Yet Elisha knew It was an easy thing for God to do.

Elisha was first a servant of a great man of God.
Elisha's character was known by many.
Elisha knew others who believed like he did.
God touched Elisha.
God spoke to Elisha.
God did the impossible, He sent water to meet their needs.
God didn't meet their needs in a little way but in an abundant overflowing way.

Our character is so important.
May others know us as ones who believe in the God of the impossible!

He loves you

Elisha said to the king of Israel, "What have I to do with you? Go to the prophets of your father, and to the prophets of your mother." The king of Israel said to him, "No, for Yahweh has called these three kings together to deliver them into the hand of Moab." Elisha said, "As Yahweh of Armies lives, before whom I stand, surely, were it not that I respect the presence of Jehoshaphat the king of Judah, I would not look toward you, nor see you. But now bring me a musician." When the musician played, Yahweh's hand came on him. He said, "Yahweh says, 'Make this valley full of trenches.' For Yahweh says, 'You will not see wind, neither will you see rain, yet that valley will be filled with water, and you will drink, both you and your livestock and your other animals. This is an easy thing in Yahweh's sight. He will also deliver the Moabites into your hand. You shall strike every fortified city, and every choice city, and shall fell every good tree, and stop all springs of water, and mark every good piece of land with stones.'" In the morning, about the time of offering the sacrifice, behold, water came by the way of Edom, and the country was filled with water.
2 Kings 3:13-20 WEB

He loves you

November 3
You give us rain

Do any of the worthless idols of the nations bring rain? Do the skies
themselves send down showers? No, it is you, Lord our God. Therefore
our hope is in you, for you are the one who does all this.
Jeremiah 14:22 NIV

God sends the rain, only He does this.
Thank you Father for the rain.
Several years ago we had had a drought in Texas for many years but now
most of the lakes are full again!
You are the one who makes the rain drops form.
You are the one who causes the rain to spill forth.
You are the one who makes the rain nourish the plants and trees.
You are the one who stops drought and brings lakes to overflowing their
banks.

*In the same way, God gives the rain when we have drought
in our lives.*

When it seems you can't go on anymore, God sends the rain!

Not just a few drops, but millions and billions of raindrops.

Enough to completely change your life

Enough to cause new life to grow.

Enough to give you a new hope and a purpose.

Thank you Father for the rain!
You are the one who does all this.

"You are my witnesses, " declares the Lord, "and my servant whom I
have chosen, so that you may know and believe me and understand that I
am he. Before me no god was formed, nor will there be one after me.
Isaiah 43:10 NIV

November 4
Finish the race

I have fought the good fight, I have finished the race, I have kept the faith.
2 Timothy 4:7 NIV

My aim is to:
Finish the race
Complete the task given me
The task is to testify of the good news of God's grace

The task is to tell of His grace
Not His laws!
His grace

Years ago there was a popular movie called "Chariots of Fire".
It was about a man named Eric Liddell. He was a gifted runner and when
he ran, he ran fast. His first love was Jesus but he knew also that God
had given him a talent, a talent to run. He actually ran in the Olympics
and won a gold medal for his country, Scotland. The one statement I
have always remembered from the movie was, "When I run, I feel God's
pleasure." It was also said that when Eric died that "all of Scotland
mourned"! What a testimony, what a life, what a race!
As we each "run our race" here on earth, may we feel God's
pleasure. God loves to watch His children doing what brings us pleasure,
using the gifts and talents He's given us.

Run, never give up!
He's waiting at the finish line for you!
Your prize awaits you. . .
Life everlasting with the one who gave everything for you.

I press on toward the goal to win the prize for which God has called me
heavenward in Christ Jesus.
Philippians 3:14 NIV

November 5
There will be a harvest

Let us not become weary in doing good, for at the proper time
we will reap a harvest if we do not give up.
Galatians 6:9 NIV

The slogan several years ago was "Just Do It"!
Keep on, you can do it! Run the race!
Now today that same attitude has been construed to mean something
else.
Just do it!
Do what feels right to you.
Don't consider the cost to you or to others.
"It's my right!" We've become a world of me, me, me!!!

Yet God says, no, it's not about you, it's about me.

My love for you
My love through you
You loving others through me

"Do unto others as you would have them do to you."

If we would only stop and listen . . . He is there

He longs to express His love to you
There will be a harvest if you don't give up

He loves you

November 6
For this reason I kneel

For this reason I kneel before the Father, from whom every family in
heaven and on earth derives its name.
Ephesians 3:14-15 NIV

For this reason....I kneel

For this reason
Is it for the cancer that has ravaged a loved one
Is it for your child who has wandered away
Is it for freedom from the darkness
Is it for provision just to feed your children

For whatever reason it is

That is your place

To kneel before the Father

Your Abba Father

The one who knows all

The one who created all

The one who provides all

He is there.
He sees you.
He knows you.
He hears you

He loves you

November 7
Every good and perfect gift

Every good and perfect gift is from above, coming down from the Father of
the heavenly lights, who does not change like shifting shadows.
James 1:17 NIV

Every good and perfect gift is from God.
He never changes.
He can only give good gifts.
His gifts are perfect.
His gifts have no strings attached.
He knows what you need.
He will only give you what is good for you.

Your Father knows what you need before you ask him.
Matthew 6:8 NIV

November 8
A warning about distorting His word

His letters contain some things that are hard to understand,
which ignorant and unstable people distort, as they do the other
Scriptures, to their own destruction.
2 Peter 3:16 NIV

Ignorant and unstable people distort the truth of God's word,
but this only causes their own destruction.
We are to be on our guard so that we won't be carried away by these
lawless people.
We are to instead grow in the grace and knowledge of Jesus.
Don't be like the waves tossed to and fro, rather stand on His word.

Believe what He says about you and for you.
Close your ears to those who are trying to change God's word.

With Him there is no shifting sand.
He is our rock.
He is our firm foundation.

His ways are right.
His ways are perfect.
His word is truth.

Therefore, dear friends, since you have been forewarned, be on your
guard so that you may not be carried away by the error of the lawless and
fall from your secure position. But grow in the grace and knowledge of our
Lord and Savior Jesus Christ. To him be glory both now and forever!
Amen.
2 Peter 3:17-18 NIV

He loves you

November 9
Repair the altar

Then Elijah said to all the people, "Come here to me." They came to him,
and he repaired the altar of the Lord, which had been torn down.
1 Kings 18:30 NIV

Before Elijah could ask God to show Himself, Elijah had to repair the altar.
Elijah knew the altar had been torn down.

Elijah then prayed for God to reveal himself to the people.
'Show your power' and God did. He not only burned up the sacrifice but
He also burned up the wood and the stones and the soil. Then He licked
up the water in the trench, the twelve jars of water.

When the people saw this they knew it was God who had shown His
power.
Their gods had done nothing!

So also we must first 'repair the altar',

the altar of our heart

Before we can ask God to reveal Himself.

We must 'sacrifice' ourselves on this altar.

Our wants and our desires for His desires.

He will reveal Himself to the world through us.

He will burn up everything in our lives

that is not for our good.

Therefore, I urge you, brothers and sisters, in view of God's mercy, to
offer your bodies as a living sacrifice, holy and pleasing to God
this is your true and proper worship.
Romans 12:1 NIV

November 10
At that moment

Jesus turned and saw her. "Take heart, daughter," he said, "your faith has healed you." And the woman was healed at that moment.
Matthew 9:22 NIV

One woman needed healing for herself.
One woman needed healing for her daughter.
Both went to Jesus.
One touched the hem of his garment.
One spoke her request to Him.

God healed both "at that moment"!
God knew about "this moment"
before the foundation of the world.
He knew "at that moment" they both would be healed.
He knows your need.
He has a moment for you too,
in which He will touch you.

Continue to seek Him
Continue to ask Him
He will be there!
At that moment

Then Jesus said to her, "Woman, you have great faith! Your request is granted." And her daughter was healed at that moment.
Matthew 15:28 NIV

He loves you

November 11
His word brings life

Now the Berean Jews were of more noble character than those in Thessalonica, for they received the message with great eagerness and examined the Scriptures every day to see if what Paul said was true.
Acts 17:11 NIV

His word is truth.
His word brings life.

It is so very important that we study the scripture, His word,
the word that He breathed life into.
But be careful why you study it.
Is it to gain more knowledge and to prove your point?
Or is it to know the God of the Bible more?
If you do not know His son, Jesus, and believe in Him
then your studies will not produce life, only works!

Once you know His Son everything changes

and this word,

His word, dwells in you.

You will be forever changed and you will have a hunger

to know Him more.

To read His word.
To find your answers in His word
To share His encouraging word with others.
His word is truth.
His word brings life.
And the Father who sent me has himself testified concerning me.
You have never heard his voice nor seen his form, nor does his word
dwell in you, for you do not believe the one he sent. You study the
Scriptures diligently because you think that in them you have eternal life.
These are the very Scriptures that testify about me,
yet you refuse to come to me to have life.
John 5:37-40 NIV

November 12
Do what pleases Him

For John came neither eating nor drinking, and they say, 'He has a
demon.' The Son of Man came eating and drinking, and they say, 'Here is
a glutton and a drunkard, a friend of tax collectors and sinners.'
But wisdom is proved right by her deeds."
Matthew 11:18-19 NIV

You will not be able to live in the world and be "of the world".
You can never satisfy the world.
One will say you are possessed.
And another will say you are crazy.
You cannot please them both.

But your deeds will show your true heart.
And God knows your heart.

Do what pleases Him.
It will draw some to Him.
Some may see and wonder
But others will see and know.

"Wisdom is proved right by her deeds."

He loves you

November 13
To walk with God

Enoch lived sixty-five years, then became the father of Methuselah. After Methuselah's birth, Enoch walked with God for three hundred years, and became the father of more sons and daughters. The days of Enoch were three hundred sixty-five years. Enoch walked with God, and he was not found, for God took him.

Genesis 5:21-24 WEB

What is recorded about Enoch:

He was the seventh from Adam.

He was the father of Methuselah, who lived longer than anyone else (969 years).

He was 65 when Methuselah was born.

He walked faithfully with God for 300 years.

He had other sons and daughters.

He lived 365 years.

God took him away.

He did not experience death.

Before he was taken away it was said . . .

He pleased God.

He prophesied about Jesus and his return and his judgment against those who have spoken against him.

This is all that is written about Enoch for us to know.

God knew something more.

He knew Enoch pleased him.

His legacy was not written down for us,

just the fact that he pleased God.

May your legacy be as such.

Even if no one ever knows what you say or do

may you be pleasing to God.

By faith Enoch was taken from this life, so that he did not experience death: "He could not be found, because God had taken him away." For before he was taken, he was commended as one who pleased God.

Hebrews 11:5 NIV

November 14
What would you have me do today?

*A discerning person keeps wisdom in view, but a fool's eyes
wander to the ends of the earth.*
Proverbs 17:24 NIV

We only have one life. We won't get to do this life again. We must keep
our eyes on the goal. We need to focus on what is really important. What
one thing would you have us do today, God? Let go of the craziness and
the hurriedness of this day and focus only on Him. He will show you what
He has for you.

"What would you have me do today?"
Those are the words on a sign outside my friend's parents apartment.
Her parents moved into an assisted living facility.
Her father was 96 and her mother was also in her nineties.
I'm sure moving from their home to this place was not the desire of their
hearts yet the sign on their door speaks volumes. They both loved Jesus
and wanted to be "Him" to the world.

God gave me a dream about this man. Even though he was bedridden on
this earth in my dream he was dancing before Jesus. It was such a sweet
dream. The next day this sweet man of 96 left this earth and met Jesus.
I can imagine that he was dancing before his Savior. He no longer had
his old and sick body, he had a new body in his forever home.

So today just ask the Father,
"Show me what I am to do today"
Don't worry about tomorrow focus only on today.
What one thing is mine to do for you today?"
He will show you.

He loves you

November 15
Be His fragrance

I have become its servant by the commission God gave me to present to you the word of God in its fullness, the mystery that has been kept hidden for ages and generations, but is now disclosed to the Lord's people.
Colossians 1:25-26 NIV

To present to you the word of God in its glory.
And in you and in all that are God's children.
He has chosen us to make known to the world the hope of glory, Jesus.

We are to be Him here!
His love. . . His hope
His peace. . .His joy
His grace
We are His reflection.
But the best part of this is we don't have to do it.
He does it through us.
We need only abide.
He will "Be" through your life.

"It is not to try to do or be some great thing but simply to have Him and let Him live His own life in us; abiding in Him and He in us, and letting Him reflect His own graces, His own faith, His own consecration, His own love, His own patience, His own gentleness, His own words in us, while we "show forth the virtues of Him who hath called us out of darkness into His marvelous light."
(L. B. E. Cowman. "Springs in the Valley." August 3)

May our lives emit the sweetest fragrance, to the world, of the ever so gentle Savior we serve.

To them God has chosen to make known among the Gentiles the glorious riches of this mystery, which is Christ in you, the hope of glory.
Colossians 1:27 NIV

November 16
To really know Him

"I know that you can do all things; no purpose of yours can be thwarted.
You asked, 'Who is this that obscures my plans without knowledge?'
Surely I spoke of things I did not understand, things too wonderful for me
to know. My ears had heard of you but now my eyes have seen you.
After the Lord had said these things to Job, he said to Eliphaz the
Temanite, "I am angry with you and your two friends, because you have
not spoken the truth about me, as my servant Job has."
Job 42:2-5,7 NIV

Job thought he knew God before but after all that happened to him God
became very real.
Job now knew God in a new and enlightened way.
Before Job had heard of God but now Job saw God, really saw Him for
the first time.

He came to know a God that had a plan for his life.
He came to know a God that wanted only the best for him.
He came to know a God that listened to his cries.
He came to know a God that spoke only truth.
He came to know a God he could trust.
He had heard but now he saw!

Be careful who you listen to!
Sometimes your friends' counsel may not be wise counsel.
When you speak, always speak His truth in love.
You may have to pray for the very friends that gave you bad counsel,
remember to do it in love and sincerity.

One day there will be a restoration for you

just as there was in Job's life.

He will work it all out for your good.

After Job had prayed for his friends, the Lord restored his fortunes and
gave him twice as much as he had before.   Job 42:10 NIV

November 17
He met me

I will extol the Lord at all times; his praise will always be on my lips.
Psalm 34:1 NIV

I got up early one Saturday morning to try to beat the heat (that's hard to do in Texas in July)!
I had finally convinced myself the weeds had to go in the flowerbed outside our bedroom window. I do not like to pick weeds! I'm not sure if that comes from my childhood or what but weeds have never been my friend. But I was determined today, so I got my glove and my tool and set out to win this battle. I hadn't been working very long when I heard the most beautiful sound, as I looked up I saw a red cardinal. He was singing his heart out. The heat did not bother him at all. He was so happy just to sing.

When I heard his sweet praise I immediately realized
God had sent that little bird to encourage me, to remind
me that there is "joy in the morning".
That praise is good.
That praise brings joy.
That I need only to be still and listen
and He will put a new song in my heart.

No longer were the weeds a chore, I began to tackle this job with a new fervor because God met me on this special morning!
And I did conquer the weeds!

He loves you

November 18
Amen to His promises

For no matter how many promises God has made, they are "Yes"
in Christ. And so through him the "Amen" is spoken
by us to the glory of God.
2 Corinthians 1:20 NIV

His promises are always Yes.
They always have been Yes.
They always will be Yes.

Before the foundation of the world He was the great I Am.
He always has been the great I Am.
He always will be the great I Am.

The great I Am. . .
God, the Father
Jesus, the Son
The Holy Spirit, our comforter.
They have always been three in one.
They always will be three in one.

God spoke the promises.
Jesus fulfilled the promises.
The Holy Spirit confirms the promises.

His promises are Yes.
We say Amen!
So be it Father

He loves you

November 19
I carried you on eagle's wings

'You yourselves have seen what I did to Egypt, and how I carried you on
eagles' wings and brought you to myself.
Exodus 19:4 NIV

In the movie "Lord of the Rings", based on the book written by J.R.R.
Tolkien, there are giant flying eagles. In one scene the eagles swoop
down and rescue the people that need help.
The eagles then carry them on their backs and they fly them far away to a
safe place. They gently land and place them out of harm's way.

That's what God does for us. He very gently bends down and scoops us
up and carries us to a safe place, a different place, a new place.

I remember being carried by Jesus for several months, it was when my
son had been diagnosed with a malignant brain tumor. The tumor was
inoperable due to the location deep between the two lobes of his brain. At
the time I thought it was more than I could bear. Yet I realize now looking
back at those long months, God did carry me. He carried me on eagles'
wings!

I was never to be the same again.
My son was never to be the same again.
I met God in an incredible way!
My son met God in an incredible way as a sixteen-year-old boy.
God carried him on eagles' wings too!

Such a faithful God we serve!

He loves you

November 20
The accents of His voice

After the earthquake came a fire, but the Lord was not in the fire.
And after the fire came a gentle whisper.
1 Kings 19:12 NIV

"Expectation quickens the hearing; and when we are truly desirous toward Christ, how quickly the accents of His voice are caught!"
(L. B. E. Cowman. "Springs in the Valley.")

I am from Texas and everywhere I go, outside of Texas, once I speak, people know where I am from!
My accent is very obvious. And as hard as I try I have not been able to change that.
I am a Texan through and through.
The father of two of my grandsons is from New Zealand. When he speaks it is obvious he is not from Texas.
Most know where he is from when he speaks but it becomes even more obvious when he says, "Good day mate"!

Our accents reveal where our home is.
God's accent reveals who He is.
He speaks in such a gentle, kind way.
There is no harshness.
There is no condemnation.
There is no hate.
There is no rudeness.
There is no self-seeking.
There is no wrong.
He only speaks love!

His only accent is gentleness.
When you expect and become desirous of Him, you will
begin to hear the gentle accents of His voice.

November 21
With Thanksgiving

For everything God created is good, and nothing is to be rejected if it is received with thanksgiving, because it is consecrated by the word of God and prayer.   1 Timothy 4:4-5 NIV

The law brings death.
But Jesus' love brings life.
Rules or laws, whatever you might call them, do not bring life.
We are saved by His grace.
It has nothing to do with our works.
God created it, we are to enjoy it.
He does tell us to be careful and refrain from excess.
But He very specifically says to enjoy what He has created.
The one key is thanksgiving!

Whatever you eat, whatever you do

Wherever you go

Do it all with thanksgiving, with a heart of gratitude.

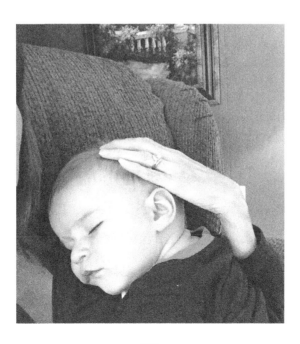

November 22
We can see clearly now

But whenever one turns to the Lord, the veil is taken away. Now the Lord
is the Spirit and where the Spirit of the Lord is, there is liberty. But we all,
with unveiled face seeing the glory of the Lord as in a mirror, are
transformed into the same image from glory to glory,
even as from the Lord, the Spirit.
2 Corinthians 3:16-18 WEB

For those that know Him:
The veil has been taken away!
There is now freedom.
We see His glory.
We are being changed as we look upon His glory.
We are being made to look like Him.
His glory is ever increasing in us.
All this is a gift from the Lord.
We can see Him clearly now.
There is no more condemnation.
There is only freedom in Him.

There was a song that was popular in the '70's called "I Can See Clearly
Now". I was reminded of this song when I thought about the words
above. There actually is truth in the lyrics to this song. When the veil is
taken away we can see clearly for the very first time. We may still see
obstacles before us but we know God has us and He will lead us. The
dark clouds are gone, the clouds, the veil, that blinded us.

*What we see now is the light, His light. He gives us a
new heart, to love as He loves. We see today and every
day after, through His eyes.
He allows us to see the rainbow and the blue skies.*

He loves you

I Can See Clearly Now
By Jimmy Cliff

"I can see clearly now the rain is gone.
I can see all obstacles in my way.
Gone are the dark clouds that had me blind.
It's gonna be a bright, bright
Bright, bright sunshiny day.
Oh, yes I can make it now the pain is gone.
All of the bad feelings have disappeared.
Here is that rainbow I've been praying for.
It's gonna be a bright (bright)
bright (bright) sunshiny day.
Look straight ahead, there's nothing but blue skies."

November 23
He has rescued us

For he has rescued us from the dominion of darkness and brought us
into the kingdom of the Son he loves.
Colossians 1:13 NIV

He has rescued us from the dominion of darkness.

I recently saw a picture that broke my heart.
It was of a little three-year-old Syrian boy who lay dead on the sands of a
beach. He, along with his brother and mother and father, were attempting
to flee their native country of Syria, a war torn country.
The father had paid someone over $6,000 to help his family escape.
The family along with others were all put in a small boat.
They were each given life jackets.
The boat capsized. They tried to hold on to the boat.
The father tried to save his family.
First the youngest little boy drowned.
The dad left him to try to save the others.
Then the three-year-old son drowned.
He left him to try to save his wife.
Then the wife drowned!
His whole family gone!

He alone survived!
In agonizing tears with heartbreaking words the father said
"The life jackets were not real!"
They had been told a lie and they believed it.
"My whole family is gone! What do I do now?"

What kind of person would sell this precious family life jackets and yet
knowing all the time the life jackets would not save them? Then I
remembered! The one who has come to kill, steal and destroy . . .that's
the one who would deceive and lie!

All I could think of is the similarity between this story and our world. What they thought would save them, the life jackets. would not, could not. They were fake, not the real thing!

How many in our world today have been told the same lie?
Do this and you will live.
Believe in this and you will have peace.
Follow them and you will find your way.
Do your own thing and happiness will follow.

All lies of the enemy!

The only one that can truly save is Jesus.
He wasn't created by someone or something.
He has always been.
He will always will be.

He is the only one that can rescue you.
He is waiting with outstretched arms.

I find hope in this.
I believe the moment the two little boys took their last breath here on earth they took their first breath in heaven. They will never see war or famine or persecution again. Ever!
My hope is that the one who rescued me, Jesus, can rescue their father too.

He loves you

November 24
Do unto others

Do to others as you would have them do to you.
Luke 6:31 NIV

I taught Kindergarten for 25 years. This was my theme, my main message. Everyday held many conflicts between children, not big conflicts but big in their eyes.
"He won't share. He took my book. I had that first. He wasn't kind to me." Each time I talked to the child I would let them tell me their version of the story. Then I would ask the other child involved their version. Many times it was that both were being unkind. Sometimes it was just one that was unkind. Each time I asked the one offended, "How did that make you feel?" After the hurt child expressed their thoughts then I would ask the 'offender', "How would that make you feel if someone had done that to you"?
Almost every time I could see the child begin to understand. They began to understand how the other person felt. Over time when there were problems I would just say, "That's a problem you are going to have to solve." Then they knew it was their job to go talk to the one they had a conflict with and work through the problem.

The amazing thing over the years I did see the children in my classroom begin to "Do unto others as they would have them do the you".

My hope, my prayer, has always been that I did make a difference in the lives of these children.
That they did remember the words I sang to them.
"I will be kind, careful and caring in everything I do.
I will always do my very best and I know you will too."
If we could just remember to ask ourselves
"How would that make you feel?"
I think we might choose our spoken words and actions much more carefully.

He loves you

November 25
Find your war room

Them that are quiet in the land.
Psalm 35:20 KJV

The movie "War Room" was a movie, written, directed and produced by two brothers, the Kendrick Brothers, who are Christians. The main message of the movie was that we are in a war and the only way through every "war" in our life is prayer. Prayer has the power to move mountains! Prayer can cease wars! Prayer can change any situation for the good. Prayer can give hope when all hope is lost. It was an amazing movie. And it did amazingly well at the box office too.

To be quiet is the key to prayer and hearing God.
We must be still, really still, not just in our body, but in our mind, in our heart to hear God.

But the thing about being still and quiet is that you won't be seen.
Others may not even notice you anymore.
Many may not even think about you.
Many may not call or ask how you are.
But God does!
He notices you.
He thinks about you.
He talks to you.
He asks how you are.

To live a life in quietness brings confidence in Jesus.
He will give you His strength.
You will see the victory!
Be quiet before man but mighty before God.

He loves you

November 26
To soothe the hearts of men

I will give thanks to the Lord because of his righteousness; I will sing the praises of the name of the Lord Most High.
Psalm 7:17 NIV

David, the little shepherd boy
David, the young boy who slew the giant
David, the compassionate king
David, the one who took Bathsheba
David, the one who had Bathsheba's husband killed
David, the one pursued by many
David, the one always running, always fighting
David, the one who fought many battles
David, the one who played and sang for God

David, a man after God's own heart

God "breathed the music of His love" through David.
David in turn has continued to soothe
the hearts of men.

I consider that our present sufferings are not worth comparing with the glory that will be revealed in us.
Romans 8:18 NIV

May our present sufferings produce in us
such "sweet, soothing music" that the world
will be drawn to you, Father.

He loves you

November 27
Jesus knew

The Lord said, "Simon, Simon, behold, Satan asked to have you, that he might sift you as wheat, but I prayed for you, that your faith wouldn't fail. You, when once you have turned again, establish your brothers." He said to him, "Lord, I am ready to go with you both to prison and to death!" He said, "I tell you, Peter, the rooster will by no means crow today until you deny that you know me three times."
Luke 22:31-34 WEB

Jesus said these words to Peter before Peter denied him.
He knew Peter's future. He knew Peter would deny him, not once but three times. Yet even though Jesus knew this He did not condemn him. He encouraged him.
Jesus knew how difficult this would be for Peter.
He knew the words Peter spoke of denial would come back to haunt him. He knew it would be so hard for Peter to get past this. So even before it happened Jesus wanted to encourage Peter. There is no condemnation for those who are in Christ Jesus. Not only did Jesus encourage Peter with his words, He also prayed for him. He prayed Peter's faith would not fail. He knew so many others would need to be strengthened by Peter.

Jesus knew!
Yet Jesus spoke words to encourage.
Jesus prayed for his faith to be strong.
Jesus prayed he would encourage others.
Even though Peter denied Jesus three times God used Peter in an incredible way to do just what Jesus asked him to do.

"Strengthen your brothers".

May we also hear the words God speaks to us.
He knows our past but He does not condemn.
His words to us are meant to encourage us so that we in turn might "strengthen our brothers".

He loves you

November 28
What are you boasting in

This is what the Lord says: "Let not the wise boast of their wisdom or the strong boast of their strength or the rich boast of their riches, but let the one who boasts boast about this: that they have the understanding to know me, that I am the Lord, who exercises kindness, justice and righteousness on earth, for in these I delight," declares the Lord.
Jeremiah 9:23-24 NIV

In today's world we have many who boast.
Because of their "knowledge"
They know more about this
They know more about that
Or
Because of their "strength"
They can run this race
They can run that race
Or
Because of their riches
They can buy this
They can buy that

But God says this about boasting.
Boast only in your understanding to know Him.
That He is the Lord.
That He exercises kindness and justice and
righteousness.
That His delight is in these things.

He loves you

November 29
He watches over you

My eyes will watch over them for their good, and I will bring them back to
this land. I will build them up and not tear them down;
I will plant them and not uproot them.
Jeremiah 24:6 NIV

My eyes will watch over them.
God's eyes will watch over you.
He will watch over you for your good.
That's an incredible thought.
The God, who created the universe and every star in the heavens,
watches over you.
You are that important to Him.
He doesn't watch over you to see what you are doing wrong.

He watches over you for your good.
He wants the very best for you!

November 30
God's protection

But let all who take refuge in you be glad; let them ever sing for joy.
Spread your protection over them, that those who love your name
may rejoice in you.
Psalm 5:11 NIV

Sometimes we need more protection than we think.
It is worth the extra time in prayer and preparation to receive that needed
protection.

I broke my foot after a fall. The break was called a spiral break, not a
normal break! It was severe enough that I needed to have surgery to
repair it. Not just to repair it but also to add some needed protection
inside my foot like six screws, a plate, biological bone and removal of
bone fragments.
I needed the extra protection inside my foot for my bones to be able to
heal right. I was given a boot to wear.
I needed the extra protection outside my foot for the bone to have to time
to heal inside my foot.

It was a pain to put the boot on. Each time I put it on, I had to velcro the
top and the bottom and put the three straps on and pump it up with air, I
was reminded of the reason for this. It is all for my good! To protect
me! To ultimately make my foot stronger!

In life it is worth the extra time in prayer
to receive the protection from God we so need.
There is a reason for every "strap" in life.
Trust God He knows.

He loves you

December 1
The one who calls you

The one who calls you is faithful, and he will do it.
1 Thessalonians 5:2 NIV

Last week I got a phone call from my second born grandson who was three at the time.
He wanted to know if he and his mama could come over and play.
I, of course, said, yes, I'll be home and I want to play.
That was the first time he's called me (with his mama's help) and I have to admit it thrilled me to hear his little voice and to know he wanted to come over and "play" with me.
He and his mama did come and we played and we laughed and we had lunch together.

He made my heart happy.
With his little voice
With his little smile
With his laughter

God is the same way, when He calls He is faithful.
Whatever He says He will do.
And when God does call and you hear His voice
it will make you happy and you will smile
and you may even laugh too.

I think the same is true when we call God.
When He hears our voice, it makes Him happy and
I think He smiles and He may even laugh, too!

He loves you

December 2
Stormy winds

Lightning and hail, snow and clouds, stormy winds that do his bidding.
Psalm 148:8 NIV

In October of 2015, hurricane Patricia became the most powerful hurricane to ever hit the Western Hemisphere. Winds were clocked at 200 mph. It was projected to hit the coast of Mexico. The potential for its damage was huge. I remember praying the night before for all those that might be in the path of this possible deadly hurricane. When I got up the next morning I looked online and read that Patricia had been downgraded to a tropical depression. It appeared that the damage that many had feared did not occur and that many, many lives were spared.
I read about the Air Force Hurricane Hunters. It is incredible what they do. They fly directly into the eye of the storm to get accurate data about a hurricane. Satellites get some data but the hunters get the most precise, up to date data. This data is then used to help analyze the potential for the storm. Amazing that men can and will do this.

Two things stand out to me in this:
One - when we pray God does listen.
The storms do His bidding.
He can and does calm the storms.
He calmed hurricane Patricia.
Two - sometimes we do have to go into the "eye of the storm" and through the storm in order to understand "the storm". Just as the hurricane hunters gathered all the data, we too can do the same thing. We can enter the eye of the storm, with God's help, and learn from it. The information we obtain may very well be just the information we need to save us (or someone else) from the next storm.
Thank you God for calming the storms of our life.

He stilled the storm to a whisper; the waves of the sea were hushed.
Psalm 107:29 NIV

He loves you

December 3
A mother's ponderings

After three days they found him in the temple, sitting in the middle of the teachers, both listening to them, and asking them questions. All who heard him were amazed at his understanding and his answers. When they saw him, they were astonished, and his mother said to him, "Son, why have you treated us this way? Behold, your father and I were anxiously looking for you." And he went down with them, and came to Nazareth. He was subject to them, and his mother kept all these sayings in her heart. And Jesus increased in wisdom and stature, and in favor with God and men.
Luke 2:46-48, 51-52 WEB

Mothers love to watch their children.
Mothers love to see their children listening.
Mothers love to know their children are growing in wisdom and knowledge.

But mothers also get very anxious when they don't know where their children are.
How kind it was of God to let Mary see her son listening and watching and learning.

And how reassuring it is to be reminded
that they are His.
Their Heavenly Father watches over them.
He never sleeps nor slumbers.
He is always with them, always!

What a treasure it is for a mother to store up memories of her children.
How reassuring it is to know God has our children in the palm of His hand.
Mothers have a special place in God's heart.

He loves you

December 4
Remember how He told you

In their fright the women bowed down with their faces to the ground, but
the men said to them, "Why do you look for the living among the dead?
He is not here; he has risen! Remember how he told you,
while he was still with you in Galilee."
Luke 24:5-6 NIV

Why do you look for the living among the dead?
He is not here.
He is risen!
Remember how He told you.

How often we look for answers among the things that have no life.
In our possessions
In our jobs
In our plans
In our past
In our future
Yet Jesus says look to me for life.
I am the one who provides.
I am the one who gives hope.
I am the one who paves the road for you.
I am the one who takes away all your sins.
I am the one who has come to give you life and give it more abundantly.

Remember how He told you!

"The Son of Man must be delivered over to the hands of sinners, be
crucified and on the third day be raised again."
Then they remembered his words.
Luke 24:7-8 NIV

He loves you

December 5
I will remember for you

Then I thought, "To this I will appeal: the years when the Most High stretched out his right hand. I will remember the deeds of the Lord; yes, I will remember your miracles of long ago. I will consider all your works and meditate on all your mighty deeds."
Psalm 77:10-12 NIV

Recently I went to a funeral for a dear friend's mother. It was such a sweet service listening to her grandchildren talk about how special their Mimi was and how much she loved them unconditionally.

Several years ago I went to this same friend's funeral for her dad. Once again, it was such a sweet service with his grandchildren telling of their love for their granddad. One thing was different though, my friend's dad had Alzheimer's. He had been affected by it for several years but in his last year of life it had gotten really bad. They eventually had to put him in a home for Alzheimer's patients. He could not remember even basic things like who people were, where he lived, what he was supposed to do nor much of his past. One of his grandsons wrote a song honoring his granddad. The name of the song was, "I'll remember for you." The words were so touching and meaningful. I wept as I thought of the meaning behind these words. Even though their granddad couldn't remember, his grandchildren would never forget what he did and the impact he had on their lives!

I believe the same is true for each of us, when we feel like we can't remember, or the pain is too much, or the road seems too hard, God's word remembers for us. His word reminds us of His great love for us, of His great plans for us and of His great hope for us. Take a moment to meditate on His word, He will use it to help you remember!

Psalm 77:13-15

He loves you

December 6
Speak the truth in love

Instead, speaking the truth in love, we will grow to become in every
respect the mature body of him who is the head, that is, Christ.
Ephesians 4:15 NIV

How often do we speak the truth in love?
We so often have this need to speak.
We have an inner desire, that is sometimes driven by self, to just speak.
We think we have the answer to others problems and they need to hear
the truth through us.

Those of us who know Jesus do know the truth.
We have His word, which is all truth.
He lives inside of us and He is truth.

Yet, we often do not speak this truth in love.
We say 'God is love' but our actions, our words, are far from that.

The world does not want more truth.
They want more love, Christ' love revealed through us.
Think before you speak.
Always, always, speak in love.
Then Christ' truth through love will be revealed.

If I be lifted up I will draw all men unto me.
John 12:32 NIV

He loves you

December 7
The things God has prepared

However, as it is written: "What no eye has seen, what no ear has heard, and what no human mind has conceived"---the things God has prepared for those who love him
1 Corinthians 2:9-10 NIV

The things God has prepared for those who love Him:
No eye has seen
No ear has heard
No human mind has conceived

I have seen the most beautiful flowers with their vibrant colors.
I have seen the most amazing butterflies with their perfectly symmetrical wings.
I have seen the majestic mountains and the unending oceans.
I have seen the trees that seem to tower to the skies.
I have seen the beauty in the eyes of my children and grandchildren.

I have heard the sweet song of a bird.
I have heard the sound of holy voices singing as one to God.
I have heard the gentle voices of my grandsons whisper, I love you.
I have heard the roar of the waves in the ocean storm.
I have heard the rhythmic beating of the NICU machines keeping my tiny grandson alive.

But the amazing things I have seen,
the incredible sounds I have heard
pale in comparison to what God has prepared
for me, for us, for those who love Him.

He loves you

December 8
He did not open His mouth

He was oppressed and afflicted, yet he did not open his mouth; he was
led like a lamb to the slaughter, and as a sheep before its shearers is
silent, so he did not open his mouth. He was assigned a grave with the
wicked, and with the rich in his death, though he had done no violence,
nor was any deceit in his mouth.
Isaiah 53:7,9 NIV

He was oppressed
He was afflicted
Yet He did not open His mouth

He was led like a lamb to the slaughter
Yet He did not open His mouth

He was assigned a grave with the wicked.
He had committed no violence.
Yet He did not have any deceit in His mouth

In all of this Jesus did not open His mouth
until the very end when they had nailed his hands and
his feet to the cross and had placed a crown of thorns on
his head and even pierced His side.
In His final breath He spoke and His words were full of
such compassion when He said,

"Father forgive them
for they know not what they do!"

He loves you

December 9
God knew you

Listen, dear friends. isn't it clear by now that God operates quiet differently? He chose the world's down and out as the kingdom's first citizens, with full rights and privileges. The kingdom of God is promised to anyone who will love God.
James 2:5 The Message

"God had complete foreknowledge when He created us. Our infirmities, insecurities, and insufficiencies neither surprised Him not repulsed Him. They were all part of the human package. Yet we wonder why He would choose us?
The answer is because He delights when hearts so prone to wander choose Him. What would be His greater source of joy—for perfect people to do perfect things? Or for pitifully self-centered, world-centered humans to fight the daily battle to be God-centered? Beloved, our victories bring far more delight to God than our defeats bring disappointment."
(Moore, Beth. "Believing God Day by Day." November 19)

God knew you before He created you.
He knew everything about you.
He knew every word you would ever speak.
He knew every thought you would ever have.
He knew every decision you would ever make.
He knew and yet He loved you still!

He loves you

December 10
You are special

I will praise You, because I have been fearfully and wonderfully made.
Your works are wonderful, and I know this very well.
Psalm 139:14 NIV

"Though he lived several thousand years before Charles Darwin, a simple shepherd's inspired appreciation for the wonders of human existence far surpassed the human hypotheses of an acclaimed scientist who convinced much of the world that he had the answers.
While Darwin sat at his desk and reduced all creation to simple blobs of protoplasm, the outstretched DNA in his body could have reached back and forth to the sun about fifty times. Charles Darwin was fearfully and wonderfully made. He just never knew it. So are you, Dear One."
(Moore, Beth. "Believing God Day by Day." November 30)

There is no one made just like you.
No one with the exact same DNA
No one with the exact same gifts
No one with the exact same talents
No one with the exact same purpose
You are totally unique
One of a kind
You are fearfully and wonderfully made!
May you begin to realize just how special you are

He loves you

December 11
God's word is not chained

Remember Jesus Christ, raised from the dead, descended from David. This is my gospel, for which I am suffering even to the point of being chained like a criminal. But God's word is not chained.
2 Timothy 2:8-9 NIV

God's word is not chained.

When His word goes out it has such power
The power that can change a person's heart forever
The power to move mountains
The power to give life to the dying
The power to change the course of a man's life
The power to resurrect the dead
The power to breathe life into the hopeless

Devour His word.

Breathe His word.

Speak His word.

Live His word.

Believe His word.

Reflect on what I am saying, for the Lord will give you insight into all this.
2 Timothy 2:7 NIV

He loves you

December 12
Your weapons

A champion out of the camp of the Philistines named Goliath, of Gath, whose height was six cubits and a span went out. He had a helmet of brass on his head, and he wore a coat of mail; and the weight of the coat was five thousand shekels of brass. He had brass armor on his legs, and a brass javelin between his shoulders. The staff of his spear was like a weaver's beam; and his spear's head weighed six hundred shekels of iron. His shield bearer went before him.
1 Samuel 17:4-7 WEB

Goliath was a giant of 9 feet 9 inches tall.
His armor weighed 125 pounds.
The point of his spear weighed 15 pounds.
Yet, none of this was protection enough.

David was a young shepherd boy, the youngest of four brothers.
His job was to tend the sheep.
He learned to trust God, while tending these sheep.
He learned that, with God's help, he could slay a bear and a lion and he did.

David trusted God.
He knew the battle was not his but God's.
He tried to wear Saul's armor but he was not used to it, it did not feel right.
The only thing that he took was his sling and five smooth stones.
He took what he was familiar with.
He took what he trusted.
His God and his weapon.

It is important to know what our weapons are.
We have to be familiar with them in order to be able to
use them properly when the battle comes.
And it will come.

Then David said to the Philistine, "You come to me with a sword, with a spear, and with a javelin; but I come to you in the name of Yahweh of Armies, the God of the armies of Israel, whom you have defied. Today, Yahweh will deliver you into my hand. I will strike you, and take your head from off you. I will give the dead bodies of the army of the Philistines today to the birds of the sky, and to the wild animals of the earth; that all the earth may know that there is a God in Israel, and that all this assembly may know that Yahweh doesn't save with sword and spear; for the battle is Yahweh's, and he will give you into our hand."
1 Samuel 17:45-47 WEB

Sometimes you may be forced to stand alone,
above the crowd, totally dependent upon God.
He will give you your weapons.

He loves you

December 13
The trumpet call

For the Lord himself will come down from heaven, with a loud command,
with the voice of the archangel and with the trumpet call of God, and the
dead in Christ will rise first. After that, we who are still alive and are left will
be caught up together with them in the clouds to meet the Lord in the air.
And so we will be with the Lord forever.
therefore encourage one another with these words.
1 Thessalonians 4:16-18 NIV

We've had two of our sweet grandsons, along with their mom, at our
house for about a week. It's been fun to listen to them talk. Yesterday the
three year old, said, "I thought Jesus was coming with that thing". While
he was saying this he held up his hands like he was blowing a trumpet.
I thought to myself, how cool is that! Then I thought, oh wow, did God tell
him something I don't know? Is Jesus coming soon? Either way I loved
that he had thought about these things.

One day Jesus will return with the trumpet call. The dead will rise. Those
who are still alive will be caught up in the clouds and meet Jesus in the
air. Are you ready? Do you know Him?

I'm so thankful my grandson reminded me of this. His words so
encouraged me.

For here we do not have an enduring city, but we are looking
for the city that is to come.
Hebrews 13:14 NIV

He loves you

December 14
His ears are attentive

For the eyes of the Lord are on the righteous and his ears are attentive to their prayer, but the face of the Lord is against those who do evil."
1 Peter 3:12 NIV

I have this picture in my head of someone cupping their hand around their ear so that they can hear better. I am also reminded of a game we played when I was little. We would sit in a circle and whisper something, a word or two, to the person next to you and they would whisper what they heard to the next person and so on. When it got to the last person they would speak out loud what they heard. It was never the same as what the original word or words were.

So often we think we hear but we really don't because our ears are not attentive to what is being said, we just aren't listening.
So often God speaks but there is such noise from our world we don't hear His gentle whisper.
So often we hear incorrectly because we already have some preconceived idea of what is going to be said.
The amazing thing is God always hears us.
He doesn't have to cup His ear.
He doesn't have to clear His mind of the world's clutter.
He doesn't hear what others say about us.

He just listens!
He is always listening.
He is so attentive to you, only you!
He hears your every prayer.
He even hears the groanings of your heart, when it is too hard to even speak.
He hears!

December 15
My people have forgotten

"My people have been lost sheep; their shepherds have led them astray
and caused them to roam on the mountains. They wandered over
mountain and hill and forgot their own resting place."
Jeremiah 50:6 NIV

So many have become like lost sheep.
They've turned to their own ways.
They don't know which way to go, whether to the right or the left.
Their shepherds have led them astray.
So many, who proclaim to be shepherds, don't even know their own path.
How can they lead others!
So many, who proclaim to be shepherds, are listening to their own voice.
How can they lead others!
So many, who proclaim to be shepherds, don't know Your voice, Father
How can they teach others to hear Your voice!
So many sheep are just roaming
They take a stance here
Then they take a stance there
They have no firm foundation.
They have wandered over mountains and hills.
They have no resting place.

You, Father, have a resting place for each of your sheep.
A secure and safe place
To lie down in green pastures
To walk beside still waters.
To run in open meadows.
Only God can provide this resting place for you.
He has it ready for you!

He makes me lie down in green pastures, he leads me beside quiet
waters. Psalm 23:2 NIV

December 16
Their sins will be remembered no more

Then he adds: "Their sins and lawless acts I will remember no more."
And where these have been forgiven, sacrifice for sin
is no longer necessary.
Hebrews 10:17-18 NIV

God has this amazing ability to know all
Yet He also has the ability to remember no more!

How can He be all knowing and yet remember no more
Because of what Jesus did on the cross.

Your sins are not only forgiven, they are remembered no more.
What was once visible and seen,
has now become invisible never to be seen again.

What was once dirty and ugly and stained with blood,
has now become clean and perfect and white as snow.

Though your sins were as "scarlet they shall be as white as snow"!

Jesus covered all your sins!
God sees them no more
Nor does He remember them
Nor does He remind you of them

It is finished!
Now see yourself as He sees you!
Beautiful and clean and new
His bride

He loves you

December 17
To be separate from God

He will punish those who do not know God and do not obey the gospel of our Lord Jesus. They will be punished with everlasting destruction and shut out from the presence of the Lord and from the glory of his might on the day he comes to be glorified in his holy people and to be marveled at among all those who have believed. This includes you, because you believed our testimony to you.
2 Thessalonians 1:8-10 NIV

Hell is a choice.
There are those who want nothing to do with God.
They are choosing their own eternity.

God is a loving God.
He lets every man choose his destiny.
He is so gracious He will not "make you go with Him".
It is a choice.

But for those that choose to be "away from God", their eternity is hell.
There are only two choices:
To be with God or
To be away from God

One choice is an eternity in heaven, with God.
The other choice is an eternity in hell, without God.

We get to choose.

Choose for yourselves this day whom you will serve.
Joshua 24:15

He loves you

December 18
I can run

I run in the path of your commands, for you
have broadened my understanding.
Psalm 119:32 NIV

There was a time that I did not know His path.
All I knew was the path that I chose.
It always, always lead to a dead end, with much hurt and heartache.

Then there came a time that I saw His path.
He shed His light for me that I might see His path.
But I only saw this path as a narrow path that I had to walk very carefully on.
I carried my past with me down His path, never realizing I was not supposed to.
Never fully realizing that I had been made totally new!

Then there came a day that I began to see His path was very broad,
filled with all kinds of incredible pleasures for me to enjoy.

Now He has "broadened my understanding"!
I know His freedom
Now I can run!

"I can run and not grow weary
I can walk and not faint"

Oh, the depth of the riches of the wisdom and knowledge of God! How
unsearchable his judgments, and his paths beyond tracing out!
Romans 11:33 NIV

He loves you

December 19
Come

"Come," he said. Then Peter got down out of the boat,
walked on the water and came toward Jesus.
Matthew 14:29 NIV

Come, He said.
Come, He still says.

Come all who are weary and burdened and you will find rest for your soul.
Come, He says.

Come to me all who are thirsty and drink from my cup.
Come, He says.

Come and let me love you.
Come, He says.

Come and I will give you life forevermore.
Come, He says.

Come I will restore your hope.
Come, He says.

Come and we can dance and sing and laugh together.
Come, He says.

Come, I am waiting.

He loves you

December 20
He knows what you need

On the first day of unleavened bread, when they sacrificed the Passover, his disciples asked him, "Where do you want us to go and prepare that you may eat the Passover?" He sent two of his disciples, and said to them, "Go into the city, and there you will meet a man carrying a pitcher of water. Follow him, and wherever he enters in, tell the master of the house, 'The Teacher says, "Where is the guest room, where I may eat the Passover with my disciples?"' He will himself show you a large upper room furnished and ready. Get ready for us there." His disciples went out, and came into the city, and found things as he had said to them, and they prepared the Passover.
Mark 14:12-16 WEB

The room was made ready even before the disciples asked.
Jesus knew their need even before they did.

He goes in advance of you.
He prepares a table for you.

There will one day be the ultimate feast with Jesus.
We will never leave Him.
But we must remember that even now He goes in
advance of us.
His preparations are always ready.
He knows what you need.

He loves you

December 21
All of creation

For the creation waits with eager expectation for the children of God to be revealed. For the creation was subjected to vanity, not of its own will, but because of him who subjected it, in hope that the creation itself also will be delivered from the bondage of decay into the liberty of the glory of the children of God. For we know that the whole creation groans and travails in pain together until now.
Romans 8:19-22 WEB

Creation waits.
Creation was subjected to frustration.
Creation will one day be liberated from the bondage to decay.
Creation will be brought into freedom and glory.
Creation groans as it waits.

When I look outside in my own backyard at all God has created, I am blown away by this thought. All of this beauty that I see is in bondage, it is decaying. It is not as God meant it to be. That thought just astounds me.

When I look at the incredible beauty of just one little yellow swallowtail butterfly with its very intricate, symmetrical detail and color, I think God intended much more for even this little part of His creation. How could there be more beauty in one small insect? Or in one beautifully fragrant gardenia flower? Or in one towering majestic pine tree? It's an amazing thought to me. Yet one day creation will no longer be waiting. One day creation will no longer be subject to frustration. Creation will be liberated from all bondage of decay. Creation will be free and glorious! There will be no more groans of pain or sadness or death or dying!

Or wounded butterflies!

He loves you

414

He loves you

December 22
Walls are coming down

All of your men of war shall march around the city, going around the city once. You shall do this six days. Seven priests shall bear seven trumpets of rams' horns before the ark. On the seventh day, you shall march around the city seven times, and the priests shall blow the trumpets. It shall be that when they make a long blast with the ram's horn, and when you hear the sound of the trumpet, all the people shall shout with a great shout; and the wall the city shall fall down flat, and the people shall go up, every man straight in front of him."

Joshua 6:3-5 WEB

God had a plan.

Joshua and the Israelites needed help.

God shared His plan with Joshua.

Joshua believed God and shared God's plan with the Israelites.

The Israelites listened, obeyed and trusted their leader.

They did not question that the walls were securely barred.

They did not question how the walls would come down.

They did not question how Jericho's kings would be delivered into their hands.

They did not question how the Jericho's fighting men would be delivered into their hands.

They did not question why they had to march for seven days.

They did not question why seven priests were to carry trumpets of ram's horns.

They did not question why the ark was being carried around too.

They did not question why they were to march seven times around on the seventh day.

They did not question why the priests were to blow their trumpets on the seventh day.

They did not question why they were to give a loud shout on the seventh day.

They did not question anything.

They just obeyed and trusted.

Francine Rivers wrote in one of her books about the walls of Jericho coming down. She said that when the Israelites (who were great in number) marched around the city that the continual marching for seven

days could have shaken the ground so much that the walls began to
loosen making it easier for the walls to fall down.
The walls did come down!
God knew, Joshua believed, the Israelites trusted
and the walls came down.
In the same way, we are not to question, just believe and keep marching.
In His time the walls will come down.

I love this song by Cody Carnes.

Walls are coming down
"We are daughters and sons
Singing as one
We've got a hope now
Walls have tried to divide
But nothing can hide the power that we've found
You are walking with us and all of the walls are turning to dust
They are falling down
Sing praise, we sing praise
We fill the skies with songs from our hearts
Sing praise, we sing praise
'Til enemies know how faithful You are, O God
High We lift up Your name put darkness in chains
You go before us
Love is swallowing fear and all of the walls will soon disappear
they are crumbling down"

He loves you

December 23
When I Am Afraid

When I am afraid I will trust in you. Psalm 56:3 NIV

Just as mothers love to wrap their arms around their children when they are afraid,

Your Abba Father loves to wrap his arms around you.

Just as mothers love to calm the hearts of their children.
Your Abba Father loves to calm your heart.
He loves for you to run to Him.
His arms are open wide!
He loves you so.

He loves you

December 24
Someone will be listening

They returned from the tomb, and told all these things to the eleven, and to all the rest. Now they were Mary Magdalene, Joanna, and Mary the mother of James. The other women with them told these things to the apostles. These words seemed to them to be nonsense, and they didn't believe them. But Peter got up and ran to the tomb. Stooping and looking in, he saw the strips of linen lying by themselves, and he departed to his home, wondering what had happened.
Luke 24:9-12 WEB

After you've seen Jesus you will want to tell others what you've seen. Many will not listen or believe, but someone will hear and believe.

Peter listened and believed!
Peter ran back to the tomb to see for himself.
He wanted to know if what they said was true.
He did not see the angels, but he saw the evidence that was left.
He saw enough to make him wonder what had happened.

Peter, the one that denied Jesus, was the one that really listened and believed!

Always be faithful to tell others what you've seen
Tell your story
You never know who will be listening

He loves you

December 25
God's unending love

And to know Christ's love which surpasses knowledge, that you may be
filled with all the fullness of God.
Ephesians 3:19 WEB

"God's measureless love is like the ocean. Through the windows of
earthly life we catch a gleam. From the valleys of trouble we glimpse it
near the shore. On the sands of hope we see it, wave on wave. From the
headlands of faith we view a broader tide to the line that blends eternity
with time. Our happiest days are islands set in its boundless breadth. Yet,
as with the ocean, we have never seen it all! Even eternity cannot reveal
its greatness to the wondering hosts of heaven, nor all the universe
exhaust the fountains whence it flows.
(L. B. E. Cowman. "Springs in the Valley." November 16)

You cannot see the depth.
You cannot see the width.
It seems to never end.
That's the way God's love is!
There is no end to His love.
You cannot measure it.
It goes beyond all depth.
It goes beyond all height.

And I pray that you may be strengthened to comprehend with all the
saints what is the width and length and height and depth, and to know
Christ's love which surpasses knowledge, that you may be filled with all
the fullness of God. Now to him who is able to do exceedingly abundantly
above all that we ask or think, according to the power that works in us, to
him be the glory in the assembly and in Christ Jesus
to all generations forever and ever. Amen.
Ephesians 3:18-21WEB

He loves you

December 26
Pick up your mat and walk

A certain man was there, who had been sick for thirty-eight years. When
Jesus saw him lying there, and knew that he had been sick for a long
time, he asked him, "Do you want to be made well?" The sick man
answered him, "Sir, I have no one to put me into the pool when the water
is stirred up, but while I'm coming, another steps down before me."
Jesus said to him, "Arise, take up your mat, and walk."
Immediately, the man was made well, and took up his mat
and walked. Now it was the Sabbath on that day.
John 5:5-9 WEB

"Do you want to get well"?
Those were the words Jesus spoke.
It seems like a rather strange question, doesn't it?
Surely, the man wanted to get well.
He'd been an invalid for 38 years!
Surely, he wanted to be free from the crippling illness.
That is all he had ever known.
Jesus spoke these healing words, "Get up! Pick up your mat and walk."
The man listened, received Jesus' words and he was healed.
Then and only then could he pick up his mat and walk.

I wonder if there are people that do not really want to be healed, not just of
physical conditions but of emotional and spiritual hurts too. Sometimes it
seems for some it is just easier to stay the same. Their habits are well
established. Their thoughts are well planted. Their emotions are solid.
To actually listen to His voice might mean you have to do something. It
might mean He wants to cure you of all your pain and hurts and change
you. But it also might mean you would have to do something,
"Pick up your mat and walk".

Jesus loves you that much that He's willing to say it over and

over again to you.

You only need to listen and obey.

Pick up your mat and walk!

December 27
Tell your story

Jesus did many other things as well. If every one of them were written down, I suppose that even the whole world would not have room for the books that would be written. John 21:25 NIV

Jesus did so many things during His 33 years on earth.

If it were all written down the world would not have room for all of these books. I wonder what it would be like if we each told our own story of all that Jesus has done in our lives. How many books would be filled then? Tell your story. Write your story down. Share with the world what God has done for you. You never know who your story will encourage.

Two can defend themselves. A cord of three strands is not easily broken. Ecclesiastes 4:12

December 28
He sees your every step

His eyes are on the ways of mortals; he sees their every step.
Job 34:21 NIV

I remember when each of my three children took their first steps.
How exciting it was for me their mom.
Their first step represented so much. . .
Strength
Normalcy
Independence
Courage
Progress
The ability to help themselves

Now that I am older I've felt this same joy when I've watched my three grandsons take their first steps.
I have had those same feelings again. They can do it! They did it!
Such joy and such pride.
I love looking at their little faces and seeing their excitement when they realize they did it all by themselves.

He sees their every step.

He sees your every step.

Whether you turn to the left or to the right He sees.

When I think of the verse above I am astounded by the fact that God sees not just our first steps but our every step. He knows the path I take. He smiles when I take my first steps down a new path, a different path, a path that is filled with faith. He loves to see me trust Him, knowing if I do start to fall when I am taking "new steps" He will be there to catch me.
What a loving Father I serve.

December 29
He sees the big picture

He was looking forward to the city that has foundations, whose architect and builder is God. Hebrews 11:10 NIV

He sees so much more than we see.
He knows what He has prepared for us.
He knows what will make us content and happy for all eternity.
Could it be that He is preparing us, equipping us now for what we will be doing with Him for an eternity?
Our time here is not wasted and yet it is only the introduction to the actual "book of our life" that will be lived out for all eternity.
Let your introduction be one of greatness in Him, the architect and builder of all eternity. Let His dew from your life fall on others.

December 30
Everything will be made new

One of the elders answered, saying to me, "These who are arrayed in white robes, who are they, and from where did they come?" I told him, "My lord, you know." He said to me, "These are those who came out of the great tribulation. They washed their robes, and made them white in the Lamb's blood. Therefore they are before the throne of God, they serve him day and night in his temple. He who sits on the throne will spread his tabernacle over them. They will never be hungry, neither thirsty any more; neither will the sun beat on them, nor any heat; for the Lamb who is in the middle of the throne shepherds them, and leads them to springs of waters of life. And God will wipe away every tear from their eyes."
Revelations 7:13-17 WEB

He has washed our robes and made them white in the blood of the lamb.
He will shelter us with His presence.
Never again will we hunger.
Never again will we thirst.
The sun will not beat down on us, nor any scorching heat.

The lamb will be our shepherd forever.

Jesus will lead us to springs of living water.

God will wipe away every tear from our eyes

forever and ever!

Amen and amen

He loves you

December 31
Dew of the morning

But your dead will live, Lord, their bodies will rise
Let those who dwell in the dust wake up and shout for joy
Your dew is like the dew of the morning;
the earth will give birth to her dead.
Isaiah 26:19 NIV

One day all those that have gone before us will rise
We will be taken up to be with Jesus for all eternity.

We are not there yet.
We have work to do on this earth.
So many do not know Jesus
So many have no hope
So many are in desperate need of help
So many need to know the love of a Savior

So many need to hear of His love
So many need to see His love shown through others
So many need to feel that someone cares
So many need to taste His goodness
So many need to walk a new path

If you are one of those, my prayer is that you will open your heart to Him
The one who gave it all for you
The one who loves you unconditionally
The one who forgives your every sin
The one who is all you will ever need

The one who is like the "dew of the morning".

Making everything new!

He loves you

May these words be like new falling dew,
refreshing the hearts of all who read.
May they be like a splash of the fragrance
of Jesus upon your life.
May you be forever changed when you feel
His gentle touch upon you.

In Jesus name,
From a daughter of the one true King,
Mary Ann Grady

May God give you heaven's dew and earth's
richness, an abundance of grain and new wine.
Genesis 27:28 NIV

I am a daughter of the King.
I am a wife of a husband who loves me like
Christ loves the church.
I am a mother to three
"fearfully and wonderfully"
created gifts from God.
I am a "Mamae" to four precious grandsons.
I am a friend who loves to do crazy things.
I am the one who loves to laugh,
even when I shouldn't!
I am growing more in love with Jesus each day.
I am watching and listening for Jesus' return.
I am waiting in great anticipation
for my eternal home.
But, until that time, I want to be like dew,
"refreshing the hearts of the saints".

He loves you

More than you could

ever imagine